WHY WON'T

THE WORLD

EVER

CHANGE?

WRITTEN
BY: PAUL SCHMIDT

EMAIL: pierre424286@yahoo.com

WEB: oneinus.com

A BOOK OF GOD-INSPIRED CHAPTERS

FORWARD

AND

ACKNOWLEDGEMENTS

In writing this book, it is my desire that every person can read and understand the ideas and the thoughts that lie within. Over the last year, I have read many books about our Lord and Savior, many of which I could not understand. God's message is so clear. God's message is also easy to follow. God desires every man to understand His good news. We, as humans, go to great lengths at times to complicate God's written word and what God wants to say to each of us.

Many of the ideas and thoughts in this book you can find in other writings and in other books. Like I said previously, I did a lot of reading during this last year. My hunger and thirst for the Lord was and still is unquenchable.

I am writing this book because God talks to me daily. I hear the voice of God. What a wonderful thing it is to be able to hear and talk to God every day. God desires to have that type of relationship with everybody.

This relationship also has its responsibilities. Over this last year, since I accepted the Lord as my Savior, I have done my best to follow all the instructions that the Lord has entrusted me with. The biggest part is being the Lord's scribe and writing this book.

In the beginning, I had no idea that there was going to be a book. I was never very good at writing more than a couple of pages at a time. I thought I was just reading and taking notes to learn about God.

Then, through the Church that I attend, I was invited to go into the prisons and minister the Word of God. So as the Lord gave me books to read out of the local library, I would take notes and I began to write what the Lord would tell me to write; and then, we would go into the prisons and I would read those writings.

I started to carry pocket notebooks wherever I went to write notes as God spoke to me. I would write notes as I heard other preachers preach. I wrote notes as I listened to TBN. I wrote notes anytime I heard someone talk about God. I just wrote notes all the time. I actually probably have at least two dozen notebooks filled with just these notes.

When I began to take these notes, what I did not do was document which preacher said what or what quote came out of what book. Like I said before, I had no idea that there was ever going to be a book. God led and I followed without question. One day, God took all those writings and notes that I had been saving and God put them together in this book.

Many of the ideas and thoughts in these writings are not new. Other writers, other men and women of God, have already preached and written many of the ideas that you will find here.

This book is inspired by God. God had His hand in everything written on these pages. I could not have found or known what to do with what I had found without God. God put this book together, and now God has put this book into your hands to read. Only God knows why. But there is a reason why you have this book. I do not and I no longer even ask why.

I want to make sure that everyone is given proper credit for their work. I have tried to do my best. I would like to acknowledge three authors that the Lord led me to when I was selecting books to read in the public library; Deepak Chopra, Neale Donald Walsch, and Caroline Myss.

I have read many of the books written by these three authors and you will find that many quotes and ideas expressed in this book come out of their books.

Following this introduction, I will list as many as I can remember of the books I used as references. A few of the books I read when I went back to the library, I could not find again. I hope no one takes offense to me using parts of their writings in this book.

I believe that the words already written by these three authors must be said over and over again until the majority of us receive the message, the good news of God. The more of us talking and writing about bringing the world back to Christ, the better.

It is my wish for people to read this book and to start talking to each other about the ideas presented in these pages. I would like to start people talking about Christ not only on Sunday, but on the other six days of the week as well.

Our country is in a mess and it is my wish to reverse the direction that our country is now going in; that direction is away from God. In America today, we seem to be running away from God as fast as we can go.

It is my deepest desire to hear the name of Jesus being mentioned from Monday through Saturday in conversations, as much as the name of Jesus is talked about on Sunday.

The world as we know it today does not work and as the Apostle Paul wrote, "There is a better way."

I know there is a better way.

WHEN ENOUGH OF US BECOME

THE LOVE OF GOD

IN THE WORLD TODAY,

ALL THE PROBLEMS

OF THE WORLD

WILL

DISAPPEAR!

CHAPTER ONE

WHAT HAPPENED?

WHAT REALLY DID HAPPEN?

How did this great country of ours get into the mess that we find ourselves in today?

We fell asleep! We really did, literally, we fell asleep. We became complacent. How did this world, how did the United States, grow so far away from God so quickly? How is it possible that we let these things happen? And believe me when I say this, we did let these things happen.

At one time in this great country of ours, the words "In God We Trust" really did mean something. To the vast majority of us today, those are just words on the back of our money. Words that some people want to see removed from that very same money. Words that some people want to see removed from our public speech altogether.

Those four words are rarely spoken outside the Church anymore. And very few people really put any faith into those words. But those four words are the main idea that this great country of ours is built upon. For most people, they are just a group of meaningless words, "IN GOD WE TRUST".

In a world where profanity in our speech is becoming more and more acceptable, everywhere and anywhere, in a world where the "N" word is said constantly, anywhere and everywhere, with no thought to the word's true meaning - why is it that we want to strike anything having to do with God from public view or public speech? How has the spoken word of God become more offensive to people than profanity?

How is it possible that we let prayer get voted out of our schools? How is it possible that God can no longer be talked about in our schools? The Ten Commandments cannot even be mentioned or displayed in public places?

How is it possible that the Pledge of Allegiance can no longer be said in our schools? We can no longer sing "God Bless America". How is it possible that Christmas has almost been eliminated from our schools? How is it possible that we have a court system that, time and time again, rules against anything Christian and anything having to do with God? Why do we stand by and do nothing?

I read yesterday that a judge had ruled in America that we cannot have a national day of prayer because it is unconstitutional. How can this be? And where is the outcry from the people? Why do we just lie down and let these rulings happen? And how did we let this happen? Yes, we did let this happen, again. Once again, we fell asleep.

How is it possible, in a country where ninety-two percent of all people say that they have heard of God and seventy-five percent of all Americans say that they are Christian, we have killed fifty million innocent babies since abortion became the law of the land? How did abortion even become the law of this land? We fell asleep, again. How does abortion stay the law of this great land? Are we still asleep even today?

In a country where seventy-five percent of all the population say that they are Christian and an even more important number, fifty-three percent of all Americans, say that God is very important in their everyday life, how did the family in America, which was once this country's backbone, become so eroded and so unrecognizable? We have families with no fathers. Single parent households in America now number fourteen million. We had 750,000 teenage mothers last year alone. Too many children are having children. How does this happen? We fell asleep and did nothing.

Four out of ten Americans attend a Church every Sunday. 104 million Americans attend some type of Church every Sunday morning. In the last presidential election, 123 million Americans voted. 104 million attend Church. 123 million voted. So how did abortion become law if we did not fall asleep?

Our television is full of shows doing paternity testing because women do not know who fathered their children. How does that happen? We no longer have married families. We have babies' fathers and babies' mothers. This is my baby's mother; not let me introduce you to my wife and the mother of my children. What has happened to the family in this great country of ours? Are you starting to see a pattern developing here? Do we really believe that God is pleased with our choices and the way we have distorted the family?

We have sex without any consideration for the children that we might be bringing into this world. How is it possible for women to have five children by five different fathers? How is it possible for a man to have three different women pregnant all at the same time? And he has no job. Do we really have such little disregard for the children that we are bringing into this world? Forget the fact that we have no respect for ourselves.

The answer is yes. We have no regard for the children. We have become a world that is only concerned about our own needs. We have become a nation of people who are only interested in pleasing our own selfish desires. We want what we want and we want it now; who cares about the consequences. Someone else will clean up my mess. Someone else can take responsibility for what I do.

Do we really believe that God is pleased with the state that our country is in right now? America is in trouble because the family is in trouble. The true strength of this country lies within the strength of its families. And right now, the strength of this once great country of ours is deteriorating as fast as the family in America is becoming unrecognizable. Are we kidding ourselves when we say that we are still a God-fearing nation?

Are you starting to wake up yet? Or better yet, have any of my words disturbed you yet?

We all know that the world today, the world as we currently know it, does not work and that many things must change. With all its great technology, with all its great inventions to make our lives easier, the world is not a better place. It has become much worse. The world today is more corrupt, more immoral, and more dangerous than ever before. Many things in this great country of ours must change and have to change!

Let me give you another statistic that I learned just today. One out of four girls in this country will be molested; one out of four. That number alone stopped me in my tracks. And if that number did not make you stop and think, where will this act take place? In their own home and by a family member. The world today is a far worse place than it ever has been and for most of us we just keep turning a blind eye to what is going on.

We did the worst possible thing that we as people could ever do. We did nothing. We who claim to be Christians became an invisible society. We were around. You could see us every Sunday filing into Church buildings, but as soon as church was over, we became invisible all over again until the next Sunday. Monday through Saturday, you could never find a Christian.

Early in my professional career, someone taught me the word *tacit*. I ask people all the time if they have ever heard of the word or know the definition. Maybe one out of ten has heard and knows the word *tacit*. The definition that was taught to me was "you give your approval to something by doing nothing." By not saying anything, you in all actuality have said, "It is ok." And that is exactly what we have done in America. We gave our approval to everything, tacitly.

By not saying or doing anything, we have given our approval. Abortion is ok. No prayer in school is ok. No Christ in Christmas is ok. No National Day of Prayer is ok. Teens having children is ok. No father in our families is ok. All is tacit approval.

All the conditions of the world, which were created by us, exist today: hunger, poverty, disease, famine, war, intolerance, and the list could go on and on and on. It's not because they cannot be fixed, but because there has not been a collected will from us to fix them.

The greater the problem, the greater the collected will it would take to fix the problem, the more people it will take to make the change. But if chosen, there is nothing going on in the world today that we cannot change and that we cannot fix!!!!

When your determination is greater than their resistance, when your resolve is greater than their stubbornness, then people around you will become like you. You, as a single person, can change the habits of the people around you. Let me say that again. You, as a single person, can change habits and you can make a difference. One person can change the world.

Your determination must be greater than their resistance and/or their stubbornness to change.

The world is exactly the way it is today not because God wants it this way. That's far from the truth. The world is the way it is because we want it this way! We want the world this way. We like the world the way that it is. We have become used to it. It's easy. We choose for the world to be the way that it is today. It is our choice.

If we did not want the world this way, we could change it overnight. Yes, that quickly. We could eliminate the pain, the sadness, the suffering in a blink of an eye. We could end depression, recession, and oppression tomorrow. We could eliminate starvation, poverty, and hopelessness and they would never return. It is our choice which way we want the world to go.

700,000 Americans on any given night are homeless. Approximately two million Americans were homeless last year. 700,000 Americans were homeless last night. That number alone is staggering.

If those numbers alone did not give you pause, then almost one million Americans slept on the street last night. I would hope that number would cause you to stop and think. How can that happen in America? Almost one million of my fellow countrymen had nowhere to sleep last night. As I slept in my nice comfortable bed last night, there were people, many people, sleeping in the cold, on the sand, under the boardwalk in Atlantic City where I live.

My heart melts when I read those numbers. For one night, I was one of that 700,000. But only for the grace and mercy of God, it was for only one night. It was a very tough night and I learned and I felt.

The unemployment number is at fifteen million. In 2007, the number of people living in hunger and in poverty was seventy-five million. That's in America alone. How do these things happen in a country that is so rich, so ambitious, with so much know-how? Maybe it's because our leaders only want to point fingers at each other and we keep waiting for the leadership in this country to fix things. Remember the word *tacit*!

So if we could change all these negatives, why do we not? Because we make the choice everyday not to. The real truth is that we really don't want to. Individually, we might want to fix some of the things on the list; maybe all. But as a group, as a society, as a nation, as a world, it is obvious that we do not want to fix a thing. If we wanted it fixed, it would have already been done. We have the knowledge. We have the skill. We have the technology, the resources, to fix anything and everything.

We want to blame God for most of the problems that we have caused ourselves. It's easy to say that all these things are God's fault. It's easy to blame God for what we have done.

We must someday look into the mirror and put the blame and the responsibility for all the ills of the world on the shoulders onto whom it belongs: us. We caused the problems, but we can also fix every problem.

I completely believe that the world will turn around. That we will wake up as a collective people and ban together to fix the Earth and make the Earth the place that God intended it to be. God intended for the Earth that we are living on to be the Garden. Yes, that's right I said The Garden of Eden. God also intends for the Kingdom of Heaven to reside upon this Earth. I know that this will happen. It's not too late. It's never too late.

This book is dedicated to that change. I believe the world will change one person at a time. It's that principle of one who touches one who touches one who touches one. Will you be the one that I touch who will go out and touch another? That is my wish with this writing, for one to touch one who will touch another.

I see churches, upon churches, upon churches filled every Sunday with people worshipping and singing praises to our Lord. I see men of God preaching the word of God to these same people, but yet we still walk around with unforgiveness, jealousy, envy, hatred, and anger in the world today. Inside of our Churches, we breed the worst intolerance. There are religions that will not even tolerate another religion.

We fill arenas, stadiums, and concert halls with tens of thousands of people night after night after night, to listen to preachers preach the word of God. People come down the aisles in waves when the preacher gives the altar call, but still the world does not change. There is hunger, poverty, homelessness in every city in America. People are hurting and in desperate need all over the world. Why?

Why do we choose to say that we believe in God, but yet, we choose to live our lives so far below the word of God? Why do we live our everyday lives, the Monday through Saturday life, so far below God's standards? Why does the world not change?

People attend Church on Sunday for a multitude of reasons. We attend church for a few hours every Sunday to fulfill an obligation, to say to ourselves that we are doing the right thing, so that we can make ourselves feel good, to be seen by others, or because the wife made me.

Who do we think that we are fooling? One hundred and sixty-eight hours in a week and you think spending two or three hours a week in church is all God wants? Why do we think that we can please God by giving God the leftovers of our lives? Is everything else we do really more important than God?

In America, four out of ten people spend their Sunday morning in a Church. People attend Church for every other reason than to build a relationship with their heavenly father.

For a few hours on a Sunday morning, people change their behavior to what they think God would like their behavior to be. But as soon as the service is over and they leave the building, they go right back to being that same person they were before they entered church just a few hours before. No repentance here.

People leave church and cuss. People leave church and go have a drink. People leave church and gamble. People leave church and still dislike their neighbor. People leave church and still harbor grudges. People leave church and still have deep hatred in their hearts. People leave church jealous of the very same people that they were just worshipping with.

People leave church carrying their same mess with them. People leave church exactly the same person as when they entered that morning. No repentance. No change. No true worship. No sincerity to find God. For the majority, we leave church every Sunday still carrying the same sin with us out the door.

How can this be possible? The reason is simple, because we come to church on Sunday for all the wrong reasons. There is no purging today in the body of Christ. There is no renewing of the mind. There is no made-up mind. People in church on Sunday have become lazy. We have become complacent. We think that we already know everything. We come to church for a feel good not because we want to do any work, especially when that work has to do with ourselves.

We come to church for the atmosphere, for the singing, for the show, because our friends are here, because I'm keeping my wife off my tail, because I like how the preacher preaches, because I need to be seen, because my parents made me. We come to church for every reason, but the right reason.

We bring sin into the Church with us on Sunday and we leave Church on Sunday carrying that same sin right out the door with us. We know no repentance.

We should never be the same person coming out of Church on Sunday as that person who went in.

Some people cannot even get out of the building before they start spreading rumors and gossiping about the people they saw at Sunday Service. Who do you think that you are fooling? Not God!

Churches are filled to the rafters with people who think that a couple of hours on a Sunday morning is all it takes to get into Heaven. They sing the hymns. They read the word. They can even quote some scripture. They might even give a tithe, thinking that they have done their duty for the week. Let me ask you a question: Are you singing about a Heaven that you might not even be qualified to see?

So many people are going to Church who have not seen Jesus in many, many years. So many people are going to Church every Sunday not knowing the love of God. So many people use their bible only as a fashion accessory. So many people today who have no relationship with the Father, or the Son, or the Holy Ghost.

So many people in the world today have a religion but they do not have Christ. They can tell you all about their religion. They spend lots of time studying their specific religion. They can tell you every custom. They know every holiday. They know all about religion, but they do not know Jesus. Because when you really get to know Jesus, you discover that Jesus wants nothing to do with religion.

Jesus did not die on the cross so that you could have your particular religious beliefs. Jesus did not die on the cross so that you can have your favorite, manmade denomination. If only the Church today and especially church folk could get this one fact. This is and never will be about your denomination.

Jesus died so that I might know Him. Jesus died for a relationship, a relationship between God the Father and you and me; an intimate, personal relationship. Jesus died on that cross so that we might know the power of His resurrection. Jesus died for people, not for religion. When will all these different denominations get and understand why Jesus died for you and me?

Almost everyone in the world today knows of God, but very few truly know God, and fewer yet have ever felt the presence of God, and even fewer yet hear His voice.

Everyone knows the name Jesus. Almost everyone knows His story. But so few of us who know the name really know the man. Everyone knows of Him, but so few ever take the time to really get to know Him. And even a smaller few of those who know Him will follow Him to become His disciple.

I went out to lunch today and I had just been seated at my table when I heard, from a few tables away, a woman say how much she loved Jesus. My soul soared. I always get excited when I am out among the world on a weekday and I hear the name of Jesus being spoken. How few times this ever happens when I am out and about. As I continued to eavesdrop on their conversation, what the same woman said next saddened me greatly. In her next sentence, she said the "S" word, and then a few sentences later, she said the "F" word. I have heard this same type of talk before and I always ask myself what church could this girl attend that would condone such talk. But we have church upon church upon church full of people every Sunday who know the story but have never met the man.

Let me ask you a question? If every church building was to disappear overnight, could you sustain a relationship with your heavenly father? Would you even know where to find him?

There is one more staggering number I want to give you here. I have said earlier that seventy-five percent of all Americans say that they are Christian. In 1997, that number was eighty-five percent. In the last twenty years, ten percent of the population has left Christianity. Ten percent may not sound like a lot, but that is ten percent of all Americans. That is a lot of people who once said that they believe now say they no longer believe in Christ. Christianity is not losing these people to other religions, but people are rejecting Christianity altogether.

People see church or religion as a place where they are told what they can and cannot do. The church is just another house full of rules. Church leaders are seen as bosses just barking out orders. They see the members of these churches as hypocrites. The church has these rules that the majority of the members do not even follow. Many of these so-called church leaders are not even following the rules. You try to beat me up with rules that you yourself do not even follow.

They see the leaders of the church as beggars with their hands out, only speaking about God for the money that they can get out of an offering plate. So many people are hurting and in desperate need, but we have church leaders who are living life large. Most people who will not enter a church tell me that the number one reason they will not come in is because all the church wants is their money.

Let me clear something up, right here, right now. God does not need your money. God does not need your money to get His work done. God needs you, not your money. We tithe to God because of our faith, because of our great love for our Lord. The God I serve isn't in need of anything. The God I serve and love is not a needy God.

God is "THE GREAT I AM".

I have not read the entire New Testament word for word, but I am pretty sure that Jesus delivered the Word of God, traveled from city to city, healed the sick, fed thousands, took care of all His disciples, and Jesus did all that without ever asking anyone for a nickel. I get so upset watching Christian television, always with our hands out. It's man who has made God a peddler. It is man who has made God a beggar.

The Church once again has turned so many people off and turned so many people away because all it talks about is money. Have you heard people say, "I love Jesus, but I really dislike Christians"? I hear ministers say all the time that "I need your money to take the word of God around the world." I have attended churches where passing the plate once a service is not enough. I have been to services where the pastor has announced a specific number that is to be reached and no one leaves until that amount of money is given. God is not taking hostages. Lately, I have heard pastors plead for millions because of shortfalls in their particular ministries. With all this talk about money in the church, all we have managed to do is confuse the masses about the truth in God's word. Confusion is a great tool of the devil and the devil is using it masterfully.

I am going to say exactly what God said to me in church one Sunday morning. If God truly means for your ministry to go where God wants it to go, then God will, no God already has, made the provision for you to be there. It's easier to beg for money than to seek the way of God. It's easier to beg for money than to live by faith. We like easy. To put yourself out there and live by faith; that's not always easy, but it is the kingdom way. Go spread the Word of God and stop making God a beggar.

God is no longer about the law. Jesus came and fulfilled the law for us. God is all about grace and mercy. We must stop beating people up with a law that we do not even follow. We must stop being so judgmental in our churches. Jesus accepted everyone. Why, in the very same buildings that we call God's house, have we become so judgmental toward the very same people that Jesus helped the most. It's amazing how quickly we become so high and mighty. How quickly we have assumed the roles of the Pharisees and Sadducees. We must teach all people about God's endless grace and God's bountiful mercy. We must teach people about God's saving grace and God's saving mercy.

We need to stop thinking that we are better than everyone else just because we wear a suit and tie and attend church on Sunday. No one is better than another. We have all; every one of us has sinned and fallen short of the glory of God. Jesus did not say "some" or "a few". Jesus came to save us all; every person walking on the face of this Earth. We have all sinned and fallen short of the glory of God. We must reintroduce people to the risen Christ and to the Kingdom that Jesus came to establish. We must introduce people to God's grace and God's mercy.

America is not turned off to Jesus. America is turned off to the church and all of its traditions; all of its hypocrisy; all of its judgments; and of course all of its talk about money.

Let me give you one more staggering statistic. Seventy percent of people who say that they are Christian do not attend Church on Sunday, except for the major holidays. Most people today feel that they do not need the Church and that the Church today has nothing to offer them. Let's be real; the Church today is not giving people a reason to need the Church.

People in the church have become more judgmental than ever before, driving many people away from Christ. There are divisions among all the different religions. Divisions in what we believe. Divisions in what the Bible says. Divisions between the denominations have become deeper and more rigid than ever. These divisions are manmade and only confuse people, keeping people away from God. Many people I speak with want to know Jesus but they are confused as to how. People think that they have to choose a denomination in order to find Jesus. Man has confused them by inventing all these different denominations and religions. They become so confused by all the choices that they get frustrated and give up on ever finding God.

I do not know a church that will say it, but many, many churches, many of the denominations today, practice exclusion. We only want to worship with our own kind. With people who believe exactly as I believe.

Jesus came to this Earth to reconnect the body of Christ - one body. Not to start your denomination.

When are we going to get it? When will we truly begin to understand the Word of God? There is only one God! There is only one Bible! There is only one faith! There is only one kingdom! There is only one way to get into Heaven! There is only one way!

We need to teach people about God's grace and God's mercy. We must stop preaching at people, stop confusing people, and start teaching people about the love of God, about the Kingdom of God. We have way too many preachers and not enough teachers. Preaching behind a pulpit on Sunday morning is the gravy, not the meat and potatoes of the gospel. Not enough of the leadership in our churches understands this fact. The "meat and potatoes" is in the going out among the lost. Going out and finding the lost. We must go into the world, go into this world today, right now as teachers of the Word of God, as teachers bringing the good news to a lost people. We must follow and begin to live the great commission that Jesus gave us. We must teach.

In the book of John, Jesus meets a man named Nicodemus. Nicodemus was a very religious man. Nicodemus was probably one of the most religious men of his day. Nicodemus had studied and was highly educated about his particular religious beliefs. Nicodemus knew every religious law and he worked hard every day to follow the letter of the law. Not the spirit of the law, but the letter of the law and the sad thing about Nicodemus was that Nicodemus really deep down knew nothing about the God that he worked so hard to follow. Nicodemus had no relationship with his Heavenly

Father. Nicodemus knew everything about religion, but Nicodemus knew nothing of the personal, intimate relationship that God so desperately desired to have with Nicodemus.

How many of us are just like Nicodemus? We know and even practice our religion with the same zeal just like Nicodemus. We know everything that there is to know about being a Baptist, being a Catholic, being a Buddhist, and being a Muslim. We spend years studying each of our own particular religious beliefs. We follow every law and practice every custom that we have been taught. But yet we have no relationship with our Father.

God made man for relationship, an intimate one-on-one relationship to be shared between you and God. This relationship is so special that no two relationships with God are the same. My relationship with God will never be the same as is your relationship with God. God desires that type of one-on-one relationship with every one of us.

Many people today believe that God has become irrelevant in our world. God's teachings are no longer valid. God's teachings no longer apply today. It's a different world. Most people today believe that they no longer need God in their everyday lives. Funny, how we need God when the emergency comes.

People in the Church live their lives just like the people outside the Church. Let me give you two examples of that fact. The divorce rate is the same in the church as it is outside the church: fifty percent. For preachers, their divorce rate is twenty-five percent. Let me give you one more statistic. Fourteen percent of the women who are having abortions say that they attend church. We no longer practice the word of God, even in our churches.

The world, and especially America, is in the mess that it is in today because the Church is in the mess that it is in today.

The unsaved world sees no difference between the lives that they are living every day and the lives that the Church folk are living every day. And you know, except for Sunday when we are filing into our Church buildings, they are right. Monday through Saturday, we live almost exactly the same lives. That reason alone is enough for people to see why they no longer need the Church. The Church has failed to do its part to show the world Christ, and so, the world and especially America is in the worst shape ever.

The devil lives on every street corner. Just visit my city, Atlantic City if you need to see a visual example of that fact. But if you were to look closely, there is almost a Church building on every street corner. Once again you can see this in my city of Atlantic City. So the question is, "How is it possible that the devil is living so large right next to a Church building?" In America today, we have plenty of religion. And we have plenty of religious people. But we have no Jesus. We have churches on every street corner but our hearts are far, far away from God.

We have confused religion with a relationship. We profess Christ but we do not possess Christ. We confuse religious ceremony with having a relationship with Christ. We attend church because it has become a show, because we have become part of that show, because church has become a spectacle, because church entertains us. Not because of the power and the presence of God. Not because we are there wanting God. Not because we are there waiting upon the Lord. Not because we want to repent. Not because we want to be made new. Not because we want to be filled with the Holy Ghost!

We attend church because we feel an obligation. We join a church because we like the way the preacher preaches; no conviction. We join a church because the choir sings my favorite church songs. My friends attend this church. It's the biggest church in the city. They asked me to be an usher. All the wrong reasons to attend a church on Sunday.

The gospel is not something we come to church to hear. The gospel is something that we leave church to tell. Who this week did you share the good news with? We stand around the water cooler at the job talking about the great football game that we watched on Sunday. Why is it that no one is ever sharing around that same water cooler the great preaching that they heard on that same Sunday? Is it that we put more value on a sporting event than we do on the word of God?

Some of the greatest opposition to change has always come, and will continue to come, even today from organized religion. This was true in the days of Jesus and it is still true; and I believe this opposition is even stronger today. The lines between Baptist and Catholic; Catholic and Muslim; Jews and Islam; Mormons and Methodists; these to only name a few; are more entrenched than ever before. My way is the right way and my way is the only way. It always has to be my way.

The major denominations preach every Sunday that we, as individuals, must change but they as a religion continue to go on business as usual - day after day, month after month, year after year, decade after decade, century after century.

Many churches and the organized religions are so steeped in tradition that they cannot change. They won't change. They do not believe that they need to change. They are so intolerant of others, so quick to judge others. I'm right. You're wrong. So hypocritical. Jesus came to save everyone. Let me say that statement again, because not everyone will get the major implications, and the major significance which that one statement has on the world. Jesus came to save everyone. No you were not the only one who Jesus came to give salvation to. Jesus came to save the entire world. Not just your denomination. Not just the people you fellowship with on Sunday morning. Jesus came and died to save us all.

So many times, I truly wonder if we are all reading the same Bible.

Not much separates the actions of the church from the actions of the world. Many people say they do not attend church because they see no difference. You know, there is one difference. The people living outside the church live in sin and they know it. The people in the church live in sin and they won't, for one second, admit the sin in their lives. Or worst yet, when church folk finally do admit the sin in their lives, they want to try and justify their sins.

Many leaders of these different religions really deep down see no reason to change. My religion is right why should I change? Is it not funny that these are the same people standing in the pulpit every Sunday preaching that we as individuals must make a change in our lives.

Our prisons are full to capacity. Seven million Americans are either behind bars, on parole, or on probation. 2.2 million Americans are either in a jail or in a prison. And we believe the answer to our overcrowded prison population is just to build more prisons. When are we going to get tired of business as usual and try a new solution; a solution that really works?

Crime is everywhere in our inner cities. Violence has become so bad in some cities that people are afraid to go out at certain times of the day, or to go into certain parts of their cities at all.

A woman is raped in America every forty-eight seconds. Drugs and alcohol are rampant in our society today and have almost become an acceptable part of our everyday lives. I hear people say that we just need to give in and make drugs legal. What right minded person can actually believe that making drugs legal is the right solution? If we are going to try a solution let's try one that we know is going to work. Gun violence in our inner cities is as much a part of life as eating dinner. People use profanity today as a part of their everyday speech without giving it another thought. Too many people cannot even form a sentence without using profanity. When did all this become acceptable conduct?

What this generation finds acceptable today becomes the norm for the next generation. Are we really happy with the things that we are passing on to the next generation?

Our country is as immoral as it has ever been. And as a society, we seem very proud of that fact. Immorality has become the biggest threat to our country today. Immorality is a disease spreading like wildfire. Pornography, gambling, casual drug use, alcoholism, violence, have all become rampant in every part of our society, as well as single-parent households, teenagers having children, and abortion. How far from God will we let our country go? Where are all the Christians? Where is everyone who is attending all these churches on Sunday morning? Where are you on Monday morning at the water cooler? Why is no one speaking up? Remember the word *tacit*?

Let me give you another example of our immorality and how we have become so proud of our immoral nature. On my drive to work this morning, I noticed a new billboard along that highway. It read:

"Life is too short
       Have an affair"

It was an advertisement for an internet online agency for married couples to have an affair. How low in the gutter have we gone? How low will we go to make a dollar? We are now advertising to married couples that it is ok for them to have an affair. Have we really become that selfish?

What has happened to the holiness of marriage? What happened to the sanctity of marriage? What has happened to the vows that we say to God in marriage? Do we not mean anything that we promise anymore? What happened to until death do us part? I know that we live in a disposable society. Is marriage just one more thing to us that has become disposable?

Do we really take everything in our lives as being only temporary? I can still remember a time when our word used to mean something. Not anymore! I remember, very vaguely, when a man's handshake and a man's name had value. That's long gone too. I was walking down the street in Atlantic City and I saw an advertisement for a night club that said, "Come celebrate your divorce with us." Is nothing permanent for us any longer?

What has happened to the family in America? What has happened to America? Do we really believe this is the right way to go? Do we really believe that things are better today than in past days? We are so proud of our sins. We brag about them. We wear our sin like they are a badge of honor. And then we wonder why it feels like God has turned His back on us, or that God is so far away, or that God never hears us.

Does anyone dispute the fact that the family, and specifically, the sanctity and the purity of marriage in America - how God sees and defines the marriage contract - are under serious attack? The devil has broken out every weapon in his arsenal to completely wipe out and destroy the family in our great country. The family was what our country was built upon and a strong family unit used to be the backbone of this great, God-fearing country. Do we not realize that once the family is destroyed in America, our country will not be far behind? The devil is trying to destroy this country by breaking its back!

We have a serious crisis of leadership in this country. We have a serious crisis in the character of the people who are supposed to be leading this country. Does anyone tell the truth anymore? Does anyone lead by example anymore? Do you trust the people who are leading this country?

Our leaders have a lack of morals. Our leaders have no integrity. Our leaders lie. Our leaders have affairs. Our leaders deceive and steal. Our leaders cheat. Our leaders manipulate. Our leaders are users and takers. It's to the point where you can no longer believe anyone just by what they say. We have to have visual proof. The people that we have entrusted in Washington to lead this great nation are leading us. They are leading us right down the road of immorality.

What is truly amazing to me is that if they do come clean - and trust me, most only come clean after being caught - all they want to do is justify their lack of morals and lack of integrity. Our leaders in this country want you to believe that a greater good is being achieved by what they do. Our leaders want you to believe that a little lie and a little deceit for the right reasons are ok. It's justified. Telling lies, cheating others, deceiving people, causing people to hurt is never ok under any circumstance!

When will we stand and say enough is enough? Or are we just as corrupt and immoral as our leaders? It's ok for them to lie because I'm a liar. It's ok for them to cheat because I'm a cheater. It's ok for them to hurt whoever because I do the same.

When will we become a nation of truth and honesty again? When will we stop doing business as usual and start doing business God's way?

Immorality has seeped its way into every part of our society and we just sit back and accept it. We need God to take the lead back in this country. If left unchecked, immorality never fixes itself it only goes from bad to worse.

We have been taught to fear the atomic bomb. We have been taught that, in the wrong hands, someone will blow up America and that will be the end of us. Wrong. It was not the atomic bomb that brought down the great Roman empire. Greed and its appetite for immorality which ultimately destroyed Rome. Fear the immorality that is consuming America. Immorality is the crack in the foundation that will bring down this great country of ours. Wake up, America!

We have war in many parts of the world going on right now. The threat of terrorism is more real today than ever before. The world is a scary place. Things are not better as far as man learning to get along with his fellow man. We are more intolerant, with a shorter fuse, quicker to become angry with each other, more so today than ever before.

As a country we talk about help, but are we really helping anyone? President's promise, Politician's talk, Preachers preach, and yet nothing ever changes. Everything just stays at the status quo. Everything just stays the same.

The better question is: Is anyone really trying to make the world a better place? Or is it just all talk? Is it just me or does it seem like everyone is just satisfied with the way that things have been going? Are we really happy with the country that America has become? Is it really easier just to keep going along with the flow? Am I the only one who sees that nothing ever gets fixed? The problems in this country that we have had for the last twenty five years; we still have today. Why is that? Does no one really care?

We talk about the poor. We talk about solving homelessness in this country. Do we really believe that these problems are getting better? Are we really reaching out to those who need the most help? It's Super Bowl week, and as I was driving home one afternoon, I was listening to sports talk on the radio. They have just built a new football stadium in Dallas where this year's Super Bowl will be played; 1.2 billion dollars was spent to build this stadium. Most of that was tax payers' dollars. My question for you to think about is: Could that amount of money have been used for a better purpose?

It is never that we, as a nation, do not have the money, the resources, the energy, or the talent to fix any problem. We do! We have everything we need to fix everything that we choose to fix. We can solve all the world's problems if only we wanted to. That's right; I said we do not want them fixed.

What happens is that we, as a collective people, turn our backs and we choose not to fix poverty or homelessness or the fact that people have no work. Instead of fixing or solving the issues that could change this world, we choose to spend 1.2 billion on a football stadium. We can fix the world's problems if we would only unite as a people to solve them. Unity is the key and we refuse to unite. We would rather bicker and squabble over our differences than unite to really fix anything. Just look at our politicians in Washington!

IN UNITY, WE CAN CONQUER ALL THINGS
IT IS IN THIS UNITY THAT ALL THINGS CAN AND
WILL BE FIXED

The world, as we know it today, does not work for the majority of us. Many of us live our lives in constant, everyday fear. Not knowing what tomorrow holds or what is around the next corner for us. So much loneliness in the world. So many people searching for answers. So much hurt. So many wounds that may never heal. No stability in our lives. No one is truly happy.

Contentment, restful peace, being at ease - do you know where these can be found? I believe that, deep down, most people know that there can be a better way. There is a better way. People want a better way to live their lives. People want contentment.

Everyone is looking for something else. Why am I here? What am I here for? What purpose does my life hold? I feel like I am here for a reason, but what is it? What will my life amount to? Will my life ever mean anything? So many people are looking for the meaning of their life.

Most of us want to do something meaningful with our lives. But what is it? The majority knows that their lives are missing something. The majority knows that there is a big hole inside of them. What is it that is missing? For many of us, we are missing contentment with our lives.

For all the hundreds of thousands of people who say they believe in God, or who say that they are Christian, people are not living their lives by what they hear or what they read about in the Bible. People today use Jesus to make them feel good for a couple of hours every Sunday. It's a commitment that they fulfill every week. But on Monday morning, they go right back to being that person the world really knows them to be. No one puts the words they hear on Sunday into practice on Monday at the office. Most people, if asked on Sunday evening, could not even tell you the message they had just heard that very Sunday morning.

Why do we choose to live our lives so far below the level of God's words? Why do we choose to be less than what we can be? Why do we choose to give God the leftovers of our lives?

Monday through Saturday, we give the world the best we have. We get up Monday morning, go to work and give our boss our hundred percent. On Sunday, maybe if we are not too tired to get up out of bed, we drag ourselves to church and give God a couple of hours of our time. Why do we give God our leftovers? The better question is: do we really think that God is happy getting the leftovers of our lives?

Why do we choose the dark over the light? Why do we choose to be deceived rather than live in the truth? How can we say that we believe on Sunday, but on Monday, live our lives so far away from the Word of God? What kind of impact is the church really making on the lives of the people attending these churches Sunday after Sunday?

Too many church folk, and I include the leadership of our churches, are too busy talking about faith and belief and not busy enough putting their own faith and beliefs into action. Our Church leaders lack influence because their own walk on Monday does not match their talk from Sunday.

My question is: are the leaders of our churches showing the example, living the example, being the example? To be a true leader of the faith, it is not nearly enough to only speak about the word. You must become the word. As a man of God, God lives inside of you. The kingdom resides inside of you. It is your duty to your King to show the world, every minute of every day, the character and likeness of your King.

In our world today, there are not enough examples of our Lord walking around outside of the church for people to see and feel. We must become the examples. We must be accessible for people in the world to feel, to touch, to talk with, one on one, as the examples of a living Christ. That is exactly why Jesus said for us to be in the world but not of the world. Too many church folk still think that they can be both.

Most church folk seem happy to hang out in their buildings, playing church. We have built these great church buildings to show off to the world. We put Christ on as a suit of clothes when we enter church, and then we take Christ off as we leave the building, leaving Jesus inside the building until the next Sunday when we put Him back on again. There is no example for the world there. It's that example that the world is dying to see.

One touches one who touches one who touches one. That is exactly how we will win the world for Christ. The world needs physical examples of Christ to touch. This cannot be done over the internet, or with a tweet, or on Facebook, or even with a text. The world is starving for the doers of the world, not the talkers.

Jesus came to this Earth, said what He said, did what He did, performed miracles, healed the sick, raised the dead, even raised Himself from the grave, so that we might know who Jesus was and by knowing who Jesus was and by knowing who Jesus is, we would discover who we are.

Too many church leaders are in the mode that we have built these multimillion-dollar buildings and now the people should come to me. These buildings have become our golden calf, our tower of Babel. God is not into the building. Actually, God wants nothing to do with your buildings.

Jesus appointed the twelve, designating the apostles, and He sent them out to deliver the gospel to the people. Jesus sent them out and He gave them all authority. Jesus gave to each of them His power. We must go out and find the lost sheep. How self-righteous it is of us to think that the lost sheep are going to find us.

I was watching TBN one evening and a fact came up that almost knocked me out of my chair. Fifty-three percent of all pastors in the United States do not share their faith outside of their building. How can you be a pastor for the Lord and not share your faith outside of your building?

I was in shock and in disbelief when I heard this number. We have become so prideful that we think the lost are just going to come running to us because we have these buildings. How arrogant are we?

We have church leaders wearing all these titles, believing that they have been saved, their entire lives. Is it possible to forget what Jesus has done for you? Is it possible to forget from where Jesus only Jesus brought you from? What happened to your relationship?

God gave all of us, every one of us, a testimony. God gave you that testimony to lead someone to salvation. There is a soul out there that only you can reach. How can you save that soul if you are unwilling to share your testimony? Was it really that easy to forget the testimony that God placed into your belly? These pastors who will not bear their testimony outside their buildings, or who will only share that testimony from behind their pulpit, should be ashamed of their actions.

There are many, many people who cannot receive salvation until you deliver that salvation to them. They may never come to us. We must bring the word to them. We must get out!

No wonder we can't win the world to Christ. How can we, when over half our leadership won't come out of their buildings and give a testimony for their Lord, when over half of our leadership has forgotten from where the Lord has brought them from, over half have forgotten what the Lord what only the lord could have done for them. No man did it! It was only God! How could you forget?

Jesus came and walked the Earth. Jesus came and touched people, walked among people, physically touched people. Jesus came and taught mercy, forgiveness, longsuffering, tolerance, meekness, goodness, but yet none of these exist as a rule in the world today. When will we wake up and live as Jesus taught us? What will it take for us to take Jesus back into the streets?

When Jesus came to Earth, He spent the majority of His time serving others. Jesus walked the Earth asking the people He met:

What can I do for you?
Can I teach you?
Can I heal you?
Can I feed you?
Can I free you?

People are so confused today. They know about religion but they know nothing about God. People today want to see God. If I could only see God, then that would clear up my confusion.

We, the majority of America who say that we know Christ, are not showing the world God. We are not being that living, breathing example of Christ that the world wants to see. We are not out among the people asking the one question that really matters:

What can I do for you?

People are tired of the talk. People are tired of being preached to. People want to see a result. People really do need help. People really do want to see God. People, deep down, really do want to believe. They want to believe that Jesus still lives.

God lives in each of us. We must show the world God. But we are living so far below the example that Jesus gave us. We are not showing people the characteristics of God. We cannot show people what we ourselves do not possess.

We talk love
But we do not show love
We talk forgiveness
But we do not forgive
We talk about giving
But we do not give
We talk about the poor
But we do nothing to help them
We talk about the homeless
But we walk right by them on the street
And this list could go on forever

Why is the world not changing? Because all we do is talk. We love to talk. We have become good at talking. Let me tell you what I have observed about our talk. It is your talk that makes you fake. For so many of us, and this includes the majority of our so-called leaders in this country, your talk does not line up with your actions. It is so much easier to fake your talk than to fake your actions.

We talk about giving, but we really give nothing.
We talk about forgiveness, but in all reality, we forgive no one.
We talk about sacrifice, but we refuse to compromise.
We talk about making the world a better place, but in actuality, all we really do is point fingers and place blame

WE TALK SO MUCH AND ACCOMPLISH SO LITTLE

Why does the world not change? Because we, as the body of Christ, are not out there doing the work that Jesus did when He walked the Earth. Jesus gave witness to the Kingdom of Heaven. Jesus came in a body to be the living witness. Jesus gave testimony. Jesus came to bring the Kingdom to the Earth. Jesus not only talked the word, but Jesus was the doer of the word.

We talk about the Kingdom but the truth is that the majority of us are waiting to die to see the Kingdom. It was God's intention all along for the Kingdom to be here on the Earth. Right now. When are we going to stop talking about the Kingdom and start living in the Kingdom today? The problem is that the majority of us have no idea how! How do I live in the kingdom?

Jesus came as love into the world and it is the love of Jesus that is going to save this world. When you learn about the love of God, you will begin to understand the Kingdom of God. To show the love of God to every person that you see, that's kingdom living. That is how you live in the kingdom. God is love and to walk in the kingdom is to give away the love of God which lives in you.

The world can continue to go down the same path that it is going on until we destroy ourselves and every living thing on this planet, which we will eventually do, or we can learn how to love each other as Jesus loves us - unconditionally, no strings, no questions asked.

Why is it that we will trust a man
But we can't trust Jesus
Why is it we will believe a man
But we cannot believe Jesus
Why is it that we will listen to a man
But we won't listen to Jesus
Why will we read and believe the history books that men write
But we refuse to read or believe the history book that Jesus wrote

So many people have become bored with the church because the church today does not address the problems of the people. The church today does not offer people in need any answers or solutions.

Jesus came to teach us and to show us what it is possible for us to do. When we are born again, we become brothers and sisters of Jesus. We become part of the family. We have everything inside of us that Jesus had. Greater works we shall do. We can change the world when we realize who we are and the power that lives inside each of us. We can make the world a better place for everyone.

A world that gives
Is better than a world which only takes
A world that forgives
Is better than a world full of anger
A world that heals
Is better than a world that can only hurt
A world that tells the truth
Is better than a world full of mistrust
A world which only loves

Is always better than a world full of hatred
A world led by the laws of God
Is better than a world of war and chaos

I hope the writings in this book will inspire people to get out and, through their actions, make this world a better place for everyone.

Let me give you one more question to think about:

What would happen to the Earth if you choose to live every minute of every day to the level of your belief and trust in God?

When enough of us become the love of God in the world, then all the problems of the world will disappear!!

As you read these pages, let me give you one more thing to think about:

All the ills of the world can be traced back to our unwillingness to sacrifice.

CHAPTER TWO

SEARCHING FOR A PLACE

CALLED "THERE"

Traveling around, trying to find love
My one and only dove,
Like an angel from above
But it's like an endless search
I've given up
'Cause I can't seem to meet any girl I can trust
All these girls seem so fake now
Felt love once,
But I'm so far away now
Try not to settle
But can't seem to see any way how
Loneliness is a hole,
And I can't see no way out
I've given up
Forget them, then turn them way out
Searching for love like looking for a needle in a haystack
Worthless little girls
I can never lay back
'Cause they buckle under pressure,
Never really got my back
So I sleep with them
Just to get my swagger back
Without feeding the need I lack,
Like a crack head without his crack
Not a sex fiend
But you get what I lack
So I'm going to do me
Till I get a room full of green
Without one once of greed
Freedom's all I need

Jonathan McGuckin

There is so much loneliness in the world today. I read this poem, written by a friend that I work with, and I was instantly struck by all the loneliness, the heartache, and all the pain that was in this writing. The morning I read this, I read it over and over again. I felt the pain in every word. And as I read the poem over and over again, I was filled with such emotion. I felt all the loneliness and all the pain because throughout my life I too have known such pain and such loneliness.

People are truly suffering and they feel that they have been abandoned. This poem talks to and about so many. And then it struck me how we think that we are the only one. No one else can possibly know how I feel because I am the only one having these feelings, going through this situation.

Nothing is further from the truth! So many people are hurting. So many people are hurting in silence. We smile on the outside, only to have a war going on within. We feel as if we are being torn apart on the inside. So many people are in such deep agony.

I felt that exact way once in my life, for a very long time. We suffer all alone. No matter how we try to surround ourselves with people, we still feel all alone. I was ashamed of my suffering and I did not want anyone to know. We have no idea that the sufferers in the world today are probably the majority of us in this world. I was just so stuck in this moment, the flood of all the pain from my past, as I read the poem over and over and over again.

Everyone is searching for this place called "there". It's this wonderful, magical, mystical, and very elusive place; we believe that when we get to "there", our lives will be perfect. We have this fantasy in our minds that when we arrive at that place called "there", our lives will be so full, so complete, and when we arrive, we will have everything we ever wanted or needed to fill our lives. Everything is perfect at this place called "there".

If I could only make a little more money, then I'll be there.
If I could get a better car, then I'll be there.
If I could only find a job, then I'll be there.
If I could get a better job, then I'll be there.
If I could find Mister Right, then I'll be there.
If I could only win the lottery, then I'll be there.
If my parents would only accept me, then I'll be there.
If I could only get over my addiction, then I'll be there.
If I could only find someone to love me, then I'll be there.

So many if's all along that road to "there". What is your "if"?

So much hope and so many dreams. All our answers to those dreams rest on us finding this place called "there". So much hope and so much confidence we place in people and possessions to help us find this place called "there". If only I could get to "there", this hole inside me would be filled.

We all know that this place called "there" actually exists. It's not a fantasy. It's not a dream. We really believe in that place called "there". "There" is a real place where all our expectations will come true. Our lives will be perfect when we finally arrive at that place called "there".

We all know of people who have gotten "there". We know that they have found the exact place that we are looking for. They look happy. They look content. They look like they are having that happy and wonderful life that we want. But are they really?

This has been my story my entire life, desperately searching for that place called "there". Constantly searching, everywhere I could, year after year, never giving up seeking contentment in my life. Searching for peace, and trying everything to find that peace. Constantly searching and trying every idea just to find a way for that war that was raging inside me to be over. I just wanted the pain to end, and for the sadness to stop.

Every year, I would tell myself that this was going to be the year. This year, I am going to find that place called "there". This is the year that I really will find happiness. This is the year all the pain goes away. This is the year that hole inside me gets filled. This is the year the emptiness goes away.

I would make goals for myself, make New Year's resolutions, and set up action plans for the upcoming year. All that just to find that place called "there".

More years than not, I would achieve the goals that I had laid out for myself. I would make more money. I would buy a new car. I would take the family on a great vacation. I would invest and save money. I would get healthy. I always got things done, but when I sat down and looked at my life, I still knew that something important was still missing. My life was never complete.

I had accomplished my goals but the pain deep inside me would never go away. I was never satisfied. Isn't that one of the things that the world promises us; satisfaction. We really believe that when we get to that place called "there", we will be satisfied. We will become content. Everything will suddenly make sense. We will find everything at the place called "there". All the things that will make our lives complete. Everything that we have been so desperately searching for will be found at that place called "there".

There was always this battle raging inside me. On the outside, I looked happy. On the outside, I looked successful. But inside, I was hurting and hurting bad. I was still not "there". For some reason, I knew my body was not whole. Not complete. I felt this big hole inside of me and the pain was still there.

Another year had gone by and I was still not "there". After years of doing this, of just going round and round, I began to feel as if my life was a failure.

Understand that, during all this time, I was married to a woman I loved very much. I had a son whom I would die for in a second. We lived in a beautiful home in the suburbs. My wife and I both had management jobs making excellent money with great benefits. We had money in the bank. We took nice vacations every year. We had what America would call "a great life". But for me, there was always something missing.

I knew I was missing something; something that would make me, as a person, complete. What that was, I had no idea. Nor could I find what it was. But I was never truly happy with the life that I was living. There was a pain I had inside me. There was a hole. And that hole was growing.

I was never raised to be a failure. My father was a very strict man. I had been raised under great expectations and failure was never an option. So this feeling that my life was failing weighed very heavily on me. I already had one marriage end in divorce; a major failure. So when my second wife walked out on me, after fifteen years of marriage, that failure was too much for me to bear. That was six years ago when I tried to commit suicide for the first time; all because I could not find that place called "there".

When that suicide failed, I gave up on life. We usually give up on life when we come to that painful realization that no one cares about us any longer. We tell ourselves that we have become unlovable. No one will ever love me again. I had arrived at that point.

I even gave up trying to find that place called "there". I just completely gave up. I no longer cared about anything. I know that there are a great many people who either have given up or want to give up on life. Loneliness, depression, nowhere to turn, no one to turn to, not knowing what to do, not caring about what to do. I had joined the land of the Zombies, just walking through the world, just going through the motions.

That's what I did for many years, going from job to job, paycheck to paycheck, sleeping, working, sleeping, working. If there were a lot of days where I didn't have to work, I would just sleep. I had given up. I considered myself a failure at life because that is what I had been taught to believe. I was a failure.

"Success"

My whole life, I had been taught one of two things. In this world, you are either one of two people. You are either successful in this world or you are a failure. The world only sees you as one of two ways. There is no other way for the world to see you. You are one or the other.

My father had raised me over and over again to believe this exact philosophy on life; success and failure. This was the way my father judged me and in my father's world, there was only one option. Success was the only option. There were winners and losers and his son could never be a loser.

My biggest failure in life was that I could not keep a wife. My mom and dad were married for forty-five years until my mom passed away. There was no room in my father's world for a son who was divorced twice. To my father, that made me a failure.

Of course, my divorces were not my only failures in my father's eyes. There were others. Not as big, but they were failures in my life all the same. Many of these failures having to do with not doing what my father had expected of me to accomplish. All I ever wanted so much was to please my Dad. All these failures were mounting up inside of me. These feelings of failure were the war that was raging deep inside of me.

The world traps you into this thinking and it does it early, that you are either a success or a failure. This is exactly how the world puts you into bondage, exactly through this way of thinking. We are brainwashed into accepting and then passing along to the next generation, this winner and loser mentality. That's how you become a prisoner of the world. You buy completely into this belief of success and failure. And of course, which of us could ever be a failure?

How does the world measure success?

Success in the world is totally dependent upon what you possess. You become the sum total of your possessions. And if you have less than me or if you have nothing, then you are a failure. Think about that. How do you define success? Money, cars, women, jewelry, bank accounts, title, job, houses just a few of the ways that success is measured in the world.

We look at people whom we really do not even know, but we judge them as a success or failure just by what they possess. He who has the most must be the most successful. But is that statement really true?

When you have totally bought into the world's way of thinking, when you have completely become a prisoner to the world's system, when your entire life is built around what you possess, then the world will set you up for the biggest lie of them all:

SUCCESS = HAPPINESS

WHAT A LIE!!!!!!!

How many of us completely believe this equation? How many of us have bought - hook, line, and sinker - into this way of thinking?

Here, I have another equation for you:

POSSESSIONS = HAPPINESS = SUCCESS

THIS EQUATION DOES WORK, BUT IT ONLY WORKS FOR A MINUTE.

This second equation is only a temporary fix. As quickly as you buy it or gain possession of it, you lose interest in it. Then you have to have a newer one, a bigger one, a better one, a faster one, a younger one, a blonder one, more than one. The fix that we think will fix you for life only fixes you for a minute.

The only solutions you can get from the world are temporary. They may fix your want, your need, your heartache, your emptiness, but only for a minute. The world has you trapped on a treadmill that will never stop, but someone does keep turning up the speed a little bit at a time.

How far will you run? How fast will you run? And for how long will you run? We will run from one possession to another, from one woman to another, from one fix to another, from one scheme to another from one drink to another, from one high to another. How fast will you run? For how long can you run?

After you buy that brand new, shiny, beautiful car, once you get over that initial excitement of that brand new, beautiful car, once that new-car smell has evaporated from your nostrils, after you have driven all your friends around in that brand new, beautiful car, then you will find the hole inside you still exists. Your life is still not complete. That brand new, beautiful car with all its fancy gadgets, with all its bells and whistles, did not fill the hole inside of you. That new car only satisfied you for a minute.

And when you find that possessions do not fill the hole, many of us turn to drugs and alcohol to fill the emptiness in our lives. The world tells you that drugs and alcohol will numb the pain that we feel inside of us. We do all these things to ourselves to try and cover the hole. To try to fill that empty spot that we have deep inside of us. But we still cannot find that place called "there".

Jesus tells us:

And Jesus said unto them, "Watch out! Be on your guard against all kinds of greed;
for a man's life does not consist in the abundance of his possessions." (Luke 12:15)

Let me give you a new equation:

POSSESSIONS = SUCCESS = HAPPINESS ≠ THERE

But I do have great news. Now I can tell you how to find, and how to get to, that place called "there". I found the way to "there". Fifty-four years of searching, right in front of me the entire time.

I tried, over and over and over again, to find my own way there. I tried my own way, my own will. You cannot find the way there on your own. God is the only way to "there". Jesus tells us, "I am the way, the truth, and the light" (John 14:6). God tells you, "I am the way to that place called there."

Pick up the Bible. Read the book. This is the road map. The Bible contains the map that shows the exact location to that place called "there". Your soul is what has been empty inside you. Your spirit has just been lying inside of you, waiting for a breath. Your soul is the hole that you have been unable to fill. The things of the world can never permanently satisfy the cravings of your soul. Nothing of this world can revive your spirit. This connection between your soul and your spirit is what your life has been missing.

Take the Bible and fill your soul. Fill yourself with the truth and bring your spirit back to life. Invite God in. Invite God to come and live in your heart. Let God send to you, His comforter, the Holy Ghost. Let the Holy Ghost come into your life, and show you the way. God will fill your life and you will never feel empty again.

Let the Holy Ghost into your life and fill your entire body. Your search for that place called "there" will be over for good. God is the difference. God is what has been missing in your life. God will come and fill that hole. Nothing of the world can give you what God can give to you.

All the possessions, all the drugs, all the booze, all the women, all the wealth, all the fame, all the fast cars, all the so-called fun of the world, will only fill that spot, that hole, that used to live inside of you for a minute.

God will come and fill your life for eternity. God will give you things the world can never give you. Agape love, peace, and joy are all free gifts from God. God will complete your life. It's God who fills your life with meaning. This was everything that I had been searching for, year after year - everything that I knew that I had been missing.

I am now full. I am missing nothing. God came in and made my life complete. God gave me a reason to live every day. The world only gave me a handful of empty promises. The world put me in bondage. God gave me freedom.

Right now, I only want more of God. To continually walk in His presence and every day to learn more about my Lord. In 1 Corinthians 12:31, the Apostle Paul writes, "I come to show you a better way." God came into my life and God has definitely shown me a better way to live.

Where once my life did not work and my life had no meaning, now God is in control of my life, and for the first time, life makes sense and I look forward to every day. God has taught me how life can and does work. God has given me purpose and destiny - a purpose for my life that I have been searching for my entire life. Only God is capable of doing that, Only God.

I vow, for the rest of my days on this Earth, that I will serve my Lord. These days are no longer mine. Each day belongs to God. It is only because of God's grave and the mercy of God that I am still here today writing His words. These days, I belong to God and I will serve Him mightily

CHAPTER THREE

WHY DO BAD THINGS HAPPEN?

THERE IS NO PROMISE TO BE HAPPY HERE ON EARTH, BUT JESUS PROMISES ETERNAL JOY IN HEAVEN

PEOPLE ASK THIS QUESTION ALL THE TIME:

If God is so wonderful, if God is truly such a loving God, then why does God let all these bad things happen? Why would God let bad things happen to the innocent?

So often, the individual asking this type of question is asking such a question to justify their own disbelief in God. They are looking for one more reason to justify, in their own mind, why they should not believe. Many times, they use this question because they think that they will trip up or stump the person who is trying to witness to them about Christ. For the most part, the person using this question has become bitter about the circumstances of their own life and they are really looking for someone to blame for what has happened to them.

Let's first start with this statement:

God does not just let anything happen. If God did do it, then there is a plan. There is a purpose. There is definitely a reason. God always has a master plan. God is the author and the finisher. God has a plan for our lives. Most of us will not submit to God's plans. Our minds may never fully understand the plan that God has for each of us. But God definitely has a plan.

I am also here to tell you another startling fact. Almost all the pain, almost all the misery, almost all the heartache, almost all the suffering that happens today in the world is caused by you and me. Yes, by us. The pain is caused by our own inability to sacrifice. The suffering is caused by our own inability to seek compromise. The heartache is caused by our own inability to love each other unconditionally.

We make the choices. We make the decisions. We decide every day how it is that we want to treat each other, how we are going to deal with each other, how we are going to live with each other. Man, throughout the years, has come up with some pretty despicable ways in which we choose to deal with and treat each other. Man, left to his own device, will come up all on his own with many of the ways that we chose to deal with each other on a day by day case by case basis.

What are some of those ways that we have come up with to deal with each other every day? Well let's see we have come up with rape, murder, robbery, assault, torture, drunkenness, slander, backstabbing, forcing our own will upon another. It seems as if we like and have come to accept the overall violent ways in which we seem to deal with each other every day. Our society today accepts all the violence as just part of the everyday living experience.

Let me make one thing very clear right now. God is not into these things and God has nothing to do with these acts and many more the hideous ways that man has invented to interact with his fellow man. This is how we have chosen to deal with each other on a daily basis. We choose to use these acts to deal with each other every day. These despicable acts, each and every one, are a manmade invention that has come out of a mind that is unwilling to sacrifice, a mind unwilling to compromise. A mind that is unwilling to live a life devoted to love first.

People often ask about the innocent. Why would God let bad things happen to a little child, or to a newborn baby? Or even to a child not yet born? Many of these innocent children get caught up in the same mess that we get our own selves into. These children get caught in the decisions that we make over our own lives. Decisions we make without ever thinking about consequences. Sometimes yes, God does take a child.

There is an ultimate plan, a higher plan. If it is the hand of God, then God has a reason. We may never know why, but God always knows and has a reason why.

Believe me when I say this: each of us chooses the life that we live. We make the choices. If we chose to abuse ourselves with drugs and alcohol, if we chose to abuse ourselves with tobacco, if we continue to abuse ourselves with unhealthy habits and unhealthy lifestyles, then these choices and the consequences that follow are ours and ours alone.

It's the free will of man, which was one of God's gifts to man, which has also gotten us into so much trouble. It seems as if man's choices, man's use of his free will, have been more of a curse than a blessing.

Every man is free to make all his own choices in this life. God will give you everything but God will not choose for you. You are free to choose, but you do not get to choose the consequences of that choice. Every choice has a consequence. Every choice causes a reaction. We do not spend enough time thinking out the consequences of our decisions. We never think about the effect that our decision will have on others. We never think about how the ones that we say that we love the most will have to share in the consequences of our decisions; even the innocent.

Bad things happen most often because we want to choose. We want the control, all the control. We want to control every move of our own lives. Every movement, every decision that we make has a consequence. Most often, we have no control over the consequence of our decision. We control the decision, but we have no control where that decision will ultimately take us.

And where those decisions take us, the consequence of that decision is often life-changing. Those consequences might be ok if they only affected our lives, but those consequences quite often have a ripple effect on a multitude of other lives. It's sad when our consequences affect the innocent and even sadder when those consequences hurt the ones who we are supposed to love.

God gave us free will because God wants us to take that free will and choose to love Him. Whatever we choose, God will allow. Whatever direction we choose our lives to go in, God will allow. God's greatest hope is that we will choose to love and to surrender our lives to follow Him, but that has not been the case for many of us. Left to our own desires and decisions, we can and will get ourselves into some really messed-up situations.

What gives God His greatest joy? When you take your free will and choose to love God with all of your heart, all of your mind, and all of your soul.

Hurricanes, tornadoes, earthquakes, wildfires, floods, most and many of these are caused because we have mistreated and abused the Earth that God has given to us. It's easy to blame God for all the bad that happens to us, but once again, it's about the choices that we have made and the choices that we will continue to make which cause us the most harm.

It was always God's original intention for us to live in the garden, the Garden of Eden, and we were to never die. Death was never a part of God's original plan. Sickness was never a part of God's plan, either. It was God's intention for us to live in perfection and to live forever as his children:

In the beginning, God made the Heavens and the Earth and God saw everything that he had made and behold it was good. (Genesis 1:31)

The penalty for our sin is death:
Wherefore, as by one man, sin entered into the world, and death by sin; and so death passed upon all men, for that all have sinned. (Romans 5:12).

When Adam sinned, death became part of life. But even in death, man has choices. So much of death, the way that we die, we like to put the blame on God. It's easy to blame God. Make God the scapegoat for our decisions. It's convenient and blaming God gets us off the hook. By placing the blame on God, we are not forced to look into the mirror to find who really is at fault or who is really responsible for the death that we have caused. By placing the blame on God, we are not forced to own up, or even find out, who the real person is that has been making all the decisions for the life that we are living and the death that we are causing.

I know what you are thinking right now, "But I have not or I am not causing anyone to die." Are you so sure about that? What decisions are you making over your own life or the lives of others that may be causing their premature death? But because we can blame God, use God as our scapegoat, we can walk away guiltless, with a sigh of relief, thinking all along in our minds that this bad thing that happened was not even my fault.

People die and we say that it was God's will. You hear that all the time. It must have been their time. It was God's choice to take that person. But I want to caution you that many of the things that we want to blame God for, God has no hand in. God never had anything to do with it at all. Why, are we so fast to blame God and the Devil gets off scot free? I never hear anyone blaming the Devil for all the bad that happens in the world today.

People smoke and wonder why they get cancer
People fill their bodies with greasy fast food and wonder why their arteries are clogged
People stay angry their entire life and wonder why they have heart attacks
People work long hours, with little rest, under great stress and wonder why they have a stroke
People worry themselves to death

We drink, we smoke, we do drugs, we refuse to exercise, we eat horrible things, we worry constantly, we put ourselves under great stress, we do not rest properly, and then we wonder why our bodies fail us.

I heard Pastor John Hagee say it best. We work and ruin our health to make a boat-load of money. And then we are forced to spend the boat-load of money to regain our health because of the work we did to make the money. Tell me the logic in that!

I was flipping through the television one evening and a news story struck my interest. Another young man had been stabbed to death and his parents were being interviewed on the news program. The young man's father while being interviewed by a reporter was mentioning how wonderful a young man his son was and that it must have been God's will for his son to be taken so early in his life.

This was not the will of God. This was one man choosing to exercise his own free will over another man. A man chose to kill another man in an act of senseless violence. It is never God's will for us to act in sin. God will never use sin to achieve His will. God hates sin. God hates the sin but God loves the sinner. Once again, it's easy to place the blame on God for things that we cannot understand.

God does not have a hand in many of the things that we want to blame God for. Car wrecks, all the senseless acts of violence that we force upon each other. Child abuse, domestic violence, rape, murder, and many of the diseases that are found on the Earth today, God never had a hand in. Heart attacks, strokes, cancer, AIDs, most of the terminal diseases, depression, mental disease, and the list could go on and on and on, were never meant to be a part of God's great creation.

As I have said before, even death was not a part of God's original plan for man. God created you and me for Himself. God desired a family and God created you and me in His image. God wanted people in His own image that He could have a personal, one-on-one relationship with. And that relationship would go on and on and on and on.

It was God's intent for us to live with God, for us to walk with God, for us to enjoy God, and then for us to enjoy the garden that God created for us, forever and uninterrupted. God desired such a permanent, personal, loving relationship with man, and we were meant to live forever.

But because of a man's bad choice, we lost all our rights to the garden and we have been living in imperfection ever since. Sin broke that permanent relationship that we were to have with God. Sin came about because of the free will that God had given to man.

But don't think, for one minute, that you can put all the blame for everything that has happened on Adam. Yes, Adam did commit the first sin; the original sin. But every one of us has had the same choice, and given that choice, we have all chosen sin. Every one of us has made horrible choices. We have made the choices. We made the choice to live in sin. We have even made choices that have cost the innocent their very lives.

God allows you to make the choices. God will give you everything but God will not choose for you. God lets you make every choice - from what type, if any, relationship you want to have with Him to exactly how we want to treat each other. Right now, at this precise minute, you are as close to God as you choose to be. But you choose. God always gives the choice to you. It's always your free will.

WE DO HAVE A CHOICE, BUT NOT WITHOUT SOME AGONY   -- JOSEPHINE HART

How do we want to treat each other? It is exactly through those choices that the majority of all the bad things that happen to us come from. If left up to our own device, to our own thoughts, our own actions, it is in the way that man chooses to interact with other men; it is in those thoughts that we can come up with some really horrible, some really despicable ways to treat each other.

Poverty, war, homelessness, murder, rape, physical and mental torture, these were never to be a part of God' plan. To see the evilness that man can come up with, just look back into the history books; the sad part is that many of these evil acts were done in the name of religion.

The worst choice that we make is thinking that we can live our lives apart from God. That's the answer to the question: why do bad things happen? Because we think that we can control of our own lives. We really believe that we can make all the right choices. But what happens the minute things go wrong? We start to blame God. We blame God when the decisions that we made don't go the way we thought they would. Why, God? How could you let that happen to me? I don't understand.
Why you would do that to me? Why, God? Why?

We want to blame everyone and everything except for that person who made all those decisions: you. Taking personal responsibility and taking the time to think every decision through are traits that most of us do not possess.

We love to play the "WHY" game. Why did this happen? Why did that happen?
Why? Why? Why? We really think that we deserve an explanation for everything.
So many of us go to the grave carrying the all the whys of the world with us. It's when you think that you know better than God it's your vanity that demands an answer from God. When you put all your faith and trust in God, when you have

truly surrendered your life to the Lord, you never have a reason to ask why. God is in control. Trusting God will always require that you have some unanswered questions in your life.

I lay my "why"
Before your cross
In worship kneeling,
My mind beyond all hope
My heart beyond all feeling;
And worshipping,
Realizing that I
In knowing you,
Don't need a "why?"
- Ruth Bell Graham

In the book of John, there is the story of Lazarus. In the story, Lazarus becomes very ill. Lazarus's sickness eventually leads him to his death; but we who know the story, know that Jesus comes and raises Lazarus from the dead. We have all heard or read this story many, many times. But today, I want us to look at this story from a different angle. There is something much deeper going on in this story that I would like for us to explore.

This is also the story of two sisters, Mary and Martha. It is really their story that I want us to look at today. It is the story of the two sisters' struggle. It is the story of one sister and her wondering why. It is their struggle with their faith and their ability to completely trust their Lord that I want us to study and delve into a little bit deeper.

We can all easily relate the two sisters' lack of faith to our own shortsightedness and our shallow faith when bad things happen in our own lives. It is through this story of Mary, Martha, and Lazarus that we will learn one of the reasons why God does sometimes allow bad things to happen in our lives - even bad things to the people whom God says that He loves.

So why does God let bad things happen? Why did Jesus let Lazarus die? And Jesus did let Lazarus die. Jesus knew full well that Lazarus was sick. Mary and Martha had sent word to Jesus when Lazarus first took ill. But when Jesus received the word of His friend's illness, what did Jesus do? Jesus chose to stay exactly where He was. Not just for an hour or for another day, but Jesus remained where He was for another two full days.

But when Jesus heard it he said, "This illness does not lead to death. It is for the glory of God, so that the Son of God may be glorified through it." (John 11:4)

Jesus loved Mary. Jesus loved Martha and also did he love Lazarus. We know that Jesus loved this family because it is written so in the scriptures. When Jesus saw Mary weeping, He was deeply moved in His spirit and greatly troubled. These feelings of Jesus are also noted in the scriptures. So if Jesus felt this way toward Lazarus and Jesus felt this way towards the sisters, then why not, the minute when Jesus received word that His friend Lazarus was sick, did Jesus not rush immediately to His friend's side?

This is exactly what we would do. We hear about a close friend, someone we care for very much, quite possibly someone we love deeply - we get news that they are very sick, maybe even close to death, and we drop everything and rush right to their side. But you see, Jesus knew the big picture. Jesus knew the entire picture. Jesus could see everything in that picture and Jesus already knew the end of the story; just as Jesus knows the end to each of our own stories.

Jesus told His disciples, even before they left the city, that their friend Lazarus was only asleep:

Jesus said unto them, "Our friend Lazarus has fallen asleep, but I go to awaken him." (John 11:11)

Jesus knew of the greater glory that was to come by Him waiting and then going later to Lazarus.

In our small minds that can barely comprehend from moment to moment, we have no clue about our future; any future. We just want things fixed in our lives and we want them fixed now. We receive a bad report and we just want the result changed in our favor and we don't want to wait.

Jesus saw and knew the entire picture. Jesus knew that, through the suffering of Mary and Martha, there was a greater glory about to be seen.

When we are suffering, we just want God to take the pain away and we want God to do it immediately. But there are times when we are going to be asked to endure some pain and suffering for our Lord in order to see God's greater glory in the end.

Jesus said to pick up your cross. Did you think that picking up that cross was not going to require some pain? Jesus endured pain, agony, suffering, and eventually, His own death for every one of us. How is it possible that the majority of us who are following God think that we will never have a day of despair? God does not promise us that every day on Earth will be filled with roses, but what God does promise us is that if we will follow Him with all of our being, then eternal life with God will be ours.

We, in our small minds, could never understand what Jesus was doing. Why would Jesus wait? Why would Jesus not drop everything and come immediately when He received the news of His friend's illness? Did Jesus really love Lazarus? In this walk of faith, and because you do trust God with your life, you will rarely understand everything that God is doing.

Trust in the lord with all your heart, and never lean to your own understanding. In all your ways acknowledge him, and he will make straight your paths. Be not wise in your own eyes;

fear the lord and turn away from evil. It will be healing to your flesh and refreshment to your bones. (Proverbs 13: 5 – 8)

So just like the disciples, Mary, and Martha, because of our shaky trust, because we cannot see the whole picture, because we always have to understand everything, we question God. Where are you, Lord? Why are you not helping us? Why are you letting our brother die? Why? Why? Why?

How often have we, or have we heard people, utter those same questions? We have become so weak-minded that we are always questioning and doubting our God. But Lord, if you had only been on time, then everything would have turned out fine. When are we going to learn that God is always on time? God's timing is always perfect!

THROUGH OUR SUFFERING, WE CAN RECEIVE THE GREATER GLORY FROM OUR GOD

The burden of suffering
Seems as a tombstone
Hung around our neck
While in reality
It is only the weight
That keeps the diver down
While he is hunting for pearls
               -- Jean Paul Richter

I was reading a book that was talking about storms and how different animals react to a severe storm.

A turkey will often run and hide. Quite often, they will run under the barn to hide. The turkey is hoping that the storm will just pass him right on by. Maybe there is even a chance that the storm really does not even exist.

On the other hand, when a storm is coming, the eagle leaves its nest and flies right into the eye of the storm. The eagle knows that the storm has the potential to carry the eagle higher and higher. The storm will carry the eagle to heights that the eagle, without the benefit of the storm, could never achieve on its own.

So many times in my own life, I find myself acting just like the turkey. When the storms of my life approach, I just want to run and hide. Many times, I do try and pretend that the storm does not even exist. I try to tell myself that if I pretend hard enough and if I can hide long enough, then maybe the storm will just disappear. Maybe the storm will just go away on its own. I won't have to do anything. If I just avoid the situation, maybe it will just go away all on its own. Sounds just like the turkey, doesn't it?

But be honest with yourself. How many times in your life has that really happened? How many times has the storm just passed you by without causing some havoc in your life? How many times were you really just left alone and the storm disappeared?

None. The storm never just passes us by, but when the storm does hit me with its full force and I find myself right in the thick of the storm, I find myself crying out to the heavens every time:

Why? Why?
Why me, Lord?
Why are you doing this to me?
What did I ever do to deserve this?
Why is this bad thing happening to me right now?

Then I begin thinking and my mind gets such crazy thoughts. I must have done something bad and this is the payback. God is putting me through this storm for payback.

The answer to this way of thinking is a definite no! The God that I know and love is not a vengeful God. God will never be less than what He says He is. I know that my God is love and that God does love each and every one of us, unconditionally. God's unconditional love never ends. God's unconditional love never fails. God's unconditional love fixes everything.

Jesus loved Lazarus. Jesus loved Mary and Martha. Jesus loved them all so much that when Jesus saw them weeping, He wept. Jesus loves us so much that our pain is His pain. Our sorrows are His sorrows. Our tears are His tears. We are so precious to God and God loves us so much that whatever we are going through, God takes that pain and suffering upon Himself. God is always more than enough to meet whatever our needs might be. That is exactly why God is "THE GREAT I AM." And God makes each of us another promise: God will never put more upon us than what we are able to handle.

And in this world that is so messed up with deceit, lies, and corruption, God is the only constant. When we can count on nothing else, we can always count on God. God will always be there for us. We must walk in faith, knowing that, whatever comes along our way, the outcome is always for the glory of God. Every step that we take, we must walk in trust. Trust in the Lord our God.

God always knows the bigger picture, not just the moment that we get so caught up in. This is exactly why:

1) Things will not always happen when we want them to
2) The outcome will not always be the outcome that we want, desire, or even think is correct

However, the timing is always right with God and the outcome is always God's will and to His glory. That is the exact reason why Jesus let Lazarus die. So that Jesus could raise Lazarus from the grave and the greater glory of the Father could be seen.

Jesus could have just as easily shown up at Lazarus's bedside when Lazarus first took ill. Jesus could have healed Lazarus at any time, but that was not the bigger picture. That was not God's will at the time. Just healing Lazarus would not have fulfilled God's bigger picture. We would not have seen the glory of God if only a healing had taken place. Jesus raised Lazarus from the grave, and therefore, God's greater glory was shown to all.

Can you or are you willing to follow the Lord when God's plan looks unreasonable to you? It often seems that, in our small minds, God always shows up late, if ever at all. It seemed completely unreasonable to Mary and Martha that Jesus would choose to show up late and let their brother die. They had no idea of the greater glory that was about to be shown to them.

What seems so often unreasonable to us is only God's perfect plan. God will test your obedience. God will test your faith. Sometimes up to the very last minute. God will test your faith. Will you be able to follow God when you cannot understand? It's our commonsense verses God's omniscience. Which would you rather have on your side looking after you and guiding you through the storm?

Also keep in mind that God may never explain why. That's your faith in God at work. You must put your faith to work. Part of your faith is in the knowing that God always has what is best for you in His mind and in His heart.

God wants you to soar as the eagles soar, higher and higher. God wants our faith and our trust to soar to an all-time high. That is the will of God for every man. For every man to walk in God's glory.

Be assured that if God waits longer than you could wish
It is only to make the blessing doubly precious
-- Andrew Murray

So many people today are searching for reason and purpose. I was one of those people - lost, afraid, not knowing, always searching. Searching for reason why I was alive. Searching for purpose for the life I was living. What is it that I am supposed to be doing?

The purpose of our lives, the reason why we were placed here upon this Earth, is to glorify God in everything that we do. We are to walk in holiness and for our lives to become one with our Lord and Savior. We are to become His witness in everything that we do. Be the witness here on this Earth that our Lord lives. Be a walking witness to the love of God. Show the world God's unconditional love. Become God's love and give that away to all of man. Stop *waiting* for the miracle in your life and start *being* a miracle to the people in your life.

The spirit himself bears witness with our spirit that we are children of God. That we are children of God, and if children, then heirs - heirs of God and fellow heirs with Christ, provided we suffer with him in order that we may also be glorified with him. (Romans 8: 16 - 17)

Look at that last sentence again: "provided that we suffer with him in order that we may also be glorified with him. For I consider that the sufferings of this present time are not worth comparing with the glory that is to be revealed to us" (Romans 8: 17-18).

For three months in 2009, I lived on seven dollars. That was all the money that I had. Five days of the week, I could get a really great meal at a place that we called Sister Jean's. I would sit at Sister Jean's and I would just listen. I would hear people ask the same question every day:

Why, God?

As I continued to listen to the other people waiting for lunch, I would hear them say the same thing many times: "I pray. I ask God to do things for me. But it seems as if God is never listening to me... Nothing in my life ever changes. I never get a response from God. Why should I not just give up? I'm still homeless. I have no job. Most times, I'm broke. Why does God leave me like this? There is no God, and even if He does exist, He never listens to me."

For most of us, the only time we seem to know God is when we need His help. We use God only when we need Him. We call God like He is 911. We try to use God like He is this magic genie. Maybe if I can get God's attention, then He will grant me my three wishes.

It's easy to praise God when everything in our lives is going great, but can you praise and worship God in the midst of your deepest storm? Can you sing praises to God when nothing is going right in your life? Most of us want God to help us, but we do not want to give up our worldly ways. We want God to help us, but we want to dictate the terms of that help.

When terror strikes you like a storm
And calamity comes like a whirlwind
When distress and anguish come upon you
Then they will call upon me
But I will not answer
They seek me diligently
But will not find me
Because they hate knowledge
And did not choose the fear of the lord,
They would have none of my counsel
And despised all my reproof
Therefore they shall eat the fruit of their way,
And have their fill of their own devices.
For the simple are killed by their turning away
And the complacency of fools destroys them
But whoever listens to me dwells secure
And will be at ease
Without dread of disaster. (Proverbs 1:27-33)

"FOR HEEDLESS FOLK FALL BY THEIR OWN SELF WILL, THE SENSELESS ARE DESTOYED BY THEIR INDIFFERENCE."

-- MOFFATT

King David tells the story best when he writes these words from God:

And call upon me in the day of your trouble;
I will deliver you, and you will honor me.
But to the wicked, God says:
"What right have you to recite my commandments?
Or take my covenant on your lips?
You hate my instruction
And cast my words behind you
When you see a thief, you join in with him;
You throw your lot with adulterers,
You use your mouth for evil
And harness your tongue to deceit.
You speak continually against your brother
And you slander your own mother's son.
These things you have done and I have kept silent;
You thought I was altogether like you.
But I will rebuke you and accuse you to your face.
Consider this, you who forgot God,
Or I will tear you to pieces, with none to rescue:
He who sacrifices thank offerings honors me,
And he prepares the way
So that I may show him the salvation of God." (Psalm 50: 15-23)

I know from personal experience that God is alive and God hears everything. I know that God lives today. I have seen God. I talk with God every day, and God talks to me.

It's never that we are waiting for an answer from God, but it is that God is waiting on us. The answer is that God is waiting on us to be ready.

"Ready for what?" you ask. Jesus stands ready to help each and every one of us but only if we will surrender ourselves to Him. We must surrender all of our mess to God. Not some of it but every bit of our mess. If we want God to really help, we must be ready to give everything to the Lord.

Our Apostle tells a story of a man who fell into a very deep hole. He yelled and yelled for the people from his town to come and help, but no one would come. Finally, in desperation, he cried out to God. "Help me, God. Help me." God came to the man in the hole. God told the man that He could definitely be of help to the man with his struggle, but God also told the man that He could only help if the man was willing to let go of some things. God told the man that He would throw down a rope and pull the man out of the hole, but the rope was only strong enough to lift two hundred pounds total. The man was definitely carrying too much weight. God told the man, "Let me know when you are ready and I will toss down the rope."

The man thought and thought. He really wanted to get out of the hole, but he was also really attached to some of the weight that he was carrying. The man thought and thought, and finally, he was ready to make some decisions.

"Ok, I'll let the cigarettes, the alcohol, the gambling; I'll let all those things go. I can give those things up pretty easily, but the partying, the staying out all night, smoking weed, sleeping with all the women I want, I'm going to hang on to those. I don't believe God. That rope will lift more than what he said. Ok, God, I'm ready; toss down your rope." The Lord threw the rope down to the man and God started pulling the man out of the hole. About halfway up the side, the rope broke and the man fell back into the hole.

"I told you, the rope will only hold two hundred pounds. Those two hundred pounds was also the exact weight of the man. If you are not serious about this, then I cannot help you. I told you exactly what I can do. You called me for help, but you want me to help you on your terms. I cannot help you that way. When you get serious about your situation, call me, but you will have to let everything go for me to help you."

How many of you does this sound like? We call God for help but we only want God's help if God will agree to help us on our terms.

The man in the hole thought and thought. "I really need to get out of this hole. If I don't get out of this hole this hole could end my life. Am I ready and willing to give everything up to get out of here?" The man continued to think. Finally, he realized that his only help was coming from the Lord. No one from his town, friends, family, acquaintances, no one was coming to his aid. Everyone whom he thought cared about him had turned their backs on him. It was only him and God. The time had come to surrender all.

Again, the man cried out to his Lord, "Ok, God, I now give everything to you, all the women, all the drugs, all the partying. You can take them all. Take them all from me. I surrender everything to you." It was at that point that the Lord lifted the man out of the hole.

Are you at that point in your life where you have nowhere else to turn? Have the so-called friends in your life turned their backs to you? Are you ready to give up that weight that you are carrying? The Lord is always ready, willing, and able to help you - whatever your situation, whatever your storm, no matter how deep the hole. It does not even matter how long that you have been in that hole. But you must be ready to surrender everything to God. You must surrender it all.

Why is surrendering so important? It will never be possible for you to change your life on your own. A new car, a new house, a new wife, a new city for you to live in only changes you for a moment. You can change the scenery. You can change people, places, and things, but you still bring the same old you. Changing the things around you will never be permanent because you have brought the same old mind with you. If your mind will not let go of your past, then you become stuck and it will not matter what else that you do; you will always live in your past. You cannot move into a new future by taking your old mind with you.

WHATEVER A MAN THINKS, SO HE IS

You must surrender your past, and then let it go. When you let your past go, you are creating space in your mind, space where God can come into and fill with your future. God will fill that space with your purpose and your destiny. Many of us are so full of our past that there is no room for a future. Look at yourself. You only have limited space within yourself. You must unload to reload. Unload your past upon God and let God take that newly vacated space and reload that space with your destiny. If you cannot let go, you will be forever stuck. Some people become stuck for their entire lives. They may be eighty years of age, but they have been stuck mentally at twenty their entire life. Transformation, restoration only happens in one's life when you can surrender. Let go and let God do His work.

Here is one of my favorite scriptures:

Therefore, if any man is in Christ, he is a new creation. The old has passed away; behold the new has come. (II Corinthians 5:17)

Will you let God come in and make you a brand new person? God is ready to help every one of us if we will be one hundred percent obedient to God's word, whether we agree with that word or not, whether we understand that word or not. We must walk in faith and know that the help that the Lord will provide will always be the help that we need.

Will you understand? No. But if you have to understand, then it's quite possible you are not ready to receive the Lord's help. Just obey the word!

If the largest part of your brain is reserved for all the things that you must understand, then your walk with the Lord will always be hindered!

We want to serve God and we want to understand God with our minds. That is our nature. But serving God is not a mind thing. It's a heart, soul, and spirit thing. It's a faith thing. Trade in all your questions for trust.

GOD WANTS EACH OF US TO LIVE OUR LIVES
THROUGH HIS PROMISES
NOT THROUGH HIS EXPLANATIONS

When we go to the Lord for help, we must always approach the Lord with a pure heart; with a humble spirit. This purity of heart is what keeps many of us from really ever getting to know our Lord and our Savior. We wonder why it always seems that God is not listening. God will not do all the work by Himself. You must want to help yourself. You must be willing to put in some work even on yourself.

You cannot expect God to lift you out of your hole when you are still up to your elbows in your own mess. Sin will build a wall between you and the help of God. Your trust in God must be unbreakable, undeniable, steadfast, and concrete.

If you truly want the help of the Lord, you cannot pray to God one minute and then drink, use drugs, steal, and lie the next. We must first repent (turn away from your old ways), then believe, then walk in faith, and finally, trust completely in the Lord. If you believe, you will see the glory of God. It is time for all of us to soar in our trust. It is time for us to soar as the eagles soar.

Belief - is the consent of the mind
Faith - is the choice of our will
Trust - is the commitment of our heart

While faith pleases God and gives us the victory that overcomes the world, heartfelt trust in God brings us peace as all our strivings cease and we simply rest in God.

The Lord wants us to trust Him with all of our hearts. The Lord wants us to trust Him always, even when you have no understanding. When we do not understand and we still choose to walk with the Lord, we then find ourselves walking in total trust and obedience. We never question. We never doubt. We only trust in God.

IF THE LORD SAID IT
I BELIEVE IT
AND THAT SETTLES IT

Even in the midst of our greatest pain and suffering, our focus - our only focus - must be on the Lord. As long as we choose to focus on any other thing in our lives, we will find ourselves lost and only feeling hopeless.

GOD DOES TAKE US THROUGH
TO TAKE US TO

Take a moment and really contemplate that last statement. It said that God takes us. God does not leave us. God is always with you. Whatever it is that you are going through, God is there. Right there with you every step of the way. God takes you. God never leaves us alone in the middle of our battles. It is we who chose to leave God. Even in that choice, God will not leave you. If you will only allow God, God will take you through to see His greater glory.

Many times in my own life, I have made the wrong choice and have left God's side. For many years of my own life, I blamed God for my poor decisions. I did not try to understand nor did I want to put the blame where it really belonged, on myself. I felt hopeless. I was filled with so much bitterness and despair towards life. I felt as if I had no future. I was completely miserable with life. There was no joy. No happiness. No fulfillment. No hope that things would ever get any better.

It is hope that will get you through the worst of storms, but you must know where exactly to place that hope. Many of us place our hopes in all the wrong things.

Your hope can never be placed in people, places, or the possessions that the world will place in front of you. The world sees hope as a feeling that what one desires will happen. You hope for the things that you want to happen. There are definitely a couple of major problems with the world's definition of *hope*.

The first flaw in how the world defines *hope* is that hope cannot be attached to your feelings. Anything that you attach to your feelings is about to go on a monster rollercoaster ride - up and down, up and down. You wake up in the morning feeling great, and the world is full of hope and you are on top of the world. Ten minutes later, you get a phone call; it's bad news. Your feelings plummet, you lose hope in the situation and everything is falling apart. Feelings up, Feelings down, all in the blink of an eye. Your life is as stable as a roll of the dice. How do you like riding the rollercoaster?

The other thing wrong with the world's definition of *hope* is that word "one". When you put all your hope into yourself, we have this great ability to let ourselves down. So after we have let ourselves down, we get this great idea that I will put my hope in others. My family will help me. I have friends who will come to my aid. How many, many times have you put your hope in others only to have that hope shattered?

Friends and family not only let us down, but they hurt us. So where can I put my hope?

In the Lord. Hope in the Lord is putting your total reliance on God's ability. We place all our hopes in God because God does provide His blessings and His provisions in our lives... We place all our hopes in the promises of God. God is a promise-keeping God. God will never let you down nor will God ever leave you or forsake you. No matter how tough you may think the times are.

Our hope comes from the cross. Our hope lives in the resurrection of Jesus Christ, the resurrection power of our Lord and Savior. Our hope arises and is given life from the fact that we know that, because Jesus rose from the grave, we as believers will also rise from our own graves. Hope in the knowledge of our own eternal life. Our hope lives in pressing towards the higher mark, pressing towards that higher calling of our Lord.

The absolute knowledge that we will rise from our graves and enjoy eternal life with Jesus, that is our hope as we go through the trials, the persecution, the mistreatment, the abuse, the suffering, the endless battles, the tribulations, whatever this world has and wants to throw our way.

Before I ever knew anything about hope in God, my future looked pretty bleak. My mind was so messed up and I was in such a state of confusion. I had lost who I was and what I was doing. I had lost everything. As I looked into my future, I knew that as long as things stayed the same, then nothing was ever going to change.

I hated to go to sleep at night because I did not want the morning to come, since I knew that tomorrow was only full of more misery and pain. When I finally would fall asleep, I did not want to wake up because of the pain and misery that I was about to face. I went through years of this - back and forth, going round and round, back and forth, fighting a war within myself, nobody winning, everybody losing.

I went to doctors who only gave me pills to try to take the pain away. I only became addicted to the pills. Things never got any better. Little sleep, no sleep, the war raging inside me was only getting worse. My life was so messed up and my only focus, the little focus that I had, was on myself. I found that life had come down to just trying to make it from day to day. And then life became about just trying to make it through the day. I worked hard at hiding my pain from everyone. No one ever knew. I was always terrified that someone would discover my secret. Someone would see the war raging inside of me. I was just so very tired.

Never make life-affecting decisions when you are tired. For one, you are not in control of your thoughts; the tiredness is in control. Your mind is in a fog and it is true that you cannot make a clear decision. The answer that I came up with to solve all my problems was that I was going to end my life. The tiredness had me believing that this was really an excellent solution.

The despair had become so great that there was not one reason I could come up with to continue my life. That was my first attempt to die. Somehow, I was able to pull myself together, and on my own, I survived the first attempt on my life. Yes, I did say that was my first attempt, which means that there is another attempt to come.

Did I learn anything from my first attempt? No!

I went right back to doing the exact same things over and over again that I was doing before; the exact same things. That's what we do. We know no other way. The world has us trapped, and when we are left on our own, we know no other way. We have no idea how to change the cycle of our lives. We just keep running the race; the exact same race. We just keep doing the same things over and over again. We know no other way.

It took five more years of going round and round again before I became tired, hopeless, full of despair, and at the end of my rope, again. I was losing my way, and then I lost my job. The straw that broke the camel's back. The night that I had lost that job, I fell asleep, and while I slept, I came up with the grand idea of how I was going to end my life this time.

I took all the cash that I had, packed two bags, and went down to the Greyhound bus station and bought a one-way ticket to Atlantic City. The plan my mind had come up with while I slept that night was to go to Atlantic City, have a great time, spend all my money, and when the money was all gone, I would end my life. That was my plan. Little did I know that God was already in control and it was God's plan for me to come to Atlantic City. God had already taken control and it was He who was leading and guiding me.

That day was November 12, 2009. That was the day the Lord said enough was enough. On that day, the Lord said, "Paul, you have run from me long enough." It took another two months before I realized what was going on. That day was January 7, 2010. That was the day the Lord led me to Sister Jean's, The Apostle, and on that day, I surrendered my life to God.

Often times, the Lord will put us into a situation where we have nowhere else to turn, a situation where we have nowhere we can go, a situation with no one else who can or will help us. I was in just such a place. I had no job, no money, no car. I was in a strange city where I knew no one. I had no friends. No family close by. I had nothing. I was stuck and I was about to meet the crossroads.

God will delay His response to our needs until we run out of our own resources. As long as we have our own resources, we believe that we are still in charge. We must be broken, completely broken, before we can be fully restored. I had reached my brokenness.

Sometimes, we must exhaust every other possibility before we will fall on our knees and humble ourselves in the presence of God. Before we will fall on our knees and cry out to God. Until we know that there is no other way, God will leave us to our choices. God leaves us to our suffering to bring us to such a point of desperation, so that God can teach us a very simple truth. So that God can show us a life-changing lesson. The lesson that God wants to teach is trust.

You must finally wake up to the truth and realize that your way does not work. I had to wake up and learn that my way did not work. I had now tried to end my own life twice because I wanted to do things my way. I had to wake up. I had to discover the truth. I had to find a new way. I had to change my life. My way was only going to destroy my life. God will always give you choices. God, right now, was giving me a choice. Choose life or choose death. It was my choice. It was my free will.

I did not understand everything but what I did know was that my life did not work. I knew that there had to be another way so that my life would work. I had tried everything that I knew. It was now time to give God a try.

God had brought me to a point in my life where I had to make a decision. I had a choice to make.

Choose this day life or death.
Choose this day the light over the dark.
Choose this day to follow the truth or live in lies.

I had a choice. I could choose to continue my life as it was, and eventually, I would succeed in my pursuit to kill myself, or I could choose to turn my life over to God and learn to live life anew. I chose God. I chose to trust the Lord. I chose to become obedient to the word of God. I chose to surrender.

Sometimes, this choice requires time and suffering, more so for some than others. We can be an extremely hard-headed group of people. The Lord wants to help all of us, but God cannot help you if you must control your own life and refuse to surrender yourself to Him. So many of us will not ask for help. We are such prideful people. Humble yourself before the Lord. Cry out for His help. Wipe away your pride and ask the Lord for the help that the Lord so desires to give to you.

I heard a story about a little boy who had a sandbox in his backyard. The little boy really enjoyed playing in his sandbox. On this day, the little boy was digging in his sandbox and he found a rock in the sand. No matter how hard the little boy tried, he could not dig up that rock. The rock was large and really buried in the sand. The little boy tried and tried, but to no avail. No matter what he tried, the little boy could not dig up the rock.

All of this time, the little boy's father had been watching his son. He watched as his son tried and tried but could not move that rock. Finally, his son, defeated by the rock, decided to come into the house. As the little boy came passing by his father, his father asked him how he was doing. The little boy told his dad all about the rock in his sandbox.

The little boy explained to his father that he had tried everything that he could think of to get the rock out of his sandbox, but the rock was stuck solid. The father looked at his son and said that was not exactly true. The little boy looked at his father with a puzzled look on his face. "What are you talking about, Father? I have tried everything."

The father looked at his son and said, "But you never asked me."

That's exactly what we do in our own lives. We try to do everything on our own. We exhaust every possibility that we can think of. We want to make our own decisions and come up with our own conclusions to the situations that we get ourselves in. We want total control of our own lives and we want no advice from anyone. We think that we have all the answers.

We do have answers, but more often than not, they are the wrong answers to our problems. The answer we come up with usually only makes the problem worse. It's that control that gets us into so much trouble. We have to make all the decisions, and then we wonder how we are in the mess that we are in. We are so hard-headed and so full of pride. It kills us to ask for help.

All we ever have to do is cry out to the Lord for His help. God is ready and more than able to help us in every situation. God is "THE GREAT I AM." God is and can be whatever you need God to be. God is always more than what we ever need for God to be. Thank you, Father.

As a good soldier of Christ, you must endure your share of suffering.
(II Timothy 2: 3)

Measure your life by loss and not gain,
Not by the wine drunk,
But by the wine poured forth.
For love's strength stands in love's sacrifice,
And he who suffers most
Has the most to give.

God wants people who have been used, hurt, and defeated. Why does God allow
bad things to happen? To build your witness, to strengthen your faith and to build your love for God, that's why. To make you a powerful tool to be used by your Lord. Your

power for and from God comes from your suffering. Your praise for God comes from your suffering.

My knowing that the Lord is alive comes out of my suffering. I know that my Lord lives today. I know and have felt the love of God. I know and have felt the peace of God. I know the joy that God has to offer. How is it that I know these things? I know what I know because I have suffered.

Out of my suffering, the Lord will get His glory.

For a child of the most high God, your suffering is never wasted. Through and because of your suffering, your faith is strengthened and built. God is bigger than your suffering. Call out to God and He will carry you through. Trust in the faithfulness of God and that God will work through your struggle to take you to your purpose and your destiny. Trust God that His purpose for your life is for your ultimate good and for God's eternal glory. We thank you, Father, for giving our lives purpose. Give each of us the strength to seek your purpose for our lives every day.

Thank you, Father!

How can you know that God is a deliverer, if you are never in trouble?
How can you know that God is a healer if you are never sick?
How can you know that God is a restorer if you were never broken?
How can you know of God's provision if you never need anything?
How can you know that God is leading your way if you are never lost?
How can you know what God will do for you if you never ask?

GOD WALKED ME THROUGH IT, AND GOD WALKED ME OUT OF IT!

CHAPTER FOUR

SO YOU REALLY THINK THAT YOU KNOW BETTER THAN GOD?

For the vast majority of the world's population, the answer to that question is a most definite yes! Yes, we do think that we know better than God.

You might be asking yourself right now, "How can I be so definite with that answer?" Let me ask you another question back. Who is in charge of making all the decisions in your life? Whose agenda are you following? Whose vision is leading your way? If the answer to all those questions was "me" or "my parents" or "my wife" or "my friends", then you do think that you know what is better for yourself than God.

The world that we all live in today is such a messed-up place. It has become so confusing, such a scary place, with more problems and obstacles in our way than ever before. For almost everyone reading these pages, we have all faced the difficulties that the world challenges us with on an everyday basis. We have fallen into these difficulties, and due to these difficulties, the world has even defeated many of us.

For these difficulties to give us a black eye or, worse yet, defeat some of us, this was never God's intention when God was creating the Earth. So what happened? What went wrong? How did the Earth go from what God said was very good to the messed-up place that we all know that it is today.

Can we all agree on one thing before I go any further? God did not create a messed-up Earth.

When God was finished after that sixth day with His creation, the world was far from the state that the world is in today. The Earth was a paradise and man was left in charge of all the things that God had created.

So how exactly did the world arrive at the messed-up place that we find it in today?

And an even better question is: why does the world stay in the sad shape that it is in? Why, as I am writing these pages on December 12, 2011, is the world more messed-up than ever before?

The answer is really very simple:

"WE THINK THAT WE KNOW BETTER THAN GOD!"

We think that because we do know better that we should have the right to make all of our own choices. We should be able to choose everything. We don't even consult God. We don't even want to consult God. We just go right on ahead like we know it all and we make all our own decisions. Take some time right now and think about your own life. Who makes all the decisions in your life?

Why is the family in America almost nonexistent? How has the family become so unrecognizable? Today, we have babies' mothers and babies' fathers, and for the majority, these people do not even live together. For the majority of these people, the only thing that they have in common is a child. Sex in today's world has become almost as commonplace as eating. The world has changed its view on sex because we think that we know better than God. Women have children and do not know who fathered their child. Men today will not take responsibility for children without a piece of paper to prove their paternity. Honesty and integrity in this country has been thrown away like yesterday's trash. Without honesty and integrity, we have lost commitment. The family in America has disintegrated right in front of our eyes.

How is it possible for this to happen?

Because we think that we know better than God.

We spend so much of our time, our energy, and our resources searching for things in the world. In the next chapter, I write about acceptance, but the approval of the world is of such dire importance to each of us. We want and need the approval of others so badly. Do you know that we search for things in the world that the world is completely unequipped and unable to give to us?

The world cannot give you approval.
The world cannot accept you.
The world cannot forgive you.
The world cannot love you.

The world cannot give you the things that it does not possess.

We want so badly for the world to give us things. But the world does not have the ability. The world cannot give you what it does not have. We search and search and search for what we need to be fulfilled, but the world cannot give to you what it itself does not possess.

The world cannot give you love because the world does not know love.

Only God.
Only God will accept you for who you are.
Only God can give you approval for the things that you do.
Only God can forgive you for what you have done.
Only God can forget everything in your past.
Only God can love you no matter what.

Remember always the one who is the true source. Always remember the one who is your only truth, your only way, your only light! God is the only source for everything that you have been searching for your entire life.

We go into the prisons and preach the word of our Lord. Every time we go, the Lord always gives me a word to speak to the group. I believe that God gives me these words for the different groups that we minister to because the devil has the word in such a state of confusion. The devil loves to confuse us with the words that we speak.

Do you know that God is the author and finisher of your faith? But the devil is the author of all confusion. The devil loves to keep us confused and if the devil was to have his way, he would keep us in that state of confusion for our entire lives.

How many times have you heard yourself say, "I am so confused"? That was the devil speaking right out of your mouth!

The words you speak control your mind and it is your mind that controls your body. So what you speak is exactly the life that you are living. It is during those states of confusion that we make so many of our bad choices, or worse yet, we ask the wrong people for their advice on how we should live our lives.

We waste so much time seeking other people's advice. What would you do if you were me? Why are we asking them when they do not know what to do with their own lives? We ask our divorced friend for marriage advice. We ask our friend who can't keep a job for career advice. We ask our friend who has had ten girlfriends this year for love advice. We are going to follow their advice when their own life is in such a state of confusion. What is it about their lives that we really think that they can lead us out of our fog? But we keep searching for the answers in the world. A world that cannot give to you what it does not have itself.

Maybe I can understand the asking of advice. Maybe. What I cannot understand is when we follow that advice. It is bad enough that we asked the blind to lead the blind, but it's even worse that we let the blind man lead us out onto the highway. Why are we always so surprised when that great piece of advice turns out to be the wrong thing for us to do? Some of us even took another's advice and that advice changed our lives forever. Most of the time not for the better, either.

Confusion.

For the vast majority of us, the devil uses your life just like it is a yoyo. The devil has your life going up and down, up and down. The devil controls the string to your yoyo and the devil has no problem with:

Bouncing you up and down like a rubber ball
Having you run around like a chicken with its head cut off
Controlling your mind, keeping it racing with a million worthless thoughts
Running you ragged
Keeping you hopelessly tired

How many times do you find yourself just worn out, completely dog tired? You wake up in the morning just as tired as when you first went to sleep. That's exactly how the devil works his confusion.

It takes a lot of energy to stay and live in the darkness. Just close your eyes and picture yourself right now in complete darkness. You are put in a room that is completely dark and you have to find your way out of the building.

You're bumping your head on things.
You're running into obstacles.
You're running into walls.
You're bumping into things, hurting yourself.
You become frustrated because you cannot find your way.

The darkness is eating your energy, your want, your desire, your will.

What does Jesus in the New Testament tell us about the devil?

THE DEVIL COMES TO KILL, STEAL, AND DESTROY

It is in that darkness. It is in that state of confusion. It is when your energy is at its lowest. That is when the devil can destroy your life the easiest. Choosing to live in the darkness, you think that you are having all the fun. But living in that world of darkness and confusion is secretly, slowly destroying you. The devil lives in secret. The devil does not advertise with a neon sign: "come this way into the darkness, so I can destroy you." No, the devil does his work slowly and in secret. In the darkness, the devil can do his best work.

When you are in the world, living in the darkness, living among the secrets and the lies, your character, the true qualities that make up who you are, is made up of those things that you do in the dark.

Think of the things that you used to do or maybe that you still do in the dark.

What is it that you are still doing in that darkness that you would not want God to see?

With all that we know, many of us still would rather live in the dark. Why?

Could it be because we think that we know better than God?

Why do we choose to put so much faith in man and so little faith in God?

We make the choice to make all the decisions in our lives, but when things go wrong, who do we want to blame?

GOD.

I was the one who chose to marry that woman. In the beginning, when things were great, I would wake up in the morning giving myself high-fives because of the great choice in wives that I had made. In the end, when she walked out on me, choosing to drink rather than spend time with me, when things really went bad and that choice in wives almost destroyed my life, who did I blame now?

God.

I remember one night standing out on my back patio, maybe a month after she had walked out, just screaming at the top of my lungs towards the heavens that I was through with God. "I'm done with you, God! I want nothing more to do with you!" My wife had left me and it was all God's fault. I could not believe that God would allow something like this to happen to me. How quickly when things go wrong do we forget who was making all those choices.

How completely wrong I was. I had no right to blame God for decisions that God had nothing to do with. How many of you are just like me? We make all the decisions, and as long as those decisions are going great, we take all the credit. But the minute one of those decisions goes wrong, we blame God for everything.

It's easy to blame God. And why do we really think that we know better than God?

If it is you making all the decisions for your life,
       THEN STOP BLAMING GOD!!!

By the choices we make, we put ourselves into bondage.

1) We sleep with whoever we want to satisfy our own selfish pleasure and a child is conceived
2) We buy a home that we really can't afford and we trap ourselves under a financial burden
3) We max out credit cards buying things to feed our desires, credit cards that we have no way of repaying, trapping ourselves under another burden

4) We drop out of school, limiting our lives, because we cannot see a reason to go
5) We drive under the influence of drugs and alcohol, risking the lives of the innocent with no thought of any consequences
6) Whether you want to admit it or not, the lifestyle you are living is a choice you made, putting you subject to the consequences of that life

IT'S IN THESE CHOICES AND THE MANY MORE THAT WE MAKE FOR OURSELVES; WE CHAIN OURSELVES TO OUR CIRCUMSTANCES BECAUSE WE KNOW BETTER THAN GOD!

The devil has all the traps but we run right into them as fast as we can go. The devil baits the traps with all the fun, with all the pleasure, but never shows you the consequences until the trap has been sprung. We put ourselves willingly right into the devil's chains just by the choices that we make. We put ourselves into the bondage of the world's systems because we really do believe that we know better than God.

As we put ourselves into these traps, the devil is laughing at each of us just at the ease he had in destroying our lives. We run right to the bait and the devil just sits back and watches. The devil watches as those choices destroy lives and the devil did not even have to break a sweat.

Real faith in God, faith that is seeking the light, faith that is only seeking the truth, never plays the blame game. Real faith accepts blame. Real faith accepts responsibility. Faith that is real is not afraid to look into the mirror and find the truth. The truth does set you free. But it can only be the real truth. Real faith is not afraid to ask for and receive forgiveness. Real faith recognizes the sin that lives in our lives.

The devil will tempt you, but just because a temptation is placed in front of you, doesn't mean you have to yield; faith that is always seeking the truth never yields to the devil's temptation.

As you read these pages, God has made you promises, and through your faith, you have access to every promise of God. But what do we choose to do? We would rather live by the things that we can see than by the promises of God.

Do you know that your sight can and will deceive you? Your own sight has the ability and will fool you.

How many times have you thought that you saw one thing from far away, but when you got closer, it was something completely different?

We see things all the time that look so good to us. On the surface, it looks so enticing. All we see is the pleasure but what we see as possibly the best thing in the world, in all actuality, it's the worst thing that we could ever want. That's the wolf in sheep's clothes.

How many people have experienced what I am talking about? We go to a party; we see all the people getting high, drinking and drugging. It looks like so much fun, so we try some of the fun. It's time to go home; we decide to drive. On the way home, we lose control of our car. What looked like fun has now turned into a horror.

You saw something that looked too good to be true. It looked too good to pass up. Everyone else was doing it and having fun. So you had to have some; you just had to try some and that taste hurt you so bad.

STOP LIVING BY WHAT YOU SEE AND START LIVING THROUGH YOUR FAITH

God will move on your situation but God only moves when you move. And then when God moves, God moves to the level of your faith. Believe and let God move in your life.

For am I now seeking the approval of man or of God? Or am I trying to please man? If I were still trying to please man, I would not be a servant of Christ. (Galatians 1: 10)

But just as we have been approved by God to be entrusted with the Gospel, so we speak, not to please man, but to please God who tests our hearts. (I Thessalonians 2: 4)

Have nothing to do with foolish, ignorant controversies; you know that they only breed quarrels. And the servant of the lord must not be quarrelsome but kind to everyone, able to teach, patiently enduring evil, correcting his opponents with gentleness.

God may perhaps grant them repentance leading to a knowledge of the truth, and they may come to their senses and escape from the snare of the devil, after being captured by him to do his will. (II Timothy 2: 23 -26)

CHAPTER FIVE

ACCEPTANCE

I would like to start this chapter by asking each of you the same question that God asked of me: "Why is the acceptance of the world so important to each of us?"

It was a Sunday morning and I had just arrived at church. I was late and the church was almost full. The only place to sit was on the back row and that row just happened to be empty. So that's where I sat. When you come to our house of worship, you had better be prepared to praise and worship the Lord.

I was raised in a Baptist Church where the service was very structured and very subdued. At the church that I attend now, The Devine House of Deliverance, there is nothing subdued when we praise and worship the Lord. And on this particular Sunday morning, everyone was already singing and dancing and praising the Lord. It's wonderful to see how much people love the Lord, how thankful they are to the Lord.

But also on this Sunday morning, I was troubled. It had only been a few months since I had accepted the Lord as my savior and the Lord had just blessed me with a job and I had just gotten back to work. Thank you, Father, for the job.

On Saturday at my new job, we had just had a big all-store meeting and a few employees were recognized for their efforts. I was not one of them. So I was feeling rejected and I had gone home Saturday night feeling rather sorry for myself.

The next day being Sunday, I headed off to church, and as I walked to church, I began to speak to the Lord about my feelings.

So now, here I am, sitting on the back row all by myself, and all of a sudden, the church became very quiet. I felt something next to me. There was a presence. Someone was sitting next to me. For the next few minutes, it was God and I sitting together on the back row of my church all alone. It was as if everyone else had left the building.

As the two of us were sitting there, God turned to me and asked me one question, "Why is the acceptance of the world so important to you?" I did not say a word. I just sat there. I couldn't say anything. It was as if I was frozen. I just sat there, listening.

And then God turned to me and He said, "Why is the acceptance of the world so important, when it is I who has accepted you all along?" I was in tears. It was still just God and I sitting on the back row. I was crying, and then God was gone. Why is the acceptance of the world so important?

Our Apostle was up front and that was when I heard everyone in the church service again. They were still singing and praising the Lord. And that's when I heard the Apostle say, "Can you feel it? It's the presence of the Lord. He is here, right here with us!" I wanted to jump right up out of my seat on that back row and just tell everybody, "He is here! Right here! God is sitting right next to me. Can you see Him? God is right here next to me."

Why is the acceptance of the world so important, when it is I who has already accepted you the entire time? So simple a statement, but so true. God made everything so plain and so simple for me on that Sunday morning. I felt love from God instantly. I knew, at that moment, that God loved me and how special I was to God. In an instant, I knew that was all the recognition that I was ever going to need.

Later that Sunday, God came back and gave me a word. That word was *secure*. God said to me, "Talk to them (the guys we minister to in the prison) about the false sense of security that we think that the world will provide for us." When we are running and gunning in the world, we really believe that if we can win the acceptance of man, we will find security. I'm not talking about security as in being safe. I am talking about security as in finding peace of mind, as in finding acceptance. If we can win their acceptance, then we will be in. We will be part of the group. We will become one of the crowd. We will be just like you. Not an outcast. We will find peace and security.

You will never find security when you have to find that security in other people. When you build your life around the acceptance of other men, you are building your life like a house of cards that can fall at any moment. When that house does fall, which inevitably it always will, you get the opposite of acceptance. You get rejection. I have known far more rejection in my life than acceptance. The Lord is showing me that there are many, many people in this world who are just like me.

When we are in the world, we will do anything - and yes, I do mean some of us will do anything to win acceptance from others. Think back on your own life and what you have done for another. But just like me, the majority of you have felt the sting of rejection over and over and over again.

The world is famous for its rejection. The world is actually very good at rejecting us. The world will tell you how wonderful you are, how great you are, how much we need you, how much we love you, and the world will even tell you how we can't live without you. But in the very next breath, the world will reject you. You know you were never really that good. You know we never really loved you. You know we never really needed you. To tell you the truth, we never really liked you. Thanks, but no thanks…..

Rejection is a tool that the devil will use to get you to turn your back on God. Instead of turning towards God when we get rejected, we want to blame God for that rejection. The devil wants you to blame God. Satan knows that if he can get you to blame God for the world's rejection, then we will no longer trust God. But in reality, when you put all your faith and trust in man, you are setting yourself up for the world's rejection.

Man will turn his back on another man quicker than he can blink his eye. That's just the nature of man. It's part of our character. It's part of how we think. It's just part of the way that we are taught to deal with each other. To always be skeptical. To always have a doubt. To always put up walls. To never fully trust another person. Especially as men we are taught to hide our true feelings. Never let another see how you really feel. If you put all your trust in another person, then you are just setting yourself up to be hurt. You are setting yourself up for the big fall.

Part of man's make-up is that we can never fully make up our minds. It's hard, almost impossible, for us to make a complete, total commitment to another.

Man's mind is always going back and forth. What about this? What about that? Should I do this? Should I do that? Should I go here? Should I go there? Our mind is always questioning, always full of doubt. Our minds are always on the move, always racing, trying to cause confusion. Our minds are never at peace.

We have a tendency to over-think everything. What do I do now? What should I have done? Did I pick the right thing? Should I have picked the other one? I just can't make a decision. What should I do when I get there? What if no one likes me? What if I don't fit in? I can't decide. I need more time.

Does she really love me or is she just saying that to get something from me? Man's mind is always so full of doubt. Did I choose right? And then, in the end, when we do decide, we always want to second guess ourselves. Am I really sure? How will I ever be sure? How will I ever completely know?

Because man cannot make up his mind, we always doubt whether we can fully trust another man - even our closest friends, even people in our own family, even the people we say that we want to marry. We always have doubt. Just look at the world today, how messed up relationships are today, how messed up families are today. Friendships fail. Marriages fall apart. Families go to their graves not speaking to each other. No one completely trusts another. And it is that doubt that allows a man to turn his back on another quicker than he can blink his eye.

Acceptance is so important to us because we are so afraid of being alone. We are really, really scared of being left all alone in this world. That's why a woman being beaten by a man will stay with that man. That's why someone who knows that they are being cheated on will stay with a person who can't be faithful. We are so afraid that no one else will want us. That no one will ever want to be with us again. I even heard a woman say the other day, "I can't leave him. He is the best I'll ever do." Are we really that afraid of being by ourselves?

You ask people what their greatest fear is and they will tell you, hands down, it's being all alone. How many times have you heard someone say that their greatest fear is growing old alone?

I was flipping through the television channels one afternoon and I heard a fifteen-year-old girl say that she wanted to have a baby. When she was asked why she wanted to have a child, her answer was because she wanted attention. Her seventeen-year-old sister had a child, and the minute she became pregnant, all the attention from her parents, from friends, from other family members went straight to her. It was as if the younger sister was completely forgotten, and now, her only way of getting that attention back was to do as her older sister had done. She was so starved for attention and acceptance that the younger sister was willing to ruin her own future and to use an unborn child to get the attention that she so longed for. How many of us have found ourselves in the shoes of the younger sister? Willing to do anything for attention; for the acceptance of another.

We will sacrifice love for attention. For you who have children, acceptance is more important to them than love. They want your love but they crave attention just like a drug. We want attention so badly that we gravitate, even run, to wherever or whoever will show us that attention. Gangs, clubs, bad relationships, even the church we will run to, cling to, and gladly join anyone or anything that will give us the attention that we crave. The attention we so desperately desire becomes just like a magnet drawing us to it, even if we know the source of that attention may become harmful to us.

I made decisions, life-changing decisions, based on the fact that I was afraid to be alone. You do not make good decisions when you are making decisions out of your fear. I married not once but twice, not because I had this great undying love for these women, but because I did not want to be alone. I was willing to do anything, and I mean anything, to make sure that I would not be left alone. Think back on your own life and I am sure that I am not the only one.

My second marriage lasted fifteen years. I lived every day of those fifteen years in total fear. Fear that I would mess up and she would leave me. Fear that I would mess up my job and they would fire me. Fear that when they fired me, my wife would leave me. Fear that my best was never good enough for anyone. Fear that I would make a bad decision and my son would not love me anymore. Fear lived in every part of my life. Fear controlled my entire life. I made all my decisions based on those fears. Fear owned me from the time I woke up in the morning to the time I would go to bed at night. And as badly as I would sleep, I'm sure that fear controlled me as I slept.

I was so scared. I did many things that I necessarily did not enjoy because I thought that if I kept everyone else happy, then I could control the fear. If everyone around me was happy, they would like me and they would not leave me alone. I really never enjoyed drinking and I did not care for the taste of beer, but I drank because my wife drank and all our friends drank. I tried weed and cocaine not because I really wanted to, but because they were offered to me and I never wanted to be the odd man out. I wanted so much to be a part of the in-crowd. I lied because acceptance was so important and I did not want to be left alone. Isn't it amazing all the things that we do out of that fear. Don't tell me what fear will make you do or don't tell me that you can control that fear. I needed to be accepted so badly. What have you done in your life just to be accepted?

I was constantly afraid that I was one mistake away from losing everything, one mistake, just one bad decision. The pressure alone of having to live a life that could never afford one mistake; living my life everyday on that tightrope was a horrible burden. The pressure was tremendous and the pressure built every day. The fear was making me ill. It was affecting my health, the constant worrying. I worried about everything. I was willing to do whatever it took not to be alone. That was how I lived every moment of my life. Afraid, that at any moment, I could lose it all.

It took fifteen years, but I did lose it all, and that house of cards that I had built did come crashing done all around me. What you fear eventually does come to own you. And what you fear the most will come to pass. I know it does. It did in my life.

Even though I had tried to commit suicide twice, it was never my intent to die. I never wanted to kill myself. I just wanted someone to love me, to love me as I am. To love me with no strings attached; to love me without wanting anything. Jesus came and showed me that there was someone who could do just that. Jesus came and promised to love me with His love. Jesus promised to accept me unconditionally and Jesus wanted nothing in return.

It never mattered to Jesus what I had done in my past or where I had come from.

Jesus just wanted to love me. Jesus loves me. Right then, Jesus made me another promise that changed my life forever. Jesus promised that He would never leave me or forsake me. I would never ever be alone again.

Once again, no matter what I had done or where I had come from, Jesus promised to be with me forever. Through thick and thin, Jesus promised to be there. And, unlike man who will leave you in the blink of an eye, who will leave you over nothing; Jesus will never, never, never leave you, ever!

When Jesus died on the cross, Jesus reconciled us back to God. Jesus made it right for each of us to have that personal, one-on-one relationship with the Father. Jesus made it possible for a guy like me to never be alone again. Jesus wiped away and took all that fear away from a guy like me. In an instant, all that fear that had gripped me, and had such a control on my life for so many years, was gone. All I had to do was accept Jesus as my Lord and Savior. All I had to do was let God come into my life and be my shepherd. All I had to do was invite God in and let God be God in my life. Will you do the same? How badly do you want the fear to go away? Do you want to taste freedom in your life for the very first time? Invite Jesus in and let Jesus show you the way. I know now why Jesus said, "I am the way, the only way."

I am here to tell you, right now, that there is a way to freedom. That way is Jesus Christ.

I came to Atlantic City by myself in November 2008, carrying everything that I owned in two suitcases. I accepted the Lord as my savior on January 7, 2009, and from that moment to this very minute, I can truly tell you that I have not had one moment where I have felt alone. I know that God is always with me. I may be by myself, but I am never alone.

I wrote about the character of man, but what about the character of God? What is most definitely wrong with the world today is that we have lost the character of God. There are not nearly enough of us walking through the world as living examples of the character of God. The true character of God is in His fruits.

God is His omnipotence, His omnipresence, and His omniscience, but God is also so much more. God's character is made up of the fruits of the spirit.

But the fruit of the spirit is love, joy, peace, longsuffering, gentleness, goodness, faith, meekness, temperance against such things there is no law. And those who belong to Jesus Christ have crucified the flesh with its passions and desires. (Galatians 5: 22-24)

We, as followers of Christ, must live by his example. We must ask God daily to fill us with the character of God. Please, God, let me walk in humility and holiness - holiness to be one with the Father. It is our responsibility to show the world all of the character of God. I challenge each of you to walk in God's character and see what happens in your life.

If you want to crush the devil, then show someone love --- show someone love with no strings attached --- unconditional love --- God's love --- true love --- real love
If you want to destroy the devil, then forgive somebody --- really forgive somebody --- forgive, and then forget --- let it go forever

Get up tomorrow and show someone mercy, show someone else self-control, show someone else meekness, show everyone God's character.

If you will only give into the Lord, the Lord can do something wonderful, something marvelous; something astonishing in your life.

Life with the Lord is all about the good stuff. Give into the Lord and God will move in your life. Nothing in your life is going to work until you give in. Give into the Lord. Let it all go. Surrender it all. Give every piece of yourself to your God.

God will give you peace. God will give you joy. God will give you love, His love. God did all these things for me and God will do the same for you. God put destiny back into my life. God put purpose back into my life. God gave me the reason to live. God granted me freedom. God took my pain. God took my suffering. God took all my burdens. God can and wants to do the same for you.

I started by writing about the acceptance of the world. I wrote about the rejection that the world has shown us all, over and over and over again. I wrote about the loneliness that is caused by that rejection. But I have found a friend, a best friend, a friend who will never leave me, a confidant, a companion, someone who will always be with me no matter what I do, no matter what I say, in the good times and bad, someone that I can trust with everything, someone that I can bare all to, someone who will never make me afraid, someone who will never turn their back on me no matter what, no matter if I disappoint them, no matter if I don't do what they want me to do, someone who has no requirements of me.

I can never thank you enough for being that person in my life, but thank you, Father God, for being just that person.

I know that I am never alone.

Intimacy with my Father says that I do trust Him
And if I really trust Him, then I will obey Him
If I obey him, then I really do love Him.

God is waiting - waiting for you to choose Him, waiting to have that intimate relationship with you right now, today.

What is God waiting on?
God is waiting on you.

Why does God never give up?
Because you are His greatest treasure!!!

Thank you, Father, for waiting on me.

CHAPTER SIX

WHY IS EVERYONE SO ANGRY?

So why is everyone so angry?

It was a Thursday evening and I was attending a restoration program at our House of Worship. The program that night was addressing removing defects of character. Minister Lea, who was in charge of the program on this particular evening, was asking each of us which defects in our character we would like to give to the Lord. Hands down, almost everyone said "anger".

Why is the world so angry? We do a ministry in the local prison and I was speaking on the subject of anger one evening. As I ministered, I asked everyone to remember the last time that they had really gotten angry, downright mad, lost control. And then I wanted them to think about what they did with that anger.

As we went around the room, it did not take much for the men to remember the last time that they had gotten really angry. Many of the men had either just gotten angry that very same day or had been angry within the last couple of days. Why is it that everyone is so angry?

Let me tell you a little story that will bring to life exactly what I am talking about. I work in a restaurant where we get the opportunity to meet some really great people, but we also get to meet some not-so-great people. One evening, a gentleman, who had just finished his meal, was leaving the restaurant. He returned shortly very irate and demanding to see the manager. Actually, he was in a fit of rage.

The gentleman demanded that the manager find another person in the restaurant who had parked their car too close to his. He wanted to have a few words with what he called this "inconsiderate individual". Remember that all this person did was park their car too close to his.

Like I said earlier, this person was in a fit of rage and when the manager refused to do the man's bidding, the man went ballistic. Eventually, because the man would not calm down or leave, the manager was forced to call the police. When the man learned that the police had been called, he finally left.

A little later that same evening, a woman returned to the restaurant to inform the manager that her car had been keyed. It was her car that had been parked too close to the other car. The man had keyed her car from one end to the other merely because she had been parked too close to his. Where does this type of uncontrollable anger come from? Why is the world so full of this anger? Why do we allow this type of anger to overtake us and cause us to make some pretty foolish decisions? Do not be fooled; this anger exists everywhere and this anger is becoming more prevalent in our society than you might think.

Anger controls so many of our lives today. We fly into a fit of rage at the drop of a hat. This anger comes at us from primarily three directions. We get angry about the situations that we find ourselves in. That's pride. We get angry because we feel as if we have been offended. Also pride. We get angry because we have been hurt by another, either physically or emotionally. There are other reasons for our anger, but primarily, the anger in our lives grows out of these three areas: pride, offense, and hurt.

We get angry over the things that have important to us; the more important the issue, the greater the anger.

Most often, our anger leads us into other places, and most often, that anger will lead us into revenge. When we get hurt, we want to hurt back. When someone hurts us, we get angry, and we have to take that anger out on someone. Usually the first person we see. We go out into the world and we have to hurt someone, anyone, the same way that we have been hurt. We feel like we have been vindicated or justice has been served when we retaliate. That's revenge. No one got over on me.

But quite often, the hurt we inflict is directed at the first person we see. Most of the time, that person is innocent. They are not the one who caused the anger in our lives, but we don't care about that. We just have to get even with somebody. We snap at someone; we yell at someone; we might even hit someone or break something. It does not matter; we just want to feel better. It doesn't matter that they are not the ones who hurt us. That anger that is building up inside of us has to be let out.

Our first instinct is to lash back out at that person who hurt us, but if I can't find that person, anyone will do. Revenge takes on a life all its own. We have to get even. Some of us will let that anger build up inside of us. We will let that anger fester. We begin to plot and scheme for our revenge. If that anger is not dealt with properly and immediately, then that anger is allowed to build up and that anger will only lead us to other, more destructive behaviors.

We get angry because of offense. We get offended. Offense is a negative reaction usually to a comment or to the way that we are being treated. In today's world, we take offense so quickly, especially over words. The smallest criticism, someone says the wrong thing. Someone looks at us the wrong way. Our efforts or the things that we do are not being acknowledged. No one is noticing us. No one notices the way that we work, the little things that we do. No one notices and we take offense.

One area of offense that I hear all the time from people today is that people show me no respect. Our prisons are full today because of that word *respect*. Men and women demanding respect, taking respect from each other, instead of earning respect, or working towards the respect of each other.

You have to give me my respect. I cannot let you get away in front of my boys with showing me no respect. My pride kicks in and tells me that I have to do something. That pride leads me to anger and that anger leads me to react. It's the consequences of those reactions that change lives forever.

We have become a society that is so critical of each other. Everything has to go exactly our way or we get offended. We have to have our own way because so many of us feel that our way is the only right way. If we don't get that way, we become offended, and then we get mad. Once mad, we take our participation away or, worse yet, we become saboteurs. Someone talks badly about us and all we think about is how to get even. You show me no respect and you will probably receive a beat down.

Once again, it's all about getting even. We have to get even or be one up. To just let disrespect go shows weakness. We can never show weakness in the world today. We are taught very early in life to never show weakness. To show signs of weakness is to be a coward. Cowards never get ahead. Cowards never get what they want. Cowards never get ahead in the world. Cowards get the beat down. Cowards get whatever is left over. Men can never show signs of weakness. Women do not like cowards. That's what we are taught in the world. That's exactly what the world wants you to believe and wants you to buy into. To not retaliate is to be a coward. The prisons are full of people trying to get respect.

We just have to get even. We just cannot let that offending party walk away. Those feelings stew around inside of you. Those feelings bottled up in your gut with nowhere to go. Anger just builds, waiting to explode. That anger trapped inside of you builds to resentment. That resentment of others often leads you to violence. Are you starting to see a pattern develop?

Anger is often rooted in our pride. Someone talks badly about us and it's our pride that gets hurt. Your pride gets wounded, and then your ego kicks in. It's your ego that tells you that can't let someone get away with saying those things about you. "What are you, a weakling? What happened to your backbone? See everyone laughing at us." It's your pride that tells you that you have to take action before people think that they can walk all over you. "What are you, a door mat?" It's your ego plotting the revenge.

It's also your pride that leads you to making an instant decision, to lash out, to strike back without thinking. How many times has our first thought been the wrong thought, our first reaction the wrong reaction? When we get hurt, we just want the pain to go away. It's your ego that tells you revenge is the only way. Revenge is the only way to make the pain go away. And you do want the pain to go away, right? We get hurt and we want to hurt back, quickly.

THE GREATER THE LOVE – THE GREATER THE HURT
THE GREATER THE REJECTION – THE GREATER THE PAIN

When the hurt is that deep, when the rejection sends you into that blind fit of rage, you can change your life and the lives of many others forever. That's how wives kill husbands. Best friends can kill a best friend. Quick decisions are always selfish decisions. And the consequences of those decisions once again change lives forever.

We get angry about the situations that we find ourselves in. "I did not deserve this." "This is not how I pictured my life turning out." These are the things we tell ourselves as we look back over our lives. It's all about a feeling of hopelessness that overtakes our lives. We begin to see no future. We start to lose hope. And then, when we see that our dreams are fading away, or that those dreams are gone forever, anger really sets in.

We begin to point fingers and place blame for what we see as the failures in our lives. "They are the ones doing this to me. They are the ones holding me back. They are the ones holding me down. I could have been a success if someone had given me a chance. I never got a break in life. I never had a chance." We get angry about the things we think that we should have, but do not. We begin to become jealous and envious of others.

We feel entitled to the things that we want. We feel that we deserve the things that we see that others have. When we cannot get those things, we fall into hopelessness. Hopelessness will lead you into desperation. When you see your life slipping away, you become desperate. Desperation leads you to wanting to get even. Desperation makes us angry. At that point, we feel justified in taking from another, what we feel we so rightly deserve. See the cycle?

The longer you let that anger eat you up on the inside, the more likely that kind of anger will take you somewhere else, somewhere much worse. The next step in anger is rage. Rage will take you to places in your mind that you do not want to go. It's that rage that made that man key that woman's car. And that rage probably told that man that he was justified in that action. You become capable of creating the worst evil when rage is in control of you.

Primarily, that anger and/or rage leads us into destructive thoughts. We do not care whom we hurt. We just have to hurt to get rid of our hurt. Once that vengeance gets into your mind, that's all you seem to be able to think about.

We want revenge. We want revenge so badly that it is all we can think about. We plot. We scheme. We plan our method to extract our vengeance. It's all we can think about. Vengeance has come to control our entire lives. The rage, the plotting, and the scheming build up inside of us until we are about to explode.

Anger that is allowed to live inside of us will grow into a monster. We think that we can control the monster, but in reality, the monster has control of you. Have you ever heard the phrase, "in a fit of rage"? It is that kind of rage where husbands kill their wives, women have killed their lovers, friends have killed best friends, and a child can kill a parent.

But how is that possible? We hear in the news or read in the paper where that kind of thing happens more than we would like to think. How can you say you love someone, and then become so mad at them that you want to take their life?

ANGER SMOTHERS LOVE AND FUELS HATE

Anger holds the same passion that love holds, but anger has the unique power to turn love into hate. Anger also has the power to make you lose control. That's the monster that controls your mind. That monster will lead you into very dark places in your mind. Once there, you are capable of doing unspeakable evil. Once there, in that dark place of your mind, you alone cannot bring yourself back out. Do not be fooled; this anger can and will destroy you. Anger is a tool of the devil and the devil comes to destroy by any means possible. Once, that anger has become embedded in your mind, that anger owns you, and begins to spread like a cancer. That anger will consume every part of your being and your life.

One of those dark, destructive places that anger will take you to is isolation. Other people do not want to be around a person who is angry all the time. Isolation will take you into loneliness. Loneliness will lead you into depression. That depression will take you right into suicide.

Remember we started this by saying that anger is a tool of the devil? Can you see, by what I have just written, how the devil will bind and chain you to your anger? And once the devil has sprung his trap, the devil will destroy you. Anger is such a powerful tool of the devil. Because of your anger, the devil sometimes can destroy multiple lives. Can you see that your anger may not be the only life that you destroy?

**THE ANGER THAT YOU GIVE BREATH AND LIFE TO
THE ANGER THAT YOU CONTINUE TO LET LIVE IN
YOUR BODY
THE ANGER THAT YOU REFUSE TO LET GO
THAT ANGER WILL COME TO DESTROY YOU
AND IF YOU ARE LUCKY, ONLY YOU**

*The thief comes only to kill, steal, and destroy. I came that you
may have life and have life abundantly.* (John 10: 10)

*Be sober, be vigilant; because your adversary the devil, as a
roaring lion, walketh about, seeking whom he may devour.* (I
Peter 5: 8)

The devil wants only to destroy you. The result of the devil's
trap is your own suicide. We all know people who have
committed suicide. Even some of us have tried to end our
lives a few times. I have, twice.

Many, many of us were said to have been depressed when we
tried to take our own lives. Where exactly did that depression
come from? We just did not wake up one morning feeling
depressed. Is it possible that our depression could be linked
all the way back to the anger in our lives? Could that anger
be linked back to an offense taken by us or by the
hopelessness of a situation that we found ourselves in?

I know that when I was at my lowest, when I was closest to
suicide, loneliness had so much to do with my depression. I
was mad at the world. I was lonely. I was depressed. I was
suicidal.

WHATEVER ANGERS YOU WILL
EVENTUALLY COME TO CONTROL
YOU

So many people today are trapped in their anger. We let anger walk right into our lives because we are not taught the love of God at an early age. Let me say that again. We let anger walk right into our lives, just like it is our best friend. The minute we feel that anger coming upon us, we have to close that door. We have to know where that anger is coming from and we have to refuse to let that anger just walk its way into our lives.

How do we close the door on anger? By trading in that anger for God's love. If we were taught the love of God, if we truly walked in the love of God, if the love of God was the way that we lived our lives, then anger would never be able to creep its way into our lives. We would immediately be able to recognize anger for what it is: a tool the devil uses to devour each and every one of us.

God's love always trumps anger. God's love is the fire hose that puts out anger's fire. Anger cannot exist where God's love already lives. The love of God teaches forgiveness. Forgiveness is anger's kryptonite.

So why is the world so angry? Because we do not know how to forgive. Anger is one of the devil's favorite tools, but it is one of the devil's tools that we can turn around and use to get God's glory.

The devil can and will chain and bind you in anger. We have already seen one example as to how the devil will do just that. The devil will try to keep you chained to anger for your entire life.

We have all known, or we know someone now, who will not let go of the anger in their life. They have been mad about something or at someone for a very long time. They could stay angry about their situation for the rest of their life. We all know people who have carried this anger with them all the way to their grave. We know these people. These people could be in our families. This could even be us. We may even feel justified in our anger. We nay even think that we have a great reason for our anger.

Let me tell you, as long as you hold on to this anger, your walk with the Lord will be stopped. Not slowed down for a minute. Not postponed temporarily. But your walk will be completely stopped. You have just hit a brick wall that you cannot get around.

Anger that you allow to fester over a period of time will turn into bitterness. Where bitterness lives, love cannot. We all know that God is love. Anywhere that love cannot live, God can never live. Anger will stop your walk with God. Anger will stop you from finding your purpose and your destiny with God. Wherever bitterness is, God is not.

So if you are about to place your gift upon the altar, and remember that someone is angry with you, leave your gift there in front of the altar. Make peace with that person, then come back and offer your gift to God. (Matthew 5: 23 - 24)

If a person offends another, whether through anger or any other cause, there is no use for you to offer anything to the Lord. The Lord will not be pleased with any offering. Whoever is angry with another should first go make peace with that person. Make the wrong a right. Only then will God find your gift acceptable. People wonder why it feels as if God does not hear them when they pray. How much anger are you carrying around inside of you?

When you let that anger live inside of you, you allow that anger to live and breathe. You give that anger its life. When you choose not to let that anger go, you feed that anger and you let that anger grow into the monster that will consume your life.

Responsibility, people today will not take any responsibility. Responsibility has become a bad word in our vocabulary today. You were the one making the choices that have gotten you to the place where you find yourself today. But instead, we want to blame everyone else for the situations that we find ourselves in. It is exactly in that blaming which gives anger its life.

We blame, and then we get angry. Someone blames us and we get angry. All that happens anytime someone places blame instead of accepting responsibility is that we have given anger a foothold into our life. Blame leads to anger, which gets us into fights, which leads us to bitterness. When we become bitter for a period of time, we can learn to hate. We can hate someone or something our entire lives. People take their hatred to the grave with them.

When you learn to hate, the devil has sprung another of his traps and we are caught in the devil's web. Once you are trapped, the devil believes that he now has you and he has you for life. This is exactly why the Lord tells us to never go to bed angry. Do not give the devil a foothold on your life. Do not open the door and let the devil walk in.

Be angry and do not sin; do not let the sun go down on your anger, and give no opportunity to the devil. (Ephesians 4: 26-27)

In our blaming, we want to blame society; we want to blame other people; we want to blame our wives, our father, our mother, the economy, how we were or were not raised, our lack of opportunities, the environment that we were raised in; we even want to place blame upon God. I did that for a very long time. I blamed God for the mess that I had made out of my own life. And just as I have said earlier, my walk with the Lord was completely stopped.

It's easy to blame God for the choices that we make. You can spend your whole life blaming whoever you want, but when you truly want to get real with yourself, you and you alone have to take responsibility for all those choices that you have made. You and you alone made the choices that put your life in the place that it is at this very moment. It was your will. And those were all your choices.

We do not all handle anger the same way. Some of us yell. Some of us get very quiet. Some of us throw fits. Some of us seclude ourselves. Some of us have to break things. Some of us have to hit something. Some of us just want to be left alone. But if you have anger inside you, if you are mad right now at someone, then it is you and you alone who allows those feelings to live. You are the one feeding those feelings. You are the one who will not let those feelings die.

I wrote earlier that we can turn that anger living inside of you around and God can receive glory from your anger. Being angry is not the sin. It's what you do with that anger that will lead you into sin. Anger used correctly can help you. Yes, I wrote that. Anger can be a help to you. Anger used correctly can bring about great changes in one's life.

Since you are the one causing this anger to stay in your life, use that anger to make a positive change in your life. Get mad at your situation. Get mad at the place that you find yourself in. Get mad at your predicament. Get mad enough and use that anger as the fuel to make a change. Turn your life around by getting mad at where you find yourself. Turn that anger, point that anger, direct that anger not at someone, but at your particular situation. Point that anger and get mad at your choices. Direct that anger and take responsibility for the things that you did.

Get mad and change! Use that anger as the motivation to change your situation. Tell yourself, "I am not going back to where I was. I am not going back to the same destructive behaviors. I am not going back to do the same things over and over and over again. I am not going back to the same choices. I am not going back!" I know that my life can be better. I know that my life does not have to keep going the same way. I know that I can change. I *can* change. I *will* change my situation!

Use that anger. You can use that anger but point that anger in the right direction. Let that anger fuel the change in your life.

Know where that anger is coming from. Know that it is the devil who wants to keep you chained to your anger forever. Tell the devil:

"DEVIL, TODAY IS THE LAST DAY THAT I LET
YOU USE ANGER
AS A TOOL AGAINST ME!"

Take the responsibility for where you are in your life and take the responsibility to make the change. Get mad at what you have done. Get mad at the choices that you have made. Use that anger to change your life.

So what steps can we take when we find that anger is trying to creep into our lives?

The very first thing that I want you to do when you feel anger taking control of you is to ask God for His help. Cry out to the Lord. Speak your favorite scripture. Plead the blood of Jesus. After you have done those things, take a moment, take a lot of moments, and think of all the lives that are about to be affected, and more importantly, think of the lives that are about to be completely destroyed because of the anger that we are about to let live in our lives. Think of your life, your mom and dad, your wife or husband, think about your children; all these lives rest on the decisions you are about to make.

All the loved ones, the people we say we love the most, become most affected by our anger. It could be directly or indirectly, but we affect the lives of our loved ones because we cannot control our anger. Usually, we do not give them a choice. We drag them right into our anger. Most often, we make them live with the consequences of the actions from our anger. And when there are children involved, are you teaching your children your anger?

The second thing that you can do to rid yourself of that anger is that you must own that anger. Know that by not ridding yourself of that anger, you and you alone are the one giving that anger its life. By carrying that anger for days and weeks and months, and yes, we carry that anger for years, you and only you continue to fuel that anger with breath for it to live.

Put the blame for carrying that anger where it belongs. Put the blame squarely and solely on yourself. You can snuff the anger out of your life as quickly as when that anger penetrated your being. Identify the source of your anger. Find what exactly it is that is making you angry. Most times, it is not the obvious. Search; find the root cause of your anger. Take a time-out. Remove yourself if necessary. Words said in the heat of the moment are always the wrong words. Gather yourself. Gather your words. A quick reaction is always the wrong reaction.

The third step is to know that it is the devil who wants desperately to bind you to your anger for life. Remember that the devil's purpose is to destroy your life. Speak to the devil. Speak the sentence I gave you a few paragraphs ago:

DEVIL, TODAY IS THE LAST DAY THAT I LET YOU USE ANGER AS A TOOL AGAINST ME

Know that if you allow it, that anger will lead you directly into hatred. The devil's desire is to chain and imprison you with that hatred all the way to your grave. When we hate, we cannot love. Do not be fooled on this one. When hatred lives in your life, you cannot show love in any area of your life. You will lust after everything and love nothing. Where hatred lives, love cannot. These two cannot occupy the same space. Without love, it is impossible for God to live within us.

The fourth step is to know that you alone cannot break the devil's chains. Only God can break chains and set the captives free. Freedom, to be really free, to experience complete freedom, is only possible through Jesus Christ. We, especially Americans, think that we know freedom. We do not. The only way to experience freedom is in God. Vent your anger to God. Give that anger to God. Give the battle to God. Let God be the conqueror in your life. Let God take that anger from you. Pray to your Father and ask God to pour His grace and His mercy upon you and to help you with your anger. Hold God to His promises, His promise that He is a prayer-answering God. Know that every day that you walk with God, that day is another day of healing. Heal me, Father. Let God heal your wounds and make you whole again.

The final step is to become a person of forgiveness .With the love of God in your heart, you become able to forgive. Forgive the hurt. Forgive the offense. Just forgive. Forgive the one who hurt you. Once you have forgiven, then forget. Forgive and forget and that anger will never be able to find a home in your heart again.

When you have truly experienced Jesus as your Savior, when you know that you have that very personal very intimate relationship with Jesus Christ, when you have experienced the power of forgiveness that God gives to each of us freely for everything and anything that you have ever done, when you know that your forgiveness was bought at the cross with real blood, real sweat, real tears, you cannot help but forgive others. You feel that you have to forgive others. If you cannot offer that forgiveness to the ones who have hurt you, then you do not know the Savior that I know.

For if you forgive others their trespass, your heavenly father will also forgive you, but if you do not forgive others their trespass, neither will your father forgive your trespass.
(Matthew 6: 14 - 15)

Let me tell you right here. Without forgiveness, you will never see the kingdom of God.

Dearly beloved, avenge not yourselves, but rather give place unto wrath: for it is written, vengeance is mine; I will repay saith the lord. (Romans 12: 19 - 21)

Be not overcome of evil, but overcome evil with good

Let God fight the battles for you. It's not your battle to fight. Do not go to sleep with your anger, ever. Do not give the devil an open invitation into your life. Always be the bigger man and make the amends.

Replace your anger with the word of God, the truth and the only truth. Renew your mind daily with the word of God. For real change to take hold in your life, you must realize that things as they are going now do not work. You need someone to come and show you a new way, a better way. This scripture written by the Apostle Paul has become one of my all-time favorites:

And yet show I unto you a more excellent way. (I Corinthians 12: 31)

The way is Jesus Christ. Let Jesus into your life and let God show you His better way.

If you are having an issue with anger in your life, or if someone close to you is having anger issues, read Ephesians 4: 25-32. Read these scriptures for seven straight days and let the word of God change you and change your life.

I would like to end this chapter with a couple of verses from the Book of Timothy. These scriptures tell us how we, as followers of Jesus, must respond when we are confronted by anger.

So flee youthful passions and pursue righteousness, faith, love, and peace, along with those who call upon the lord with a pure heart.

Have nothing to do with foolish, ignorant controversies; for you know that they breed quarrels.

And the lord's servant must not be quarrelsome but kind to everyone, able to teach, patiently enduring evil, correcting his opponents with gentleness.
And that they may come to their senses and escape from the snare of the devil, after being captured by him to do his will. **(II Timothy 2: 22- 24, 26)**

CHAPTER SEVEN

THE DIFFERENCE IS GOD'S LOVE

THIS IS THE CHAPTER.

This is the chapter that changes everything. I know that we have all heard those words before, many times. But this chapter, if you allow it, this chapter will change your life. Many people claim to know how to change lives, but very few of these people live by the words that they teach. These words that follow changed my life forever.

THE FREEDOM YOU SEEK
IS FOUND IN THE LOVE OF GOD

The following words in this chapter are the teachings that God taught to me about His love. If people will take these teachings and apply them to their everyday life, then the world can and will change. The words that are about to follow in this chapter do hold the power to change you, and by changing you, the world does and will change. Please do not be fooled. We have been taught and told that one person cannot change this world. That is a lie! This world will change one person at a time. Jesus took Himself and twelve and they made an impact that still holds the power to change the world today. Read these words that follow, and then you become the teacher. Touch someone with the words you are about to read.

I do know one truth for sure; the only thing that can change this world for the better is God's love.

Today, love is so misunderstood, and for the vast majority of us, we could not even tell you what love is. For the masses, love has just become an empty word that is void of any real meaning. We say the word but the word has become meaningless. It's just a word we say to get what we want. After reading this chapter, you will know the love of God. You will know exactly what the phrase "The Love of God" means.

But the fruit of the spirit is love, joy, peace, longsuffering, gentleness, goodness, faith, meekness, temperance: against which there is no law. (Galatians 5: 22 - 23)

This is everything that God wants to give to you. When you hear that God wants to bless you, these fruits are the blessings that God wants to fill your life with. These are the fruits that your soul desires, the higher life your soul wants to live. That emptiness that we all feel inside of us is your soul crying to be fed with these fruits. These fruits the world does not know. These fruits many of us church-going folk do not know. But it is these fruits that we must begin to possess.

The reason I quote the fruits of the spirit here is because the fruits are in order. God made love the first fruit for a reason. We learn through the scriptures that God is love and that love is God. Actually, in the scriptures, the two are interchangeable. They are exactly the same. God equals love and love equals God.

Love is the first fruit because love serves as the base for all the other fruits. The analogy I like to use is ice cream. If I have vanilla ice cream, then I have the ability to make all the other flavors. If I have vanilla, I can make chocolate. If I have vanilla, I can make strawberry. If I have vanilla, I can make rocky road. As long as I have vanilla ice cream, I have the ability to make any of the other flavors.

That's exactly what love is to all the other fruits of the spirit. You cannot be meek without love. You cannot be gentle without love. You cannot be patient without love. You cannot be longsuffering without love. You must first possess and understand God's love before you can possess, understand, and learn how to manifest all the other fruits in your life.

There are many great chapters in this book with many great insights and valuable teachings, but you will never be able to control your anger without knowing God's love. You will never be able to live your life through the connection of your spirit and your soul until you know God's love. You will never be able to resist the evil of the world without knowing God's love. That is why this chapter, and the teachings that lie within this chapter, are so important.

GOD'S LOVE IS WHAT FIXES EVERYTHING!

So now faith, hope, and love abide, these three; but the greatest of these is love. (I Corinthians 13: 13)

The foundation is love. All else, everything else, is built upon that love. Without laying that foundation of love first, you cannot build. Please, stop and read that again. Without laying a foundation of love first there is nothing that can be built.

Therefore be imitators of God, as beloved children. And walk in love, as Christ loved us and gave himself for us, a fragrant offering and sacrifice to God. (Ephesians 5: 1 – 2)

Therefore, be imitators of God! Be an imitator of God. God tells us to imitate Him. That is the life that we are to live every day. Imitate Christ. We are to become more like God every day.

How exactly do we become an imitator of Christ? To be like God, we must become love. The more of God you want to become, the more love you need to be. But how do we do that if no one is teaching us how? We are to walk in love as Christ so loved and gave Himself for each of us. How can I walk in love if no one is teaching me about love? Christ sacrificed Himself for each of us, in order to show every one of us what true love should look like. Christ gave Himself to you and to me to teach us what real love should feel like. But what really is the love of God?

This chapter will teach you many of the keys of how we should imitate God and how to walk this Earth as Jesus walked, how to walk every day in the love of God, how to walk giving God's love to everyone who crosses your path.

Can you tell me what makes God's love different?

I was watching a television show the other day and I heard a guy on the show say, "I thought that love would be enough. But it wasn't. I was sure that my love would be more than enough to overcome anything. And it wasn't. I was sure that my love could conquer all. And it didn't."

How many times have we said those exact same words to ourselves? Most of the time, we are saying those words as another relationship in our lives is coming to an end. But did we ever really know how to love in the first place?

"I knew that she was my soul mate the minute I laid eyes on her." "He completes me in just so many ways." "It was love at first sight." How many times have I heard those phrases?

"I was sure that our love would be enough to get us through any rough times." I know that, in my own life, I have said each one of those statements probably many times, as I would go from relationship to relationship to relationship, wondering as I went from one to another: what just happened? What went wrong? I really thought that she was it. I thought that she was going to be the one. I thought that our love would last forever.

That's the love that we are taught in the world. We have this word *love* so messed up. We throw the word *love* around today with no meaning, with no conviction, with no commitment.

God's love is enough. God's love is more than enough. God's love can and will overcome anything and everything. Not only can we have God's love, which God gives freely to everyone, but we can become God's love. We can walk in that love and we can touch and teach everyone what it is to know God's love. We can learn the truth about love, God's love.

For those of you who are asking and for those of you who are not sure, God's love and the love that we are taught in the world are two completely different types of love. These two loves are as far apart as the farthest east and the farthest west.

The love of God and the love of man are not anywhere close to being the same. The love that we are taught in the world is nothing but lust. We lust after people. We lust after possessions. We lust after fame. We lust after titles. We see something we like, we see something we want, and we call that love. That's not love; that's lust.

What does God say about the love of the world and the lust that lives in the world today?

Love not the world, neither the things that are in the world. If any man loves the world, the love of the father is not in him. For all that is in the world, the lust of the flesh, and the lust of the eyes, and the pride of life, is not of the father, but is of the world. (I John 2:15 - 16)

What exactly is lust and what makes it different from love? As defined in the dictionary, *lust* is to have a strong desire for something. A desire is to wish or hope strongly for something to happen.

We often say what we desire is what we love. That's not true at all. What we desire, we lust after. "I really wish that I had one if those." "I hope that she will go out with me." "It would be so nice to get that." Remember that lust is a strong desire to get what it is that we want.

Lust and desire goes hand in hand and are rooted in your mind. What is preoccupying your mind? What we desire of the world we lust after and what we lust we desire. It's this preoccupation of your mind, when I have these strong desires for a particular person or possession which overtake all other thought. All you can think on is the lust and the desire. When lust is in control of your thoughts, it is these thoughts that will take you over and control your every movement. Lust is a consuming and controlling spirit which when given this kind of control will take over your mind, your heart, and your body. How powerful is lust? Just keep reading.

Desires do come and go. Does your love seem to fade quickly? Can you lose interest very quickly in something that you said you just had to have? Think back to the last time you said you really loved something. Did that love only last a minute? Was it really only a desire? Or maybe it was only something that you wished for?

Did the definition that I just gave to you describe your love? Did you only have a strong desire for what you were chasing? If it was, then what you thought was love just turned into lust.

If, by some chance, I did not get you with my first definition of lust, then let me give you a second definition. Lust is also a strong desire for the indulgence of sex. Yes, another desire, another want, another wish; to crave sex. Have you told someone lately that you love them when all you really did was lust after them? We only said that we loved them because of the sex we desired from them……

Or let me give you one better. How many of us equate sex with love? She just slept with me, so she must love me. He would not have had sex with me if he did not have feelings for me. She or he must love me. How wrong on so many levels those statements are. But many, so many of us (and yes, I was one of them on both sides) equate sex with love. We so desperately want to be loved by somebody, by anybody, that we take any attention to be loved. And for many of us, sex has become love.

How many relationships, how many marriages, are doomed from the very start because one or both of the participants believed that the sex that they were having was truly love? Done without God's love, sex is only lust!

Let me give you one more definition for *lust*. *Lust* is to want something so badly that you just cannot be happy without it. Did I just describe how you really feel about the man in your life? Or that car you just have to have? But I can't live without them.

We do not know how to truly love each other in this world today. We only know how to lust. And we have become quite good at feeding our lust. Lust is the intense appetite to satisfy only ourselves. Lust is all about satisfying my needs and my wants and my desires. Lust is all about being selfish. If what you are calling love is only about you, then it really is lust, not love.

Before I move on let me speak about this twisted feeling that the devil has laid upon so many of our young women today. The feeling that you have to give your body in order to get his heart; this feeling is never love, but only about feeding someone's lust. Love never takes from another. Love never has to prove itself by being put to the test by a man. When a man says prove it, he is speaking out of the lust that is in his heart.

It is the love of God that is going to save the Earth from destroying itself. It is the love of God that will turn us from the evil in the world and bring us back to God. People are searching everywhere for love, but what they are only finding is lust.

You may be sitting here right now reading these pages and saying to yourself, "The world that I know does not need to be saved. What, if anything, is really wrong with the world? The world I see is fine, just the way it is right now."

I used to think and believe the exact same thing. That is when I was only thinking of myself. My life was good. The friends that I had around me, their lives were good. And as long as we stayed to ourselves in our own neighborhood, we never saw the whole world as it really is. We never saw all the pain, all the hurt, all the suffering that was going on in the world. And if that pain did not touch us, then we really did think that those sufferings might not exist.

The only time that I would see such suffering was when I would decide to watch the evening news on television. Even then, the pain and suffering was only on my television set. It never seemed real to me. The pain displayed on television never touched me.

I know differently today. God took me out of my comfortable life because God had a few things to show me, a few things to teach me. It was time for some of that pain that really existed in the world to become real to me – in order for me to know that pain and for me to know the suffering of others. For that to happen to me, that pain had to touch me personally. I had to feel and experience that pain.

God has a plan and a purpose for every person's life. If you were one of lucky ones that God chose to wake up this morning, then it's only because God had something specifically that He needed you and you alone to do today. There is an assignment that God has for you every day. There is destiny written by God for your life. After God showed me what He had to show me and it was now time for me to begin to work on the assignments that God has for me. It was time for me to live my life for God.

It is the love of God that will teach us how to stop hurting one another. We hurt each other on a daily basis. You can think of all the really big hurts that we do to each other constantly, but I want to remind you right now of how we hurt each other through the words that we say. It amazes me how we do not even know how badly we hurt each other with the words that we say.

We have turned our backs on God. You may be saying to yourself that I am being too harsh, too overly pessimistic. Actuality, in my heart, I am the ultimate optimist. But as I look over the world today, all I see right now is man's destructive behavior. We have turned our backs on each other. Because we really do not care about our fellow man, we do some pretty despicable things to each other, and for the most part, we tell ourselves that our behavior is ok. We justify the hurt we cause each other out of our own selfishness and the greed to satisfy our own needs.

We are well on our way to destroying the very planet that God made for us to enjoy. Maybe this destruction will not happen in my lifetime, but it could easily happen in my child's or in my grandchildren's lifetime.

The Earth, as we know it today, could be an extremely different-looking place in a matter of a few short years, and I am not talking about life being better: terrorism, war, the atomic bomb, famine, poverty, the hatred that covers this globe, the intolerance that continues to grow. More countries have the ability to end the world today than ever before.

There is more hatred, less tolerance, less forgiveness, less willingness to live side by side with our differences in the world than ever before. We have never been a planet full of people willing to share. If you do not believe like me, think like me, look like me, speak like me, then I probably do not want anything to do with you. My way is not only the best way; it's the only way that I will tolerate. It's become much easier to see the differences in people than to find the many things that make us all the same.

It's much easier to be judgmental about people than to have empathy. Empathy means that we are forced to look at ourselves. It's easier to hate a person than to show someone love. The further that we, as a people, continue to run away from God, the more confusing, the more chaotic, the more dangerous the world becomes. It will only be God's love that will save us and pull us all back together as one people.

It is only through God's love that we will see how similar we truly are, all people, all nations, all cultures, and all religions. The entire world pulled together as one. Only God's love has the ability to accomplish this task. Only the love of God will set us free from the hatred, the discrimination, the intolerance that is breeding throughout every corner of this planet. It has always been the will of God for us to live as one people on this one planet. When God looks down upon this Earth, God only sees one people. It has always been God's will for us to live in His kingdom here on the Earth.

It says in the Lord's Prayer:
Thy kingdom come
Thy will be done
On Earth
As it is in Heaven
(Matthew 6:10)

It has always been God's intention for Earth to be an extension of God's kingdom. The only way that we are going to ever get that back, if we become God's love.

Did you understand what I just wrote? It is God's will and God's desire for His Kingdom to be upon this Earth. Does that statement surprise many of you?

What the Lord has revealed to me and what I am about to give to you, will be completely new for almost everyone who will read these pages. It was all brand new to me. It was a brand new way for me to think about love. It was a brand new way of acting towards love. It was a brand new way of giving love for me. It was a brand new way of living a life of love. Receive this teaching. Read carefully. God has a reason why you are reading this. Receive what God wants to give to you because you are about to be shown a brand new way of love: God's way.

See how much our heavenly father loves us. For he allows us to be called his children, and we really are! (I John 3: 1)

Love is not a word that we should use lightly, but we do. It saddens me greatly - now that I know what love is supposed to be, what love is supposed to look like - to hear how people so horribly distort and misuse that one little word, *love*. Words are so important, so critical to how we interact with each other. Speech is still the number one way that we use to communicate with each other. But we so misuse words, and then we overuse words all of the time.

I firmly believe that the Earth would be a better place if certain words were never to be spoken again, and then if other words were only spoken correctly, only in the right setting and at the appropriate time.

Love is definitely one of those words. *Love* is the word that we should use a whole lot less and only at a very particular time and only with very specific people. But how do I know when that time is? That is one of the biggest problems of them all. We talk love. We preach love. We say that we love. But no one is teaching us what love really is. No one is teaching what love should look like, or how love should really feel. This chapter will change all of that. Hopefully, the words in this book will teach plenty.

We have so overused the word *love*, that in the world today, this one little word that packs so much power has lost all of its meaning. We have thrown the word *love* around to such an extent that this one word has become completely watered down. And what is worse yet is that the word *love* has lost almost all of its meaning in the world today. If the word does have any meaning to you at all, that meaning is nowhere close to what God's original intentions were when God created love.

Love is only one word, but think of all the ways in which we use this one word, and more so, misuse this word. I was guilty. I used to use the word *love* all the time. "I love this. I love that. I love the other. I love this today. But I'll love that tomorrow. I love this one. No, wait a minute. I think I love that one instead." My love could and did change every minute. With every choice came another decision, to love or not to love. One word used so many different ways and with so many implications.

Our love has become so fickle. It's so wishy-washy. I could never decide what to love or for how long I might love a particular item or a particular person. Of course, when I first would say the word *love,* for all intents and purposes, I said it to last forever; but how many of us, deep down, believe that the love we speak about today is really going to last forever? For most of us, we start out with good intentions, but how many of us have really thought through those intentions. Without the thought to back up those intentions, and without any discussion as to where these intentions are about to lead us; how can we ever hope to achieve any level of commitment or permanence to our intentions.

I love you today. I hate you tomorrow. I used to tell people that all the time. Those are intentions without thought. How will I really feel in the morning? Yes, I can love you tonight, but how will I really feel in the morning? I could say that I love you today, but tomorrow, I might not even stop to give you the time of day. What was your name? Where do you live? I could tell someone I loved them and not know a single thing about them. That's what you call intentions without commitment. I could tell you that I loved you and not even be able to define the word *love.*

Just go back and reread what I just wrote. When you speak *love* to someone, that one word alone *love* should establish a permanent bond between you and the person whom you just spoke *love* to; permanence between two people. Just in speaking that word alone, *love*, you are building a permanent bond - an unbreakable, indestructible, forever partnership between two people, for better or for worse, in sickness and in health.

We say those words when we get married, but when you say the word *love* to someone, that's the kind of commitment that you are making, permanent. Love should never have become disposable; an intention without the commitment. We say so many words that we never really mean, just like the word *love*, but really the whole time, we have our fingers crossed. How many of us when we see a wedding taking place really believe that it will last for their lifetime.

I can definitely do the "better" part and the "health" part, and maybe I can do the "sickness" part, if it's not too bad, and maybe the "for worse" part, if it's only for a minute. But when you say that word *love,* there are no maybes. Once again we have intentions without thought. The word *love* speaks permanence. That was God's intentions for what *love* was to mean when God created love.

There is another difference between God's love and the lust of the world. Lust is only thinking about today. No permanence there. What can I get right now? Lust is all about this moment. Lust could care less about tomorrow. Lust wants what it wants and it wants it now. The love of God is permanent. It's forever. When God says that He loves you, then that love is forever.

It's only one small, four-letter word, but the word contains so much power. *Love* could be the most powerful word in all spoken language. To gain love, we are willing to climb the highest mountain, swim the deepest ocean, and leap off the tallest building. When love is taken from us, you can find yourself in the deepest, darkest of holes that you never thought existed. When in love, the highs are the highest. When losing love, the lows are the lowest. We will do almost anything to find love and we will do almost anything not to lose love, once found. We have all experienced love from both sides, probably more than we would like to comment on.

And how many of us treat love like it is a competitive sport? I bet you that I can get that one? We talk about love like it is a conquest. We go from one to one to another putting another notch on the belt. How many trophies do you have? Is that really what love is? Is that how we have come to define love? It's all about the sex and the trophies? How sure are you that you were just not another trophy for someone else?

Take a moment and think about love. Define the word *love* for me. Can you do it or are you at a loss for words?

The dictionary says that *love* is a strong passionate feeling towards someone. I knew all along that love was a feeling that I was supposed to have. Love was supposed to be a way that I felt. So often, you hear people speak of love being magical. You hear people say that love is such a magical force.

I knew that love was most definitely a feeling that I was supposed to have for someone or something. That's worldly love. That is the exact love that we have been taught to show each other. We are taught that love is a feeling. That's not God's love.

I was so wrong about what love actually is. I was wrong about how love should actually feel. Let me break a myth for you right now. Ever heard this one: "Love Hurts"? This is something that every one of us is taught. Love is going to hurt. Wrong. Let me break the myth; if it hurts you, then it is not love. Here's another difference between the love of God and lust: lust hurts.

When lust is involved, someone always gets hurt. Lust allows us to leave someone with no explanation. Lust allows you to stay out all night doing your own thing without any concern for the person waiting for you at home. Lust allows us to lie without conscience to insure that we get what we want when we want it. Lust allows us to be selfish when it comes to our happiness. Lust allows us to put our own needs and wants first without a thought for the feelings of others. It`s lust that allows a guy to sleep with his girlfriend's sister. It's lust that allows a girl to sleep with her boyfriend's best friend. And it's the fear that allows that boy or girl who has been cheated on to take back the offending party.

I had no clue as to what God's love really was. We hear and read those words all the time without any thought to those words' true meanings. I never knew what God's love was supposed to feel like. I never knew how God's love would make me feel. Once I understood what God's love was, how that knowledge changed my life. If we really knew the love of God, we would act a whole lot differently towards each other, and the world today would be a much different place.

Don't be fooled. Many people who attend church every Sunday, many people who read their bible regularly, many people who say that they know Christ, only know, but worse yet, only show the love of the world. They only show lust. That's all that they know. The love that they think they know is really only lust.

Until you know God, and I mean really know God, you cannot discover the true meaning of the word *love*. Many people, even church-going folk, say that they know of Christ, but they do not really know Jesus. They have no relationship. What they have is only what they have read or what someone has told them. They have never taken the time to establish a relationship. And if they do attempt a relationship with our Lord, they try to build that entire relationship in one day a week and for only a few hours on that day. And you know what is worse yet? Most of us can't even give God that much of our time on a consistent basis. What kind of relationship is that? In the world we would call that a relationship domed for failure. We say that we love God so much, but we definitely don't show our love with our time.

We say that we know God, but so few of us walk as God walks. To say that we really know Jesus is to show love as Jesus showed love when He walked this Earth. To say that we know Jesus is to become his imitator. Remember, I already said that the love we know in the world and the love of God are two totally different types of love.

The world only knows lust. I hope that you are starting to see that by now. Only through knowing and having a relationship with God will you ever come to truly know God's love. I never knew God's love until I came to really know Him, until I really came to seek Him. It is through that relationship that God will grant you the strength and the wisdom to learn about and to show to everyone the love of God. And believe me; it takes both great strength and wisdom to be able to walk in the love of God.

Until you commit to seek God diligently, read His word, pray, walk, and talk with God as a part of your daily life, then you will never be able to comprehend the teaching of God's love.

Does it really take a daily commitment to know God's love? Do I really have to spend that much time? Does it really take all that? It will take that much and maybe more. But to learn, to get to know the greatest love from the only one who can teach you about his love, the time devoted is more than worth it. I know that it is!

It took that commitment and more for me to discover what God's love was all about. Even today, I am still asking God to teach me more and to work out in me His perfect love. But the reward for diligence is to finally discover what love is really supposed to be, to get to know the truth about love. To get to know a pure love, a perfect love, an unconditional love; this reward far outweighs any sacrifice you think that you may have to make.

You will never know God's unconditional love by staying in the world away from the only one who can teach you this love.

Why is knowing God's love so important? Simple, you cannot live; you cannot experience what you do not know. The devil lives in those things that you do not know. The devil lives in the darkness. In the darkness, ignorance is bred. The devil dwells in your ignorance.

The devil does not want you to ever know. If the devil can keep you from not knowing, the devil can keep you in the darkness away from the light, away from the truth, away from the knowledge that God so desires each of us to have.

That's the prison that the devil wants you in and wants to keep you in, ignorance. Believe me when I tell you that there are many more people who are bound and chained by the devil in their own homemade prison cells, walking around freely today out in the world, than in all the prisons around the world.

The devil knows that if he can keep you trapped in ignorance, then the devil can keep you away from the abundant life that God wants each of us to enjoy.

PEOPLE ARE PERISHING EVERYDAY FOR THE LACK OF KNOWLEDGE

Why is knowing about God's love so important? You cannot give to me what you know nothing about. You cannot give away to someone else what you yourself do not possess. Why do relationships fail? Because we are searching for something in the world, or asking for something from someone, that they themselves do not have. I cannot give to you what I myself do not possess. We cannot even begin to show someone else love if we have no idea what love is really supposed to be. How can I possibly live what I do not know?

It is just not enough to finally know about God's love. That is very important. But you have to be able to download that love into your spirit and make God's love a part of your everyday life. Once you have accomplished that feat, once you yourself are walking every day in God's love, then you have to give that love away freely. You must give that love, the love of God, away to everyone that you meet. That is the most important. That is the ultimate goal: to walk every day as Christ walked, walking every step, giving the love of God away freely to every person in your path. That is a command of God.

How will it ever be possible for us to walk in God's love if we never know what the love of God is? How are we to give away this love if we ourselves do not know what God's love is? How can we teach to others the love of God if we are ignorant to what that love should look like?

We are to be the ambassadors for the kingdom of God. We are to be the examples of our Lord for the rest of the world to see.

So many people are truly hurting in this world today.
So many people are searching.
So many people have nothing.
So many people have lost hope.
So many people are in need.
So many people are looking for an answer.
So many people are looking to see God.
So many people want to feel God in their lives.
So many people crying out to God.
So many people unable to find their way.

We must show people the love of God. That is why we must know, and why it is so important for us to know, the love of God. We must be the ones giving love away. To be able to give God's love away, you must first know His love. You must first possess His love in order to give His love away. Learn so that you may give.

You cannot teach what you do not know.
You cannot give away to others what you do not first possess.

So let me start by asking you a question: How does the world know that you are a Christian? How does the world know with no communication, without you having to tell them that you are a follower of Christ? How does the world recognize that Christ lives in you?

People will know that you are a follower of God by the love that you show to them. Not by the love that you tell them about. Not by the love that you read to them that is found in the bible, but only by the love that you are willing to show to them. And you must show them that love seven days a week, twenty-four hours a day. No time off. No days off. No vacation time. The love of God must be shown every minute of every day, seven days a week.

A new commandment I give unto you, that you love one another: just as I have loved you, you are also to love one another. By this all people will know that you are my disciples, if you have love for another. (John 13: 34 - 35)

It is nowhere close enough to only attempt to show love on Sunday in church. There are already way too many part-time Christians. The sad fact is that most church people cannot even show the love of God for a few hours on Sunday morning. That's just too much to ask of them. It's amazing how we cannot even show God's love to the same people who we were just in the church service with. We can't even get out of church before we start talking about "I wonder where she was this morning?" or "Did you see what she was wearing?" or "Did you see who she was sitting with?" or "Did you hear what she did this last week?" - gossip, gossip, gossip.......

It's not enough to show love only on Sunday morning.
It's not enough to show love only in Bible study group.
It's not enough to show love only when you are with other Christians.

For a true follower of Christ, real authentic love - the love that Christ shows us - is self-sacrificing love. You do what you do; you give love with never a regard for yourself.

The love of God sacrifices.

NO CROSS   ----------------------- NO CROWN

Jesus commanded each of us to pick up our cross and to follow Him.

What are you willing to sacrifice to follow God? What about your daily life would you be willing to change to spend more time with God? Be careful what you speak out of your mouth. What cross are you willing to pick up and carry for our Lord? What will your sacrifice be? What are you willing to do today to show the love of God to the people around you? What more will you be willing to do tomorrow? What will you sacrifice to show authentic love? God gave us the greatest example of a sacrifice for love. God gave the greatest sacrifice willingly and God made that sacrifice to save each and every one of us.

For God so loved the world that he gave his one and only son, that whosoever believes in him shall not perish but have everlasting life. (John 3: 16)

No greater love hath no man than this, to lay down his life for his friend.
(John 15: 13)

So let me reveal to you the first truth that God gave to me about his love.

Love equals sacrifice.
Sacrifice equals love.

In order for love to become real in your life, your love must be willing to sacrifice. The essence of love - that part which makes love what it is - is the sacrifice. Love that is not willing to pay a price is not love. If you are not willing to sacrifice, then what you are calling love is really only lust. Lust becomes love when you begin to make the sacrifice to love.

Authentic love must be tested. For love to be real, that love must be tested. For love to be real, it must pay a price. True love, deep love, meaningful love, the kind of love that we all have longed for - for you to know this kind of love, you must be willing to sacrifice. The true test that will allow you to know whether this love lives within you is sacrifice. What are you willing to sacrifice to know and experience this type of love? Are you walking in this kind of love or has, all along, what you said was love really been only lust?

Take a moment and think back into your past and how many times your love has been tested. Is your past love life as riddled with failure as mine is? Love that cannot past the test is called what?

In one word, the difference between love and lust is:

SACRIFICE

The bible speaks of marriages being equally yoked. That yoke in a marriage that must be equally yoked is sacrifice. In a marriage there are no givers and takers; everyone is a giver. Two people equally committed and willing to always give that is the recipe for a permanent bond. The glue which holds this bond together is sacrifice.

For many we hear that word *sacrifice* and the word bothers us. Fear and worry come upon us because we really do not understand the word. Someone says to us "sacrifice" and we automatically think that someone has to die for there to be a sacrifice. Someone says to us "sacrifice" and we begin to think submission. I am not going to sacrifice my way for his way. I am not going to give up the way I think just to please them.

Then there is the group that think that in order for whatever to be a sacrifice, we have to make this grand display, this major production. We think of heroism or going out in a blaze of glory. That's what we have to do to sacrifice. I am here to tell you that in real everyday living, the sacrifice is all the little things that we do for each other every day. If I say that I love you, then I will wake up every morning with my only goal being to do everything that I can do to make your day the very best possible. I will sacrifice my needs, my wants, my desires to make your day the best that it can possibly be. And because I say "I love you", I will make that sacrifice willfully for you every day.

Lust makes no sacrifices. Lust will never entertain even the smallest of sacrifices for another. Lust is only out to get. I am in this relationship for me and for what I can get from you. That's it. That's the bottom line. I am only here with you to get my needs, my wants, and my desires fulfilled and for those to always be met first!

If you are truly honest with yourself, all the relationships that you have ever been in, you were only there because you had a need, a want, or a desire in your life that you, by yourself, could not fill. You needed someone to fulfill your desires. Lust is selfish and lust only takes from another.

In the world today, we believe that we should not have to sacrifice. Me, give up something? Give it up for someone else? Not me. I don't play that way. Love is there for me to take, and take it I will.

We, deep down, believe that we should be able to take love whenever, wherever, and however we want it. We do not believe in paying a price for love. Me pay? I just take what I want. Love is just as disposable today as is everything else in our society. We give love, and then we take our love away in the blink of an eye. We want what we want and we want that now. And for the most part, we want what we want the easiest way possible. We want the things that we want on our own terms. Forget about commitments. When things get tough, we just run away. Lust never commits.

We do not even want to work for the things that we want, including love. We just expect someone to give it to us and if that does not work, some of us will even just take the things that we think we are owed or deserve. We never give a second thought about the consequences that come out of our lusts.

Sacrifice. No way. My ego tells me that I do deserve to have what I want and I will have it. It does not matter who gets in my way or who may be hurt in the process. I want what I want, and if you get hurt too bad.

That's the way it is with worldly love. We take it because we think that it is a right of ours to be loved. We think that we deserve to be loved. We think that we are owed love. And if you won't love me, then I will find someone who will. We take, we give, and we take it away again. We treat love just like it is a game. I'm here. I'm there. I'm in love. No, I'm out of love. He loves me. No, he loves me not. Up and down. Our love has no meaning, no commitment, and no permanence. All these attributes are missing from our love because our love will not sacrifice.

LOVE = SACRIFICE

That's the difference between God's love and worldly lust. What so many people in this world call "love" is really only lust. Lust makes no sacrifices. Not a one. Lust pays no price. Lust will never stand firm when things get a little tough. Lust will always run and hide. When we make the sacrifice to love, it's harder to just walk away. Because we lust, we can tell someone that we love them tonight and leave them in the morning. Not only leave them in the morning, but justify that we did the right thing. Sacrifice is the anchor to our love. Sacrifice is what gives our love roots. With every sacrifice, love grows, love deepens; love entangles our self to another. We long for that entanglement. Without sacrifice, the love that everyone says they have is really not love at all. It's only lust!

LUST IS ONLY ABOUT SELF.
LOVE IS ALL ABOUT EVERYONE ELSE.

In the world today, love is truly only an illusion; here today, gone tomorrow. So many people use the word *love,* but they lie every time they say the word. The love lie tells you that love is only about you. The love lie tells you that love is all about your pleasure. The love lie tells you that love is there only to satisfy your desires. The love lie tells you to get all you can, any way that you can, from everyone you can. The love lie tells you that it does not matter who gets hurt as long as you are getting yours.

This is exactly the love the devil wants the world to know. This is the love that is giving the devil license to destroy the world today. This is selfish love and society today applauds and rewards selfishness. The devil laughs every time someone today uses the word *love* because the devil knows what a great job he has done in twisting the love that God wants the world to know to the perverted version of love that we show each other today.

ALL THE ILLS IN THE WORLD TODAY CAN BE TRACED TO AN UNWILLINGNESS FOR US TO SACRIFICE

THE GREATER THE ILL = THE GREATER THE SACRIFICE

I've already written this a couple of times, and I know that before the final pages are written, I will write this again:

WHEN ENOUGH OF US BECOME THE LOVE OF GOD IN THE WORLD TODAY, ALL THE PROBLEMS OF THE WORLD WILL DISAPPEAR.

If enough of us were truly concerned about hunger, violence, poverty, disease, hatred, homelessness, then these issues and so many more would disappear from the face of the Earth.

How do we go about showing this concern? How is it possible for us to demonstrate our sacrifice? The demonstration is only possible through you showing your love. If there are no visible signs, if there is no tangible evidence of your love in action, then you do not have the love of God living inside of you. If your love produces no works, then we have no love. Without that love, without the love of God producing works through you, we will never fix a thing.

How far are you willing to take your sacrifice for your Lord and Savior? What are you willing to sacrifice to gain the love of God? What commitment will you make to show your love to your Lord? Let's take a moment and let me share a story with you about sacrifice, just to show you how God works.

A few months before I started writing this chapter, God came to me to talk with me about the life of a bondservant. I had never heard the word *bondservant* before, and at the time, I really did not understand what God was trying to teach me. But I did write everything down. God was teaching me about the life of a bondservant before God taught me about His love. I know why now. Before you can completely understand love, you must first understand the sacrifice involved.

A bondservant is someone who has gained their freedom, but because of his love for his master, the bondservant takes his freedom and chooses to remain with his master. The bondservant loves his master so much that the bondservant chooses to stay with his master and to be his master's slave for the remainder of his life.

We too have that freedom and we are able to make that same choice for our Lord: to become God's bondservant.

The bondservant does not live for himself but lives completely for his master. Becoming the bondservant is a total commitment to a lifestyle of obedience to the master.

A true bondservant has no money of his own so he cannot spend freely with what he has been entrusted because it does not belong to him.

A bondservant does not have any time of his own. All the bondservant's time belongs to his master. A bondservant does not waste his free time because that time too does not belong to him. Time is truly one of the most precious gifts that we have been given by God. How we use our free time is a great indication of who we are serving or what we are worshipping. Whom do you serve with your time, yourself, the world, or are you choosing to serve God?

To volunteer to be a bondservant is the ultimate commitment that one can give. Those who choose to live the life do not live for themselves but live only for the will and wants of their Master.

LOVE = SACRIFICE

Are you willing to sacrifice your life for the love of your Lord? Are you willing, ready, or able to pick up the life of the bondservant for your Savior? What sacrifice are you willing to make?

Are you really ready to lose your life to gain your life? By your free will to choose to give up your old life to gain your new life, you can also choose to give that life as a bondservant to Christ.

But whatever was to my profit I consider a loss for the sake of Christ
What is more I consider everything a loss compared to the surpassing greatness of knowing Christ Jesus my Lord for whose sake I have lost all things. I consider them rubbish, that I may gain Christ and be found in him. (Philippians 3: 7 - 8)

God gave to man free will. What gives God His greatest joy is when you take that free will and choose to love and serve only God with all that you are, to choose to take up the life of a bondservant for your God. Can you do that for God?

So why is God's love so important? Let's look into the word of God:

We love because he first loved us. If anyone says, "I love God," and hates his brother, he is a liar; for he who does not love his brother whom he has seen cannot love God whom he has not seen.
And this commandment we have from him: whoever loves God must also love his brother. (I John 4: 19 -21)

I hear people say how much they love God all the time. But God says, and God says it very plainly, very directly, "If you say you love me, then you must love your brother." We must show love to all people. This is exactly where the world has gone wrong and this is exactly why so many people feel so far away from God. We can't show love to everyone. To get close to God, to really become connected with God, you must start to love as God loves. God makes it so easy. The words of God are so simplistic. Just love everyone. Why do we find that so hard? Even people who go to church every Sunday have a hard time with this one principal. We just cannot seem to be able to love everyone. But God says we must.

If you say you love God but harbor jealousy or envy in your heart towards another, if you covet or harbor ill feelings towards anyone, if you have anger and rage towards another, then God calls you a liar. If you cannot love the person next to you, walking down the street by you, sitting with you at work; if you cannot love the person who disappoints you or makes a mistake towards you; if you cannot show His love to the world around you, then you are a liar. So many of us look at that statement and tell ourselves, "God doesn't really mean me. God must be talking about you because I'm sure He is not saying those words to me."

God is talking to every one of us. God says, "If you cannot love him, then you do not love me. And if you do not love me, the Kingdom of Heaven you will never see!" Did that sink into you? Without the Kingdom, you cannot have eternal life. If you cannot love as God shows you love, then you will never possess God's Kingdom, and without the kingdom, you will never get the prize. What is the prize? Eternal life in Heaven. That is the ultimate goal that we, everyone, should be striving to attain every day. But if you cannot show love, the prize will never be yours. It's sad to say but this one fact alone, the love that you show to others, will keep a multitude from ever seeing the Kingdom of God.

This is exactly why it is so important, so critical, that you are making the love of God an integral part of your everyday life. If you are serious about living the life that you have right now for Jesus, then love must become the priority in your life. We must show the world God's love. We must become the demonstration of that love. The world is crying out for Jesus and we must show them the way.

There is a mandate in the scriptures for every person. Do you know what that is? Jesus commands us that we must love everyone. Leave no person out. You must love them all.

So God so loved the world that he gave his only begotten son, that whosoever believeth in him should not perish, but have eternal life
For God sent not his son into the world to condemn the world; but that the world through him might be saved. (John 3: 16 - 17)

Jesus consumed Himself, every minute of His short time on this Earth, showing love to the entire world. Jesus gave His love to everyone. Jesus is still giving His love to everyone even today. Why do we find it so hard to follow His example? If Jesus did not come to condemn the world, then why do we spend so much of our time condemning each other?

It's imperative that we must start now, showing, but not only showing, but giving God's love to everyone. Because I know that right now many of you are asking yourselves how is it possible for me to show love to every person; let me say something to you which might help.

You do not have to condone the actions of another, you do not have to like what they do for a living, you do not have to approve of how someone dresses, the length of their hair, how many earrings they have, how many tattoos are on their body, nor do you have to validate the words that someone speaks in order for you to show them the love of God. I have one more for you: It is never necessary for you to legitimate or approve of another's lifestyle, but you must show all people God's love.

I CAN LOVE YOU UNCONDITIONALLY
AS I RELATE TO YOU CONDITIONALLY

Jesus gave us the perfect example of how we are to love when He gave His love to the Samaritan woman at the well. Read the story in the John chapter four.

The church has messed up so many groups of people because of its refusal to show them the love of God. Jesus refused His love to no one. The church takes so many stances against so many groups of people. Jesus stood against no man. Jesus walked amongst all the people. Why if Jesus refused no one, are there are so many places that we will not go. So many people we will not talk to. What makes us better than Jesus?

We must stop selecting. We must stop dividing. We must stop choosing. We must stop making judgments. We prejudge so many, so quickly, deciding who we will show our love to, and who we won't. Just remember the mandate that Jesus gave to all of us. We must show His love to all people.

OUR COMPASSION MUST BE GIVEN FREELY TO EVERYONE
NEVER MADE TO BE EARNED BY NO MAN

Everyone, and I mean everyone, saved and the unsaved alike, has heard of the name of Jesus. But not everyone has felt the love of Jesus. And even fewer of us truly know the love of Jesus. That is our fault, we who say that we are followers of Christ. We are not giving the love of Jesus to the world.

Jesus does not make us earn His love. The love that Jesus has for all of us is just out there for us to take. So let me ask you: Why do you make the people in your life earn your love? And if you really inspect yourself, you will find that you do that constantly with almost everyone in your life. Why do we tell people through our actions that they must earn the love that I give to them?

Now that I have you thinking about love, let me begin to share with you some specific revelations that God has taught me about His love.

Let me share with you the second truth which God showed me about his love.

LOVE CANNOT BE GIVEN AND THEN TAKEN AWAY;
LOVE CAN ONLY BE GIVEN

Think about those two statements. Really contemplate the words that you just read. Spend some time and let those two sentences bounce around in your head for a while.

LOVE CAN ONLY BE GIVEN

Just that one sentence alone is enough to change everything you have ever known, thought you knew, or have ever felt about love. That one sentence alone will change how, when, why, to whom, and to what, we say that we love.

Love can only be given and never, never, never, ever can love be taken away. Once you say that word *love*, it's for keeps. It's forever. You can't take it back. God's love is permanent. God's love is forever. God's love never ends. When God says He loves you, it's for keeps. The love that you give must be the same. Your love must be permanent.

If you can grasp what God is trying to teach right here, if you can get the message of those two statements, if you will only embrace the love that God is showing you, if you can only put those two statements into practice in your everyday life, if you can only walk and treat everyone in your path by using the truth that God has just shown to you, then you will be on your way to taking the first steps in changing this world!!

The world will change and it will change one person at a time. One will change one who will change one who will change one. Right now, these words are changing you. By reading, you have been introduced to a new way to love. Can you take what you have just read and make this a part of your life? Are you willing to introduce and make this teaching a part of your everyday life? What are you will to change in the life that you are living today? Will you be the one to take this word and go change the world?

Security. How secure could you feel if you knew that no matter what happened, no matter what you said, no matter the disappointments, no matter the mistakes you made, once I told you that I loved you, that love, the love I give to you, was never going to go away? Permanence, Security, Peace of mind, Rest might just flood into your life. We all just want to find a secure place to lay our head. How different would the world be if we felt complete and total security in our relationships?

I know that before I found Jesus, my greatest fear, my greatest fear on a daily basis, was that I could and I would lose someone's love. I was always so fearful that the love that I had today, I would not have tomorrow. In the world, I never felt secure. Nor did I ever feel that the love that I was experiencing, at any given moment, was permanent. I feared that it was only a matter of time before that love would be taken from me. What a way to live one's life, in constant fear for one's security.

I was also so afraid to tell someone that I loved them. What if they didn't love me? What if they didn't say the words back? What if the love they had for me wasn't the same as the love I had for them? What if they did love me but I did something stupid and they would not love me anymore? All this doubt ran through my mind. Amazing, I ever said that word to anyone.

I know that I am not the only one who feels this way. I was so afraid to show love. I was so afraid to give love. I was so afraid just to say the word out loud. I was so afraid of being hurt. We want so desperately to be loved. We just want someone to love us. We want love in our lives so badly. But fear has crippled us. When you let fear in, that fear will paralyze you. Fear will keep you from living life. Fear will hold you back. That fear will keep you from joy and peace and rest. And that fear will keep you away from the abundant life that God has for you.

The spirit of fear paralyzed my life. Many times - many, many, many times in my life - I have lost someone's love; someone that I deeply loved. My second wife took her love away and I never saw it coming. That's devastation. It's when you are completely annihilated, when you lose love completely out of the blue, totally unexpectedly, completely blind sighted, that's the point when decisions are made that can change lives forever.

Someone you love suddenly dies. A family member betrays you. A spouse walks out on you. You have a blow up with a close friend and the friendship ends. You catch your wife in bed with a friend. Fathers and sons; Mothers and daughters; Losing loves like these, especially in a second, has the power to completely destroy you as a person.

Losing that kind of love is exactly what pushed me into two suicide attempts. Losing my wife's love, never feeling that I completely had my father's love, losing those types of love, the love from people for who you love deeply; when that happens to you out of the clear blue sky, deadly results can and often do occur. This is how a husband can kill a wife. A girlfriend can kill her lover. A person who has never had a suicidal thought can pick up a gun and kill himself. Lives are never the same. People never recover. I really want everyone to get this.

Taking love away; when you take your love from another, you are putting into motion a series of harmful thoughts on one end that quite often lead to deadly actions on the other. Yea, but no one ever got hurt. Just because no outside action was ever shown, you never know the death that you caused inside a person.

We damage, we hurt, and sometimes, we destroy so many people on so many different levels with the way we choose to give and take our love away. Well, I never get hurt. We give love and take love away with never a consideration or even a look back at the damage that we have caused. And some of us have hurt people plenty!

I heard a woman say the other day, "But people fall in and out of love all the time. What's the big deal?" She said it so casually, so nonchalantly, with almost with no feeling in her voice for the words that she was speaking. She said it like we should be used to it by now. How people just fall in and out of love. It happens to everyone, so just get over it.

We throw the word *love* around, without even realizing the time bombs that we have left behind in people's lives. The destruction that is about to go off at any time. One more break up. One more failed marriage. One more time my father says to me that I am a loser. One more fight with someone I love. All it will take is just one more person to walk out of my life. You could have just been that last one to push someone over to the brink of destruction. You never know.

What I do know is that these two statements hold the key to changing this world:

LOVE CANNOT EVER, UNDER ANY CIRCUMSTANCE, AT ANY TIME, BE GIVEN AND THEN TAKEN AWAY; LOVE CAN ONLY BE GIVEN

This is exactly the kind of love that God gives to all of us and this is the love that God wishes that we would show to each other. This statement encapsulates everything that is meant by the love of God. When we speak of unconditional love, this is the statement, and only this statement above defines what unconditional love must look like. If you will receive what that one statement says about love, then that one statement alone changes everything. It is the difference between love and lust.

Think of all the fear in the world that would be swept away in an instant. All the sadness, all the pain, all the anxieties, all the hurt, all the broken hearts that could be avoided and eliminated forever if we would only pledge to never take our love away once we have given that love to another.

How many suicides would be adverted? How many deaths avoided? How many lives would be changed? If everyone knew that the very minute you gave your love to them that love would never, could never, ever be taken away from them. That when you told someone, "I love you," there was nothing they could ever do to make you take that love away. You would always choose to love them the same way that God gives us His love, unconditionally and forever. I knew, the minute I discovered that God loved me, that God's love was forever.

Let me take this moment and talk a little bit about fear verses unconditional love. If asked, I don't believe that any person would choose to live their life in fear over living a life surrounded by unconditional love. Remember how I defined unconditional love: love that can only be given. The reason most of us live in fear is because we cannot be perfect. This lack of perfection makes us feel inadequate. Let me say this right now: God never expects any of us to be perfect. God wants us, as His sons and daughters, to strive every day for perfection, but God knows who we are. God is just looking for a people willing to be used, and being imperfect does not disqualify you from God using you for His purpose and glory. Just look in the Bible for so many examples: The Apostle Paul, Moses, Abraham, King David, all the Disciples - all imperfect men who were used mightily by God for His purpose and glory. And God will use you too.

So many people are searching for love, but feel they do not deserve to be loved. We have this feeling because we feel that we must be perfect for another to love us. If I were to show you my flaws, there is no way that you could ever love me. You could never love someone as messed up as me. That's the exact reason why dating is such a game. We never show all of our true self. We may show bits and pieces, but for the most part, we put on airs to cover up and to show the other person only what we think that they want to see, the part of us that we want them to see, so we can win their love. It's all part of the game. You see, we have made love just one big game. Just like playing a part in a play.

It's never until we say "I do" that the whole you is unmasked and let out to be seen. This is the fear we live in. We live in this constant fear that no one will ever love us for who we really are, so we play this masquerade game over and over again. I did all of this, but there is one more fear that I must warn you about. Once the "I dos" are said, we live - or let me say that I lived - every minute of every day with the fear that if I did something really wrong, or if I said something really stupid, that I had just given the other person the right or the excuse to withdraw their love and leave me. I lived in the constant fear that I could lose love in a second, and let me tell you that is no way to live a life.

God's love is unconditional love. Too many people have this belief that through my sins, because of what I have done, even God could never love me. We believe that we are even unworthy of God's love, and even if God did love me, I will just do something stupid to mess that up too. Somehow, someway, we have come to equate God's love and man's love as the same. We must begin to teach correctly that there is nothing, nothing that you have ever done, or nothing that you could ever do that will ever cause God to take His love away from you. That is unconditional love and that is the only love God has ever, or God will ever, pour out to us as His children. And this is the same love that we, as followers of Jesus, must begin to show the world.

But how can I do that? How can I love like God loves? How will it be possible for me to give my love unconditionally? How can I love the same people when all they want to do is hurt me? How can I love someone who does nothing but talk bad about me? How can I love somebody who may never love me back? How can I love somebody who does nothing but stab me in the back? How will it ever be possible for me to show all these people unconditional love?

Let me try to explain that to you. The third truth that God taught me about His love is:

LOVE IS NOT A FEELING
LOVE IS THE WAY I CHOOSE TO LIVE MY
LIFE
I CHOOSE TO SHOW GOD'S LOVE IN
EVERYTHING I DO

LOVE IS A WAY OF LIFE
LOVE IS A LIFESTYLE

DISCONNECT LOVE FROM YOUR FEELINGS
DISCONNECT LOVE FROM YOUR EMOTIONS

It's your feelings that want to masquerade themselves as love. Wrong. As long as your love is tied to your feelings, you will always be able to give and take your love away from the very ones you say you love the most. Your feelings get hurt; you take your love away. Someone talks bad about you; I hate that person. Someone stabs you in the back, and all you want to show is retaliation.

Your feelings become just like a yoyo. One minute, you feel good and you love everybody. The next minute, your feelings get hurt and you hate the world. It can and it does happen just that fast. We can turn our love on and off just like it's a light switch. I can love you, and then not love you in a matter of seconds.

If you give him the chance, the devil will hold the string to your yoyo. The yoyo is your feelings and the devil would like nothing more than to be in control and in charge of your feelings. The devil can cause more chaos, more doubt, and more confusion in your life when you allow the devil to be in charge of your feelings. When you attach your love to your feelings and the devil has control of those feelings, you now have the power to wreak chaos and confusion on the lives of every person that you come into contact with.

With the devil in charge, your ability to give and receive love will change every moment of every day. Think about your life for a moment. Reflect on how you give and receive love. Who is in charge? Is the love of God flowing through your life or is the love in your life bouncing up and down just like a yoyo? Be honest with yourself. In that honesty is the truth, and in that truth is freedom, and within freedom is restoration and a brand new way to live life in Jesus Christ! Learn and live and let the love of Jesus Christ flow through your life.

True love must always be stable. God tells us, "I am the same yesterday, today, and forever." If that statement does not speak stability, then I do not know what does. That means God's love is the same yesterday, today, and forever. When God tells you that He loves you, then His love is permanent, forever, and you can bank on that love because that love does not fail.

Your feelings and emotions have nothing to do with stability. The love you give to others cannot take them on a rollercoaster ride. That's exactly the reason why we are so messed up and how we can mess up so many people around us. We give them our love, which by now you know is only lust, and we take them on the ride of their lives. The love that we show people today in the world is a train wreck getting ready to happen at any second. And believe me the wreck happens just that quickly and just that often.

Do you have a person in your life who you are never sure just how to approach; especially first thing in the morning? One time, you walk up to them and they are nothing but friendly and giving. They are in a super good mood, smiling, laughing, and happy. But the next time you approach them, they rip your head off and you did not even have to say a word. You could not even get the words "good morning" out of your mouth. And as soon as you could you couldn't wait to run away from that person. As you walked away in confusion, you couldn't believe what just happened.

You may not realize it, but could this possibly be you? Do you feel like there are times where people avoid you? Do you find yourself asking, "Why are people always so defensive when they come around me?" Are you making people that way because of the rollercoaster ride you put them on? It's our feelings that are on that rollercoaster and because you have attached your love to those feelings, your love is on the same rollercoaster.

True love, the love that God gives to us, has nothing to do with feelings. God's love will never change. God gives His love freely to everyone, to the saved and unsaved alike. God loves every person on the Earth.

God gives His love to us all and He gives that love unconditionally. Make your love an action not a reaction. Choose to give your love away freely to everyone. Choose today to make love the way you live your life. Choose to love.

Choose to love everyone. When you make that choice in your life, when you choose to show love, then you will always be able to give that love to everyone, unconditionally.

Make love a decision not a reaction. Love is an act of your will, not your feelings. Choose to always show love. Remember that God gave us this gift of free will. God will give you everything but you still have to choose. Use that free will and choose to love. We make choices every day. What we are going to eat. What we are going to do today. What we are going to watch on television. Who we are going to talk to. Our day, every minute of our day, is full of choices. We choose what life we want to live. It's your will, your choice. Choose love. Make that choice. Choose love to be your way of life.

LOVE IS NOT WHAT YOU SAY WITH YOUR LIPS; LOVE IS ONLY SHOWN THROUGH THE LIFE THAT YOU LIVE!!

Love must be built. Ever heard some say, "I knew I loved her the minute I saw her. It was love at first sight." Nothing that will stand the test of time can be built in a second. What you have built in that second is an attraction. For all you people and I was one of those who have ever said that it was love at first sight, be honest and look back. Was it really love or was it attraction at first sight? Attraction never stands the test of time, and in today's world, far too many relationships are built upon an initial attraction.

Jesus teaches a parable in Matthew Chapter 24 about the wise man who built his house upon the rock, and when the storms came, his house withstood all the storms. However, there was another man who built his life upon the sand, and when the storm came, his house fell. This is exactly how we do love. When love is built upon attraction, you have built your love upon sand, and when the first argument comes, we are running away. But if your love is built upon God the rock, when the storms of life come, you have the foundation to weather all the storms and you have no reason to run.

Choose to live your life as Jesus lived His. Choose to do as Jesus did. Choose to always give the love of God to everyone in every situation. That's exactly what Jesus did. Jesus showed everyone love in every situation He came upon. Jesus came and walked this Earth to show us how we can and should live our lives. Jesus was the living demonstration of how we are to live. Make your love the action in your life.

Jesus came as a man, walked as flesh and blood, to show us men the life that we are capable of living. We can walk and live the exact same life as Christ lived!

So that Christ may dwell in your hearts through faith -- that you, being rooted and grounded in love. (Ephesians 3: 17)

We know that at the time of salvation, Christ comes to dwell in our hearts but what the Apostle Paul is talking about here is that our hearts are to become the home of Jesus. Our hearts are to be the permanent residence of Jesus. A home is that place where you love to be. It is the same with Jesus living in our hearts. Jesus loves to live in our hearts.

Love is the soil in which our lives must have their roots. The Apostle Paul tells us to be rooted and grounded in love. To be rooted and grounded in love is to take the love that God has given to you and make that love your way of life. The life you live with that love is unselfish. We live today in such a selfish world. It's a "me first" world. The life you live with God's love is a life of unselfish giving. We give with never a thought of ourselves; never a thought. We need to learn and live the word *compromise*. When you are living a life of unselfish love, you are living the life of Christ. You are beginning to live the same life that Christ lived. You are walking this Earth as if Christ was still walking this Earth today.

Choose to always give your love in every situation. As you go through your day, doing the daily things that each of us do, I ask you, no I beg of you, that in whatever situation that you may find yourself in, no matter how extreme the situation may be or how small and trivial the situation may be, before you respond to that situation, I beg of you to stop and ask yourself one question:

WHAT WOULD LOVE DO NOW?
WHAT WOULD LOVE DO NOW?

NO OTHER QUESTION AT THAT TIME SERVES ANY PURPOSE!
NO OTHER QUESTION AT THAT TIME IS RELEVENT!
NO OTHER QUESTION AT THAT TIME MATTERS!

In the beginning, a small voice will come to you. From your inside, that small voice will give you the answer to that question.

WHAT WILL LOVE DO NOW?

Your spirit is that voice and your spirit will give you the answer. When that answer comes, just do it. Don't think about it. Don't ask yourself other questions. Put that answer into immediate action. Your spirit will never give you the wrong answer to that question.

WHEN YOU FOLLOW THAT VOICE, YOUR SPIRIT, THAT SMALL VOICE, WILL ALWAYS BRING OUT THE JESUS IN YOU, MAKING YOU THE PERSON THAT GOD MADE FOR YOU TO BE!

At that moment, you are following God's purpose for your life. Continue to follow that voice inside you to your destiny.

We hear constantly in the world that love comes from the heart. I am here to tell you that true love, the love that God implants in you, comes through your spirit and rests in your soul. The true you, the authentic you, the higher you that dwells within your soul wants and desires to be a loving person. Not a lustful person, but a loving person. By now, you should see and know the difference. We all want to receive love, not lust, and we should all desire to give love to all those that we meet.

We all want to feel loved. For the vast majority of us, we have never felt the kind of love that I have been writing about. We have never felt pure, unpolluted, uncompromising love. But when you follow the voice and give away what God has given to you, His love, for the first time, you can experience and feel real love. It is in the giving that you get to feel God's love. By giving God's love to another, you get to know God's love. You feel the deepness of God's love. God's love begins to grow within you.

IF YOU WANT TO MAKE PROGRESS ON THE PATH AND ASCEND TO THE PLACES YOU HAVE LONGED FOR, THE IMPORTANT THING IS NOT TO THINK MUCH BUT TO LOVE MUCH, AND TO DO WHATEVER AWAKENS YOU TO LOVE
                    -- THE INTERIOR CASTLE STARR

Let's stop for a moment and try to give this word *love* a definition. So many people, and I was one of them, when asked what *love* is, have a hard, or even impossible, time putting a definition to this small little word. The best definition that I have found outside the bible is:

IF I TRULY LOVE YOU, THEN I DESIRE ONLY THE BEST OF ALL THINGS FOR YOU

Only the best, I should wake up every morning wanting only the best for another. That is why love should never hurt. How is it possible for us to hurt the one we say that we love, especially when we only want the best for that person?

Are you starting to see the differences between love and lust? Are you beginning to awaken to the truth?

I hear this from people (men and women almost equally): "But I really love him or her. He or she stays out all night. He or she cheats on me. He or she lies to me. They steal from me. They deceive me. I cannot trust them. I never know where they are or what they are doing. In some cases, they are abusive towards me. But I stay with them because I love them. I love them with all my heart. They are my life. And here is maybe the one that I dislike the most; I stay with them because they are my soul mate."

Nothing that I just described has anything to do with love. The world today knows nothing; let me repeat that; the world today knows nothing about love. We say we love another when all we do is hurt that person. Let me say this again right here, right now. Love never hurts. If it is hurting you in any way, it is not love. Call it what it is: lust. Love never hurts another.

Love was meant to be the giving of one person to another in a lifetime of commitment. That's right I said it, a lifetime commitment. People today can't make a commitment today that they will keep for five minutes, let alone a lifetime. Stop calling it love and call it what it truly is:

IT'S LUST!!!

They lie, they cheat, they steal, and I stay with them because I lust after them. Call it what you do, and call it what it really is; it's lust.

Real love, the love that God gives, only wants the best for another. That means love does not ever, love will never ever, cause pain to another. Love does not hurt. I do not care what the world tries to teach you. Love never hurts another intentionally. Love never causes wounds to another. I love you and I only want the best for you every day.

What is the best that I could want for you; to see that you achieve eternal life with our Lord. That is the best that I could want for you. My highest desire in loving you is that I will do everything in my power to help you reach eternal life. The opposite side of that is that I will never do anything, or place anything in front of you, that may cause you to fall. That is my pledge of love to you.

THE TRUE MEASURE OF LOVE IS NEVER BY WHAT I SAY;
THE TRUE MEASURE OF LOVE IS THROUGH WHAT I DO!!!!

The other way to define the word *love* is through the word of God. To find the truth, always look toward the word of God. To know about the love of God, look towards Jesus.

Many people read and quote the word from I Corinthians 13, and because they can quote this passage of scripture, they will try to convince you that they know all about love. Wrong. The majority of the church-going population who read this passage still has no idea what the love of God is supposed to look like; too many church folk still living in lust. They carry no love within them and have no ability to show the world the love of Christ. Let me say it like this: there are still too many church folk carrying their fourteen-pound bible around with them and they are still as mean as a two-headed snake. They have heard all about the love of God but know nothing about the love of God. They know that God loves them, but have no idea how to show that same love to a world which is begging to know that God also loves each of them.

They read the chapter in I Corinthians, they quote the chapter, but they do not live a life modeled after the words written in this chapter of the bible. We talked about ignorance a few moments ago. We can possess a ton of book knowledge in our brains and still be as ignorant as a rock in our actions. People read this chapter in the bible and still are clueless as to what the true meaning of God's love is. We can read books all we want, including the bible, but if we cannot put that reading into our expressions, into our actions, than that knowledge is useless.

Go back and read the chapter again. I don't care if you have it to memory; go back and read it again. Read it real slowly. Let the words sink into you. Let the words come to have a meaning for you. Read and stop at each verse. Let the words come alive. Stop as long as it takes for you to become one with the words, for you to become one with this truth, for you to become the love of God. Let your spirit guide you as you read. Don't hurry. Take all the time that you need. Let God teach. Let God touch you with the words. Let God put His love inside of you. Let God pour His love inside and let that love settle inside of you to become your new way of life.

How does God define His love? The definition starts in the fourth verse and ends in verse eight, but please read the entire chapter.

Using the words that God uses to define his love, let's dig deeper into each word to find the truth that will guide us as we begin to walk in the love of God. What is love?

1) Love is patient -- Patience is staying calm without complaining or ever losing self-control. Staying patient knows no time. We never lose our cool for as long as it takes.
2) Love is kind -- To be kind is to be charitable, to go out of your way for another. It is the giving of yourself for another with never one thought about how this giving might affect you. This quality of love searches out opportunities to do

good for all in need. As kindness grows not only will you see opportunity but you will begin to also feel the pain of others.
3) Love bears all things -- True love will hide and conceal all the faults of others. This is a love that never publicizes the faults or failures of others. The confidence of others is not only respected but cherished and valued.
4) Love believes all -- God's love never gets involved in idle chit chat, water cooler gossip, backstabbing, or the spreading of rumors. This is a love that only has the ability to speak positive words into another's life.
5) Love hopes for all -- Love should only want the best for everyone. We should never wish and hope for bad on anyone. We must become the cheerleaders in each other's lives. Not only cheer for those we like, but we must hope and cheer for the best in the lives of those sometimes who have hurt us the most.
6) Love endures all – This is a love which has the power to stand under persecution and ridicule. When you are walking in this love it no longer matters how the world wants to judge you. This is a love that keeps anger from harboring inside of us and protects us from doing the devil's bidding. Never give in to provocation or peer pressure. Never give in to the temptation of retaliation. Never give in to a feeling of resentment. When you are walking in the love of God, that love never ever succumbs to the power of revenge.
7) Love rejoices in truth -- Love does not take pleasure in wickedness. This love never takes any pleasure in getting even. There is a mean streak in our nature about getting even; don't buy into it. This spirit of love does not take any pleasure in another's sin. We never, never combat evil with evil.

The truth will also set you free. God's love sets you free. Freedom is found in the love of God. God's love sets you free from fear. Free from worry. Free from burdens. Free from all the things of the world that have us bound. Love can only truly be love when it does set you free.

What God's love is not.

1) Love does not envy -- Love always exalts in the success of others. Love gives honor to everyone. We honor and we respect. What God gives to my brother is for my brother, and I rejoice in those gifts which are given to my brother. I rejoice in my brother's blessings.

2) Love does not boast -- Remember that love is a free gift from God. We did nothing to receive this gift. We have nothing to be proud of in ourselves. We never have a reason to see ourselves as better than another man because of the free gift God has chosen to give to everyone. Remember that the key to God's love is that God gives us His love to give away to everyone we meet. We are to give His love away freely and without choice.

3) Love is never rude -- In every situation, the love you show to others is always courteous and considerate.

4) Love is never self-seeking -- The aim of love is to help and to serve others. Never to please oneself. True love never counts the cost to oneself. This is a love which always yields to the needs, desires, and wants of others. True love compromises. Is it always so necessary to be right, that we wound the ones whom we say that we love? The love of self destroys God's love.

5) Love is not easily angered -- Love cannot be provoked into anger but is willing to endure slights and insults. Love will take public ridicule and chastisement knowing that it is love that conquers all.

6) Love keeps no record -- The love that God gives to us always, always forgives and then forgets. If you cannot forget, then you have not forgiven. Love forgives and moves forward without ever giving another look back.

7) Love never delights in evil -- Our love must never give in to treachery, deceit, backhandedness, revenge, or cunning. The ways of evil must not ever be our ways. Love never places blame or cares about guilt. Love never suspects the actions of another. Love does

not start or spread rumors for the delight of the evil that may be caused. Love never instigates.

LOVE NEVER FAILS

God's love is a love that will last forever. God's love is permanent. God's love is eternal. God's love is the love that only goes one way. Remember this statement:

LOVE CAN ONLY BE GIVEN; IT CAN NEVER BE TAKEN AWAY

In the final verse of the chapter, the Apostle Paul writes:

FAITH, HOPE, AND LOVE THESE THREE ABIDE; BUT THE GREATEST OF THESE IS LOVE. (1 Corinthians 13:13)

These three graces of the spirit, these three fruits, are superior to the gifts of the spirit. When you possess the fruits, you will know how to handle and what to do with any gift that God may bestow upon you.

Faith, hope, and love - these three are eternal; but the greatest of these is love. So let me ask you a very important question:

WHAT WILL YOU CARRY WITH YOU INTO HEAVEN? If you said nothing, then that is the wrong answer. We spend all our time here on Earth trying to gain titles, awards, and accolades. We spend all our time on this Earth trying to amass cars, property, and money. We call this wealth. We hoard all this so-called wealth, trying to impress our wives, our friends, our neighbors, our co-workers. We want people to be impressed with all the stuff that we have. And God is not impressed with any of that stuff.

We spend all our time here on Earth trying to accomplish yearly goals, thinking that we are making ourselves better by "building a better life for me and my family." We spend so much time here on Earth trying to win acceptance and gain more friends. And in the end, not one of these things - not one of the things that I have listed above - is going with us into God's Kingdom. I have been fortunate in my life not to have had to attend a lot of funerals, but the ones that I have attended, I have never seen a truck going behind the hearse, carrying all the possessions of the deceased. "Look at all the things I have and they are all going with me to my grave." Sorry, but it doesn't work that way.

So what is it that I will take with me to heaven? What things should I be trying to gain while I am here on Earth?

The answer to the question is the same thing that we have been talking about in this chapter.

AM I GROWING IN MY CAPACITY TO LOVE?

Every year, we should be asking ourselves this question. Not "What New Year's resolution am I going to make for this upcoming year?", but "Am I growing each year in my capacity to love?" The enemy that I had last year I should be able to love this year. Success and failure must be measured in our capacity to love each other.

As we learn about God's love and put these principles into practice in our everyday lives, every year we should - no, we must - grow in our capacity to love. Not just the easy people in our lives to love, but the really difficult people. Your love must grow to cover all men. Our ability to love as God loves us should grow year after year after year after year. We must look deep into ourselves. Take inventory of the person that we are becoming. We must be able to ask ourselves the really tough questions. And then, once asked, we should give ourselves the truthful answer. That is how we are going to grow in God. That is how we are going to become as God became. That is the only way that we will become the true imitators of Christ; by growing every year in Christ. By growing every year in our capacity to love as Christ loved all men.

Faith, hope, and love, these three, but the greatest of these is love. When you take your last breath here on Earth, which will also be your first breath in heaven, you will no longer need faith or hope, because you will now be in the presence of God.

Then all that is left is love. In heaven, there is only love, God's love, Agape love, Eternal love, and Unconditional love. From that moment, when you first step into the presence of God, from that moment to eternity, you will be spending it with God and being surrounded only by the love of God. What a day that is going to be! What a prize you will be rewarded with.

There is much more that I must share with you about God's love.

The next step to mastering and understanding God's love is to learn about the four keys of love. When you make the commitment that you will make love your way of life, then you must show that love without:

1) ANY EXPECTATIONS
2) NO REQUIREMENTS
3) NEVER NEEDING ANYTHING IN RETURN
4) THAT LOVE EVER ENDING

Combine those four keys with the three truths that you have already learned about love:

1) LOVE EQUALS SACRIFICE
   SACRIFICE EQUALS LOVE
2) LOVE CAN ONLY BE GIVEN

3) LOVE IS THE WAY I CHOSE TO LIVE MY LIFE

And now, you have all the ingredients to make your love pure. This is God's love. This is the love that God gives to you. This is the love that we must learn to show each other. This is the love that will save the world.

On the first couple of pages of this book, I gave you two statements that I will keep referring back to from time to time:

WHEN THE MAJORITY OF US IN THE WORLD
BECOME THE LOVE OF GOD,
ALL THE PROBLEMS OF THIS WORLD WILL
DISAPPEAR.

ALL THE ILLS OF THIS WORLD CAN BE TRACED
BACK TO AN UNWILLINGNESS FOR US TO
SACRIFICE.

TRUE STATEMENTS!!!!!

1) TO LOVE WITHOUT EXPECTATIONS
The Webster dictionary defines *expectation* as looking for a future result. This is the <u>KEY</u> to loving as God loves. To love with no expectation. To give love so freely that you are without needing or expecting anything in return. We give someone a gift for their birthday and we automatically expect a gift in return on our birthday. It's not that we would say such a thing, but in our minds, that's what we expect. And when that gift does not come, we get offended. Remember offense and where that will take you.

God gives us His love without ever looking for a response back from us. Can you give with no expectation of any kind?

This kind of love - love that expects nothing back - this is the love that leads you into the path of freedom. The lack of expectation is the key to freedom. We talk of freedom, but we know nothing of freedom, because to truly experience freedom, you must have no expectation. As long as you must have something in return - as long as you are looking towards receiving something in the future - you have no chance of ever being free.

Freedom comes when you can wake up in the morning and the only necessity you have for the day is for God to command your footsteps. We do not realize that true freedom comes in the giving of oneself without looking for anything in return. True and real freedom is only found in a life led by God. God's love removes all expectations. We must love one another without ever looking for a response.

The freest man I have ever read about to live on this Earth was Jesus. Jesus lived His life on Earth without expecting anything from anyone. Jesus only gave and never desired anything in return from anybody. Jesus gave without ever looking for a response. This is the love that we must learn. To walk and give as Jesus did; to give love, desiring nothing in return. Not even a thank you. To change the world, we must become imitators of Christ in every way. And we must start in the way that we show each other love. To love without expectation is truly the key. We must stop with the lip service and we must begin to match the words that we speak with the things that we do.

WE MUST BECOME A PEOPLE WHO SPEAK LESS AND DO MORE

Now that I have said all that, let me spend some time talking about relationships.

How many of us go looking for a relationship, or we get into a relationship already having expectations, or we already have a future result for that relationship in our minds? If you cannot live up to the expectation that I have, then you may not be worthy of my love. If you are unable to meet my list of expectations, (oh yes, most of us have a list), if I cannot check you off on my list, then maybe you are not the one. That's how we have learned to love in the world, by you fulfilling what I expect. Fulfilling my list of demands. My list of my needs and my wants. My wish list for love. If it's not you, then I will just move on to the next one.

As a man, I can speak of my expectations. Yes, I had them. Even before I met the women, I knew what was on my list. What exactly it was that I was looking for, and as a man, the list was all superficial. She had to look a certain way. She had to dress a certain way. She had to make me look good in front of my friends. She had to be able to support herself. Well, I guess you get the idea. I don't need to give you the whole list. But if she could not pass the list, then she was out.

I use myself as an example for us men, but I know that you women have the same types of lists. Having never been shown one, I don't know what is on them, but I am sure the women's list is just as shallow as the men's list.

Expectations give rise to our fears. We only tell someone that we love them, fully expecting them to tell us that they love us back. "I love you too." Those expectations give rise to the fear that lives in our lives. We won't say the word first because of fear. What if she doesn't say she loves me back? If she doesn't say the words, then what do I do? That fear stops you from living your life. That fear will cause you to change the way you live your life.

Rejection, such a powerful word. The word alone can bring fear into some people's lives. Fear of being rejected will paralyze the way you live. What if I cannot live up to their expectations of me? It's one thing to do it for a few weeks while you're dating. It's completely another to have to live up to expectations in a marriage for life. You will stop living; stop making choices, stop making decisions, because of fear. We are so afraid, so scared of being rejected. Really, in all actuality, the real fear is not in the rejection but what happens after we have been rejected. The real fear is in being left all alone.

Because we have been rejected so much, we start building walls. Big walls. High walls. Tall walls. Thick walls. Walls made of concrete. Walls that we build between us and love. Walls between you and people. Walls between you and God. The more rejection in your life, the higher and wider the walls you build.

Know this first: that fear is a tool of the devil. The devil uses fear to keep you from God. When you are walking with God, you have nothing to fear. Jesus told us that where His love was, there was no fear. Love and fear cannot occupy the same space. You can only have one or the other. Jesus is on our side and it is that same Jesus who has already defeated the devil. The devil is defeated and we know no fear. Tell fear to get out of your life, once and for all. The love of God lives in me, so fear cannot.

And we have known and believed the love that God has for us. God is love; and he that dwells in love dwells in God and God in him.
Herein is our love made perfect, that we may have boldness in the Day of Judgment: because as he is, so are we in this world. There is no fear in love; but perfect love casts out all fear: because fear has torment.
He that has fear is not made in perfect love.
We love him because he first loved us. (I John 4: 16 - 19)

God's love, the love that we are learning about, is that perfect love. That is what God wants to teach here: His perfect love. How you too can walk in that perfect love. It is only God's love - that perfect love - that drives out all fears. Everyone has fears. We may all really want to believe that we are tough people. I fear nothing. Nothing can hurt me. Everyone has a fear, and right now, I am not just talking about a fear of spiders.

Only through the perfect love that God gives to each of us can we break the chains and the bondage of fear. Through God's love, you can be released from your fears. It is freedom that God gives to all of mankind through His perfect love. Only God can do that.

God gives to you His perfect love that will cast out all your fears and it is through God's love that the truth will be revealed.

I love you and I do not expect you to be or to do anything in return for my love!!

2) TO LOVE WITHOUT ANY REQUIREMENTS
A requirement as defined by the Webster dictionary is to be put under an obligation by another. An obligation is something that one has to do to please another.

I will love you until you do something that I disagree with. Until you do something that I do not like. Until you do something that disappoints me. Until you do something that I instructed you not to do. What requirements do you put on your love? What obligations do you put upon another so they can have your love? Love that has requirements is love that manipulates. Love that manipulates is the worst kind of love. It leaves the deepest wounds and it breaks hearts into a thousand pieces. People go to their grave with these wounds unless they are touched with God's grace, God's mercy, and God's love.

Both men and women, just like expectations, have their lists of requirements:

I require him or her to have and keep a job.
I require him or her to let me do what I want to do.
I require him or her to take care of me financially.
I require that they have their own place.
I require that they put up with my mess.
I require that they satisfy my needs.

I require him or her to have an education.
And this list can go on and on and on. I have actually seen this list fill multiple pages.

In our marriage vows, we say "for better or for worse," but when the worse comes, how many of us are running out the door?

How many of us as parents dole out our love to our children based on what their report card looks like, or how well they do in sports, or if they behave at grandma's, or how well they live up to our expectations?

We say that we love them with all of our hearts and we may never take all of our love away, but how many of us have degrees of love? I am really mad at you right now. You have really disappointed me again. I can't believe that you are in trouble again. You have really let me down this time. We tell them that we love them, but your actions show another side. Your authentic love is shown through your actions.

We require people, all the time, to do the things that we want for them to do, and if they fall short, then we withhold our love to them. "I love you if _____."
How would it be if God treated us that way? If God treated us the same way that we treat each other, then we would never feel or ever know the love of God!

God loves us all unconditionally and God requires us to do nothing for that love. When God says that He loves you, there are no requirements to keeping that love. There is nothing you have to do, and better yet, there is nothing you can do. God loves all of us. No hoops to jump through. No tricks to perform. No magic words to say. God loves you and God has no requirements.

3) TO LOVE WITHOUT EVER NEEDING ANYTHING IN RETURN

We are such needy people. We are born needy. The minute we come out of the womb, we already have needs. We spend the majority of our time thinking, scheming, and plotting as to how to get our needs met. Without God in our lives, it is impossible for us to move beyond our own needs. We go searching for love to fulfill our needs. We fall in love, hoping that other person will fill the void in our lives. What can you do for me? We may never ask that question out loud, but we sure are thinking it all the time.

How many times have you heard someone say, "That person completes me."? Really what we are saying is, "That person gives me what I need." When you must have another person to complete you, you will always judge the quality of the relationship by what you are able to get from the other person. I hate to break the bad news to you, but that relationship is doomed.

Why do relationships fail? Why do marriages fail? You are no longer able to meet the needs of the other person. I love you as long as you can take care of what I need. The minute you can no longer take care of my needs, I no longer need you and I must find another. That's how we can so easily go from one to another to another to another, because fulfilling my needs is always the top priority in my life.

Fulfilling another person's needs is just like taking drugs. In the beginning, it only takes a little effort to fulfill their needs; you can almost do anything and the need is fulfilled. But as time goes by, and the person's needs become greater, the effort it takes to fill those needs becomes huge.

As time goes on, either one of two things happens in these types of relationships:

A) You use the person up, filling your needs to the point where they can no longer fill all the needs that you have. So you, as the needy person, discard that person for a new person who can fill your needs. So you constantly are going from one to one to another to another, constantly using up and discarding people.

B) The person filling your needs eventually gets fed up and tired of feeding your needs and they discard you for someone who is less needy.

For the vast majority of people, we have come to the belief that love must be earned. We believe that we must do things to earn love. The more we do, the more you will love me. I believed this wholeheartedly when I was in the world. I believed if I could out-do the other guy, you would love me more. The problem with that thinking is that the person needs the recognition. The recognition becomes their drug, and if not recognized, they begin to feel unloved. If these feelings go on over a period of time, then resentment builds. See the pattern, or better yet, see anyone you know?

It is only through the love of God that your needs can ever truly be met and completely fulfilled, only through God.

4) TO LOVE WITHOUT LOVE EVER ENDING
Once you give your love to another, you can never take that love back. Pray carefully with God about who you give your love to. Be very careful how you use, and who you say, the word *love* too.

Remember when I said earlier that I could never put a definition to the word *love*? This is exactly why. When it comes to the four keys to love that we just discussed, I was one of those things at one time or another. My love had requirements. My love always had expectations. And my love could end in a second. I had no idea what love was and that was why I could never define the word *love*.

How many of you have children? I have a son. He is twenty-two. I regret every day that I never showed him love correctly. I did not know how. That is no excuse. I knew nothing about God's love. It was my ignorance, but my ignorance affects others.

You first learn how to love from your parents. Children may not listen, but they always watch. Your parents - these two are your first examples, your first demonstration, and your first models of how love works in the world. The type of love you received from your parents sets the stage for the kind of love that you are going to go out into the world and give. What kind of love did your parents show to you?

Will your love be controlling?
Will your love be demanding?
Will your love be needy?
Will you take people on a rollercoaster ride with the love you give?
Will your love come out of the fears in your life?
Will you take your love away from the same people whom you say that you love the most?
Will your love demand that people meet your requirements?
Before you show love, what expectations do you have?
Are you too scared to even say the word?

If you have children, just as I do, then what are you teaching your children about love? You cannot teach about love only using the words that come out of your mouth.

Remember, love is an action. Love is more than just a word that we speak. Love is a way of life. Love can only be taught through your actions. In this particular case, your actions speak intensely louder than your words. Your children will follow what you show them. They will mimic your actions. In the case of teaching love, it's one hundred percent all about your actions.

While we are on this subject of love and our children, let me throw in a thought for you to ponder:

Are you providing your children with a home, or is it just a house? Can you see the difference? There is a huge difference. Can knowing God's love be the difference between living in a just a house or being raised in a home?

In order for you to be able to start this process of loving as God loves, you must first do some things for yourself.

First you must learn to love yourself. You cannot give what you do not possess. So many people go through this life condemning themselves and without ever being able to show themselves love. Because of God's grace, God's mercy, and God's love, you can love yourself. Let me share with you two of my favorite scriptures that speak on this. When I first accepted the Lord as my savior, God led me to these scriptures so I could learn to love and forgive myself.

There is no condemnation for those who are in Jesus Christ. (Romans 8: 1)

No matter what you have done, no matter how bad your past might have been, God has already forgiven you. Not only has God forgiven you, but God sent His only son, Jesus Christ, to die on that cross so that all your sins can be forgiven. God has already forgiven you for whatever it is. No matter how big. No matter how bad. Forgive yourself and stop beating yourself up over your past. Jesus took it all on the cross for you and for me. Let it go! Forgive and forget.

Therefore if any man is in Christ, he is a new creature, the old has passed away and the new has come. (II Corinthians 5: 17)

This is a promise from God. Accept Jesus as your Lord and savior. Let God make you a new person. Hallelujah!! God will make you brand new. God will give you a brand new way to live life. Let your past go. Take the Lord up on this promise. I did and God made me brand new.

God will fill your life with peace and joy and His love. God will take away all your pain, all your worries, and all your burdens. Surrender everything from your past to God. Give God everything. Do not hang on to anything. Empty yourself of your past so that God can, and will, fill you with the new. So God can fill you with His love.

It is exactly what God did for me. I gave up everything to God and God filled me with everything that He wanted me to have. The Lord took all my bad and filled me with the good stuff: His peace, His joy, His love, His meekness, His patience. Let God do these things for you. God wants to do this for you; you only have to ask.

God is asking you right now:

WHAT WOULD LOVE DO NOW?

There is one piece to God's love that I still must share with you, one more truth. In order for you to truly love as God loves, you must be able to look beyond another's faults and see only the person's needs. This is a biggie.

We as individuals, and especially we as a country, fix very little and we solve very few problems. The reason for this is that we are too busy listing faults and placing blame. Just look at our leaders, the group of people whom we send to Washington to supposedly get things done. Look at our Congressmen and our Senators to see the example of what I am talking about in action. We spend so much of our time, energy, and resources in finding fault and placing blame that, in the end, there is nothing left in time, energy, and resources to fix the need.

Love, God's love, looks beyond all fault and only sees the need. True love, genuine love, is not concerned about anything else. You know that you are walking in God's love when you can see a need and you will not rest until that need is solved. You know that you are walking in God's love when you stop listing and start fixing.

This is the love that Jesus showed us as He walked the Earth. Jesus took care of people's needs. We must begin to take care of each other's needs. Not only when there is a disaster, but take care of needs on an everyday basis. We must do as Jesus did.

Jesus came as a man, walked upon this Earth, walked among us as a man, to show all of us what it is possible for each of us to accomplish.

You now have all the pieces as to how you can change the world. Now you know what the love of God is. You are no longer ignorant as to what God's love really is. If someone asked you, you can define for them the word *love*. Put these truths into practice. Put them to use in your everyday walk. Demonstrate these truths. Teach these truths. Give these truths away to every person in your life:

1) LOVE EQUALS SACRIFICE AND SACRIFICE EQUALS LOVE
2) LOVE CAN ONLY BE GIVEN - IT CAN NEVER BE TAKEN AWAY
3) LOVE IS NOT A FEELING - IT'S YOUR WAY OF LIFE
4) ALWAYS ASK - WHAT WOULD LOVE DO NOW?
5) ALWAYS BE LOOKING BEYOND THE FAULT AND SEE ONLY THE NEED

In the beginning, you will have to work at using these truths. None of this is easy, but the rewards are great. You will have to work hard to make these truths a part of your everyday walk. Earlier, we talked about a voice. A voice that is inside you. Right now, the voice of your spirit is just a small whisper. Your ego, which we will talk about in an upcoming chapter, now possesses the louder voice in your body.

As you put these truths into action, they will become easier and you will find yourself using the truths without even thinking about them. You will find yourself asking the question, "What would love do now?" without even thinking. Just out of instinct. The voice of your spirit becomes louder and louder until it is the loudest voice that you will hear. As the voice of your spirit becomes louder and louder, and you find that you are following that voice more and more, you will find yourself making the choice to make love your way of life. As your life is making these changes, a test will come. Remember that you are walking in love, so you have no fear. Look forward to the test and have no fear. The test, if you are truly walking in this newfound love, the love that Jesus walked in, is forgiveness. If you love, then you will forgive.

The test of love is to forgive. To love everyone is to forgive everyone in all situations, all of the time. That is what Jesus did and still does. Jesus forgives. God forgives all when asked. God forgives us because God truly does love us.

But forgiveness also has a test. The test of forgiveness is to forget. Can you forgive and then forget? You cannot forgive without forgetting. Not only does real love forgive, but love forgets. Love keeps no record, ever! One forgives to the same degree that one loves. One forgets to the same degree that one loves and forgives. The three fit together just like the glove on your hand.

Your life is changing! God's love is becoming your way of life. Is it a challenge? Yes! Will you slip? Yes! Will you continue to work on the principles? Yes! Transformation is taking place and you will see your actions rubbing off on the others around you. The world will begin to change one person at a time. One touches one who touches one who touches one. I am beginning the process by touching you. Will you be the one that I touch who will take the word and touch another?

Your faith only works through love. (Galatians 5: 6)

THE ONLY THING THAT COUNTS IS FAITH EXPRESSING ITSELF THROUGH
LOVE

Your faith can never be idle. Your faith must be put into action and that action is love. Faith and love show themselves through our unselfish service to God and man. When we choose to accept God as our Savior, we choose a life of service. Jesus came to serve, not to be served. In order to walk in the love of God, we must become as Jesus and be of service to everyone. Remember that love's principles look beyond the fault and see the need. Once you see the need, be of service to that need.

When the Apostle James wrote, "Faith without works is dead," the Apostle was telling us that the true work of our faith is our love. My faith in God teaches me about the love of God, which leads me to the works that I must do for my Lord.

It is in the work that the Lord leads me to, which produces greater love for my Lord, leading me to greater faith in my God.

FAITH PRODUCES LOVE, WHICH BRINGS ABOUT THE WORKS,
    WHICH BRINGS ABOUT GREATER FAITH,
    WHICH LEADS TO A DEEPER LOVE,
    WHICH LEADS ME TO DO GREATER WORKS.

Why is love the first fruit of the spirit? Because all the other fruits are built upon love.

You cannot be meek without love.
You cannot have patience without love.
You cannot be longsuffering without love.

You cannot forgive without love.

There are people sitting in churches every Sunday morning who say that they believe in God but cannot show the homeless the love of God. They say that they have faith in God, but they possess not the work of faith. They say they trust in God, but they can't find their way into a prison to deliver a testimony.

They say they read the bible when they are not too tired. They say they pray when the time presents itself. They tithe on those Sundays when they choose to attend church. And they believe that by the works they do for themselves, they can work their way into heaven.

I can work my way into heaven if I attend church enough times. I can work my way into heaven if I tithe enough. I can work my way into heaven by singing in the choir. I can work my way into heaven by teaching Sunday school. I can work my way into heaven with all the scriptures that I can quote. Notice all the "I's" in those sentences.

It's not works alone that will get you into heaven and it is definitely not the works that you perform for your own benefit. Look at me, Lord. Look at all the things that I do for you. These works are what the bible calls "dead works."

It does not matter how many scriptures you memorize. It does not matter how elegant your prayer is. It does not matter how much money you tithe. God is not interested in your rituals. God is not interested in what you do for show. God is interested in the life that you live. Are you living your life for me? Are you living a Godly and a holy life? Are you living a life that imitates your heavenly father? How many times in God's word does God tell us, "Be ye holy for I am holy."

Works alone will not get you into God's kingdom; it is the love you show to God and the love you show to others that allows you entrance into God's kingdom.

Your love for God is what produces the works. If you do not have the love of God, then it will not matter how much or how many works you perform, because without love, God is not doing His work through you. You are doing your own works without God. Love is the key that opens the door to the kingdom. Without God's love, you will never enter the Kingdom of Heaven.

Not everyone who says unto me, lord, lord, shall enter into the kingdom of heaven; but he that does the will of my father which is in heaven
Many will say to me in that day, lord, lord, have we not prophesied in thy name? and in thy name have we cast out devils? And in thy name done many wonderful works?
And then will I profess unto them, I never knew you: depart from me, ye that work iniquity. (Matthew 7: 21 - 23)

For I was hungry and you gave me nothing to eat,
I was thirsty and you gave me nothing to drink,
I was a stranger and you did not invite me in,
I needed clothes and you would not clothe me,
I was sick and in prison and you would not look after me.
They also will answer, "Lord when did we see you hungry or thirsty or a stranger or needing clothes or sick or in prison and did not help you?"
He will reply, "I tell you the truth, whatever you did not do for one of the least of these, you did not do for me."
Then they will go away to eternal punishment, but the righteous to eternal life. (Matthew 25: 42 - 46)

Any man who says they love God but hates his brother is a liar. For any man who does not love his brother, who he has seen, cannot love God who he has never seen.
(I John 4: 20)

If you cannot love everyone, you do not love God. If you do not love God, you will not enter into the Kingdom of Heaven. These are not my words. These are the words of God.

In this the children of God are manifest, and the children of the devil: whosoever doeth not righteousness is not of God, neither he that loveth not his brother.
For this is the message that ye have heard from the beginning, that we should love one another. (I John 3: 10 - 11)

WITHOUT MAN'S FREE WILL, LOVE IS NOT LOVE.

GOD DESIRES FOR YOU TO LOVE HIM OUT OF YOUR FREE WILL.
LOVE IS THE KEY THAT OPENS HEAVEN'S DOOR!

As the love we have just spoken of in this chapter takes hold of you and develops within you, this deeper love for God and this all-encompassing love for every man, you will know that this love is living within you because you will see some very visible outward changes in the way that you act.

Many of us say that we love Jesus, but that love is only words that we say. Until that love is demonstrated by action, the love you say that you have for Jesus is only lip service to our Lord and Savior. Does the life you live for Jesus reflect the words coming out of your mouth? For the majority, the answer is no! When your actions match the love that you say you have for Jesus, then the following four qualities will just appear in your life:

1) You will not care who knows of this love
2) You will not care what others say about this love
3) You will invest greatly in this love
4) You will put forth a great effort for this love

**WHEN THIS LOVE GROWS WITHIN ME, I DO FOR THEM
WHAT JESUS DID FOR ME**

When these things happen, you know that God's love has taken hold inside of you.

**PLEASE, FATHER, HELP ME SO THAT THE LIFE I LIVE ALWAYS MATCHES
THE WORDS THAT I SPEAK**

As I conclude this chapter, let me give you a word of warning and a word of inspiration. The world wants you to believe that this walk of love shows weakness.

The world will have you believe that if you live this walk of love, people will only take advantage of you. Jesus was pure love and the last word I would use to describe Jesus would be weak. Throughout the New Testament, I cannot find an example where anyone took advantage of Jesus. In reality, walking this walk of love takes great strength and courage. More strength and courage than any man alone could ever muster up.

But this walk of love puts you on the path to your freedom. Freedom can only be discovered through the love of God. Believe me when I tell you this: we think that we know freedom, but outside of God, there is no freedom. When you are rooted and grounded in the love of God, you cannot be contained. When you live your life in submission and obedience to God's love, there are no walls and there are no limits. Within that statement lies real freedom. This is the life that God so desires for you to experience.

Let me end this chapter on love with one more scripture:

*If I give away all that I have,
and if I deliver my body to be burned,*

but I have not love,
I have gained nothing. (I Corinthians 13: 3)

I read a wonderful interpretation of this verse which sums up
how I feel about the love that the Lord has given to me:

NO MATTER WHAT I SAY
NO MATTER WHAT I BELIEVE
NO MATTER WHAT I DO
I AM BANKRUPT WITHOUT LOVE

The nature, the essence of love is to give. Give without
thought to oneself. Just give. Jesus, who is pure love, only
gave. Jesus gave and continues today to give us everything.
Be a giver. Be as Jesus who came to serve and not to be
served. Walk out of oneself into the love of God and into the
unselfish giving.

Love, when it is given to you from God, is the only possession
you will ever have, that the more of it you give away, the
more of it you will receive in return.

WHEN YOU HAVE NOTHING LEFT BUT LOVE
THEN FOR THE FIRST TIME
YOU BECOME AWARE
THAT GOD'S LOVE IS ALWAYS
ENOUGH

AND THAT IS THE LOVE THAT WE HAVE BEEN
COMMANDED TO SHOW THE WORLD

What than shall we say to these things? If God is for us, who
can be against us?
He, who did not spare his own Son but gave him up for us all,
how will he not also with him graciously give us all things?

Who shall bring any charge against God's elect? It is God who justifies.
Who is to condemn? Christ is the one who died--more than that, who was raised-- who is at the right hand of God, who indeed is interceding for us.
Who shall separate us from the love of Christ? Shall tribulation, or distress, or persecution, or famine, or nakedness, or danger, or sword?
As it is written, "For your sake we are being killed all the day long; we are regarded as sheep to be slaughtered."

No, in all things we are more than conquerors through him who loved us.
For I am sure that neither life nor death, nor angels, nor rulers, nor things present nor things to come, nor powers, nor height nor depth, nor anything else in all creation, will be able to separate us from the love of God in Jesus Christ our Lord.
(Romans 8: 31 - 39)

**THANK YOU, FATHER, FOR TEACHING ME
     ABOUT THE GREATNESS OF YOUR LOVE.**

-

CHAPTER EIGHT

RESIST NOT EVIL WITH EVIL

You have heard that it was said; you shall love your neighbor and hate your enemy. But I say unto you, love your enemies and pray for those who persecute you. (Matthew 5: 43 - 44)

You have heard that it was said, an eye for an eye and a tooth for a tooth. But I say unto you, do not resist the one who is evil. But if anyone slaps you on the right cheek, turn to him the other also. And if anyone would sue you and take your tunic, let him have your cloak as well. And if anyone forces you to go one mile, go with him two miles. Give to the one who begs from you, and do not refuse the one who would borrow from you. (Matthew 5: 38 - 42)

My question is, after reading these two sets of scriptures: Why is it that we choose to live our lives so far below the word of God?

The words of Jesus are so simple and yet so explicit: Love your enemy. Pray for the ones who persecute you. Give to all who ask. Lend to those who have great need. Which of those commands do we not understand? We must not understand any of them, because none of these happen as a rule in the world that I live in today.

Why is it that there are so many things in the word of God that we just flat out refuse to follow? I am not just talking to the unsaved part of the world here, but I am asking bible-toting, church-going, so-called Christians: why do we not follow the words of God? I see people going to church every Sunday professing their love for Christ. They know the word of God, but just can't seem to bring themselves to follow the teachings of Jesus.

Why is it that we think that the Bible is a buffet line where we can pick and choose the things that we like and the things that we don't? We want to pick and choose which words of God we will follow and which words just do not apply to us.

These teachings do not apply to me; that's exactly what we tell ourselves. We may never say that out loud. We will never say that to another person, but that is exactly what we tell ourselves in our minds. I'll follow this, but this teaching over here, I really don't think Jesus meant it for me when He was talking about this. How else do we justify the picking and choosing that we do as we decide which words of Jesus to follow?

Can Jesus really expect us to love everybody? How is it possible for me to love my enemies? There is no way that I'm going to turn my check when I get hit. I just don't get all this. How can I ever love my neighbors as I love myself? Has Jesus ever met my neighbors? Have you seen the people that I have to work with?

When you detach love from your feelings, and you truly begin to know and feel the love of God in your inner core, then you can and do make love your way of life. Instead of waiting for someone to do something to win or lose your love, you just naturally show them love without anything having to happen, without ever expecting anything to be returned. Because the Holy Ghost has come into your being and taken up residence inside of you, you become able, with that help, to show everyone love in every possible situation.

STOP MAKING LOVE A REACTION AND A REFLEX;
STOP MAKING LOVE SOMETHING YOU HAVE TO THINK ABOUT;
AND START MAKING LOVE YOUR FIRST ACTION

Because the Holy Ghost has invaded your soul, the lust that you have always known in your past is becoming infused with the love of God, which is flooding every inch of your being. Things you used to do in your past no longer interest you. Things that used to make you happy and bring you pleasure no longer even raise an eyebrow. Your entire life is changing because you have chosen to make love your way of life.

Our standards - because we are followers of Christ, because we are disciples of God - must be higher than the standards of the rest of the world. When Jesus came and walked this Earth as a man, Jesus taught a higher standard. If you have any doubts read the Sermon on the Mount found in Matthew chapter five. If your standards and the world's standards are the same, then your impact upon the world will be none. We show the world the love of God by returning, in every situation, good for evil. Jesus' response to evil was to always trump evil with His love.

LOVE ALWAYS SHOWS MERCY
LOVE ALWAYS FORGIVES
LOVE ALWAYS FORGIVES AND FORGETS
LOVE ALWAYS GIVES WITHOUT MEASURE

Love always gives without measure. Let's talk about that one statement for a moment. The world has to measure everything. I do more than you. I work harder than you. Mom loves me more than you. I am better than you. I am Dad's favorite. They love me more than you. I know more than you. I have more than you. I am prettier than you. I dress better than you. I am richer than you. My house is bigger than yours. The world has to measure everything.

By measuring, we force people to live to a certain standard in order to be accepted. So you can be in the in-group. Because there are people who will not be able to meet the standard, we create division. By measuring, we place people into groups. You belong to this group and you belong to another group. My group is better than yours. It is through division that conflict develops.

Evil breeds in these divisions. The worst kinds of evil - hatred, jealousy, envy, coveting, discrimination, selfishness, and pride - are all bred within and between these groups. God's love is never found in these divisions. Actually, God's love tears down these divisions between people. God's love is given without measure because God only sees one people. God created all of us in His image, so to God, we are all the same. God only sees one. The divisions are completely manmade out of our own selfishness.

It was always God's intention, and still is God's desire, for His people to be one. For all of God's children to be united in complete unity, One Earth, One People, One Body, One Bible, ONE SALVATION and only One Way to Heaven. That's unity. There is a great strength in unity. One can save a hundred. Two can save a thousand. In the kingdom, there is supernatural power in unity. The world has never known this type of unity. If we could only come together as one body - all the followers of Christ, all the believers, all the disciples - if that could happen, then I believe Jesus would return tomorrow.

The only hope that evil has to survive is through the divisions it causes. Evil divides us through these divisions. Evil takes our power away as it divides us. Evil conquers and destroys each one of us in these divisions. God knows no measurement.

It was the evil in man that began the divisions and those divisions still continue today. We are more divided, more entrenched in those divisions, and divided in more ways, than at any other time in our history. What's sad is that these divisions even exist in the church.

It is the evil nature of man that is causing the divisions right now in the world today.

And it's that same nature that will not even begin to let those divisions go; even if we know that coming together is for our best. We cannot see the world as one. To even speak of all people as one on the Earth gets a hearty laughter from most of us. We firmly believe that getting this world together will never happen.

Just look at our own country. We cannot even see ourselves - the most enlightened and most educated people on this globe - as one America. The races, the discrimination, the horrible ways that we still treat each other because we still have race discrimination, class discrimination, wealth discrimination, sex discrimination. We know that discrimination is a thing of the past, but we just will not let it go. Until we can get past this, we will never solve poverty, homelessness, crime - the problems that really matter. We are so blinded that we do not see that it is the divisions that create poverty and homelessness.

We cannot even see America as one Nation under God. If you look back at the history of this great nation, whenever we unify, our greatest strength and our greatest ability to overcome the obstacle comes to the forefront. There are so many divisions in our own country: horrible divisions, deep-rooted divisions, inbred divisions, divisions that have been passed down from generation to generation, divisions that have lasted for centuries. We cannot even see us in the church as one body.

We label each other, put each other into groups because someone thinks that they are faster, prettier, smarter, stronger, have more, more chosen than someone else. We select and exclude by gender, by race, by religion, by nationality, by language. We select and exclude by whatever barrier we can come up with.

It is exactly all those divisions that gives the devil his power to kill, steal, and destroy us. The devil divides, and then the devil conquerors.

These divisions have not made the world a better place. Just look at your world around you. We even place divisions upon the people that we say we love. I love you more than you. I love you, but only like you. I love you this much.

God gives to every one of us all of His love. God does not love any one of us more than another. God gives all of Himself, His love, His wisdom, His knowledge, His power; God gives it all to everyone. God gives all of Himself away to everyone without measure. God wants you to have everything that is for you. God excludes no one and God holds nothing back from anyone.

You therefore must be perfect; as your heavenly father is perfect. (Matthew 5: 48)

The word *perfect* here does not mean what we think that it usually means in the world: to be sinless or flawless. That should be our goal, but realistically, that goal is unattainable. What Jesus is talking about in this scripture is that we should be perfect in our love for each other. That is attainable.

We must love all those who hate us, pray for all those who persecute us, and show kindness to both friend and enemy. Jesus not only said that we must do this, but this love that we must show is a command from Jesus Himself.

A new Commandment I give to you, that you love one another: just as I have loved you, you also are to love one another. By this all people will know that you are my disciples, if you have love for one another. (John 13: 34 - 35)

So many people really believe that the teachings of Jesus do not apply today. I hear people say all the time, "It's a different world today. It's impossible for me to live my life by the words of Jesus. Don't you know that the Bible was written two thousand years ago? The teachings of the Bible will never work in today's world." I hear people say these things all the time. Why even try? The Bible is so outdated.

That last statement is so far from the truth. Every teaching - let me repeat that again for you really hard-headed people, every teaching - in the Bible is as real today as it was two thousand years ago. How much better the world would be if only we would choose to follow the teachings of Christ our Lord!

I read the book *The Kingdom of God is within You* by Leo Tolstoy. It is truly an amazing read and it becomes even more amazing when you realize that Tolstoy wrote this book over one hundred years ago. Not only was Tolstoy speaking about the times that he was living in, but his book so describes the times that we live in today. Tolstoy describes so accurately and so vividly the times of today. Tolstoy was brilliant and many of my comments and ideas expressed in this chapter come directly from reading his book.

We have all heard the saying, "An eye for an eye." But when it comes to repaying evil with evil, an eye for an eye only makes us both blind.

To resist evil with evil fixes nothing.

Tolstoy was teaching that when you choose to attack another and cause injury, then it is you who have ignited a feeling of hatred in that other person. Feelings that, if not attacked, might never have manifested themselves until you provoked them. That hatred from your attack is the root of evil.

When you are attacked, your first reaction is to retaliate. Retaliation is the beginning of evil, the greater the attack, the greater the need to retaliate. You feel as if you must retaliate, and quite often, we do this retaliation immediately. You feel that you must repay the evil done. That's the world that we live in today, an eye for an eye. We hit them back, and in most cases, we hit them harder when we retaliate. I can never let the world see me as weak. I can never let anyone think that they might have gotten one over on me. So in the end, we repay the evil done with more evil.

We fight evil with evil, but we tell ourselves that we are defending ourselves. I am defending my honor. I am defending my manhood. I am defending what is mine. Justification for the evil we commit. Another way we justify evil is that we tell ourselves we are just getting even. We try to make the evil that we do sound as if it's ok. However, the minute we make the evil in our lives ok, the devil knows that he has a way into our hearts.

In all actuality, the retaliation that follows - you hurting another because they hurt you first - is only setting free evil into the world. The initial injury, as unjustified as it may be, did not set evil free. It's in the retaliation. That same evil that you believe you are ridding yourself of in the retaliation - you are really setting that evil loose upon the world.

Evil never ends evil. Evil for evil never rids itself of the evil. In the getting even, your thought process is: well, he hurt me first; I retaliated and that should be the end of the story. Everyone is even. But in all reality, in your retaliation, you have only managed to set off a string of events in which the evil will continue until everyone is destroyed. He hit me. I hit him back. He goes and gets his family. When he comes back, I pull my gun, and we are off to the races. No one wins this race until someone is destroyed.

What is the end result of a war? The eventual destruction of another, of everyone. An eye for an eye never makes us even. Evil does not get even until someone is destroyed.

Evil cannot vanquish evil. Satan cannot drive out Satan. Fighting evil with evil only produces more evil. Fighting evil with evil only opens the world to unending evil. If you just need an example, look at the world which we live in today. Across the globe, there is far more evil in the world than peace and tranquility. And that evil that is already set free into the world only grows greater every day.

There are more threats of violence and destruction at every corner of the world; far more threats of terrorism exist on every continent today than ever before. The world is more dangerous and it is all because we have taken the stance to fight evil with evil.

The act of nonresistance is possible because of God's unending grace and mercy. Nonresistance is possible because the love of God lives within you. Jesus instructs us never to return evil with evil. Retaliating evil with evil only makes us both evil and it allows that evil to feed and grow stronger within us. The evil that is consuming us takes us away from God. That evil blocks your purpose and destiny.

The true nonresistance of evil (i.e. showing evil only love, patience, mercy, and kindness) is the only way to rid the world of evil. Is that not what Jesus did when He walked the Earth? Through the gifts from God is the only way that we will free the world of the evil that already thrives within it. Only the love of God - only that love living inside and thriving inside the majority of us across this world - is what's going to free this world of its evil.

Remember the words I wrote on the beginning pages of this book:

WHEN THE MAJORITY OF THE WORLD BECOMES THE LOVE OF GOD, ALL THE PROBLEMS OF THE WORLD WILL DISAPPEAR!!!

Evil will most definitely be one of those problems which will disappear from this world forever.

Jesus shows us, as His followers, as His disciples, how we are to respond when we are confronted by the evil of others.

In retaliation, we are never to strike back, even though that is our natural reaction.

But what you must know is that, as a believer of Christ, you are no longer natural men and women. The Bible tells us that our weapons are no longer carnal in nature. In our accepting Christ as our Savior, we become spiritual in our being, and our weapons are now spiritual in their nature. We must always be moving in the spirit, living in the spirit, so our nature does not slip back to its carnal nature. We must stay connected to the love of Christ, always being the love of Christ to stay spiritual and denounce evil.

We must be the ones showing evil the good. In the Book of Romans, Jesus gives us five examples of how we are to react when we believe that we have been treated unfairly, unreasonably, or even when we have been confronted by the evil in the world.

Repay to no man evil for evil
But give thought to do what is honorable in the sight of all
If possible, so far as it depends on you, live peaceably with all
Beloved, never avenge yourselves, but leave it to the wrath of God
For it is written, "Vengeance is my, I will repay, says the Lord."
To the contrary, "If your enemy is hungry, feed him;
If he is thirst, give him something to drink;
For by doing you will heap burning coals on his head."
Do not be overcome by evil but overcome evil with good.
(Romans 12: 17 - 23)

Repaying evil for evil is such a common practice in the world that we live in today. I know for sure that many of us have practiced this repaying of evil at least once or twice in our lives. Vengeance, we do so much enjoy seeing people get what we think that they deserve. We take great pleasure in seeing people get even. This type of delight should never find a home in the heart of someone who says that they know the love of God.

We as Christians should never provoke or entice anyone into committing an act of evil. We, as the examples of Christ to this world, must always love peace, be making peace, or be at peace. Our souls should only find rest in one of those three states.

When we have offended someone, or someone has offended us, then we must do everything in our power, working tirelessly, for a peaceful resolution to the offense. We must be the better man. It is our duty because we know the love of Christ; we must take the initiative to exhaust every possible solution to resolve the offense. We must always be the first ones with our hands extended in friendship and apology.

Many people believe that by doing this, not repaying evil for evil, not retaliating, you are showing a sign of personal weakness. I know that this is not true. There was nothing weak about Jesus.

Take a second and contemplate each of the following statements and you will see what I mean when I say that:

IT TAKES GREATER STRENGTH TO SHOW LOVE
INSTEAD OF ANGER

IT TAKES GREATER STRENGTH TO FORGIVE
INSTEAD OF STRIKING BACK

IT TAKES GREATER STRENGTH TO FORGET
INSTEAD OF FEEDING YOUR HATE

IT TAKES GREATER STRENGTH TO BE THE FIRST
TO STRETCH OUT YOUR HAND IN FRIENDSHIP THAN

TO PUT YOUR HANDS IN YOUR POCKETS AND WALK AWAY

In Romans 12:20, when the Apostle Paul writes, "for by doing so you will heap burning coals on his head," the Apostle is speaking that we will not destroy our enemy through acts of violence, but we will convert them through our love. We should become so charitable towards our enemies and shower that enemy with so much kindness, that our enemy becomes ashamed of the hostility he ever showed to us. What a concept!

In verse twenty-one, the Apostle then writes, "be not overcome by evil." If my bad mood puts you into a bad mood, then you have been overcome by the evil that possesses me. If you truly walk in the love of God, that spirit of love should be able to change and control the atmosphere in any room to the favor and glory of the Lord. The love we carry should always overtake, not be overtaken!

Why do we find the teachings of Christ so hard, almost impossible to follow? Why are the teachings of Christ so misunderstood? Many of Jesus' teachings have become muddled, obscured, altered, corrupted, and some of the teachings have even been lost. I heard one preacher call this "Watered Down Christianity".

We water down the words of Jesus to bring the teachings of Jesus down to our level in order to make them easier for us to follow. We bring God's standards down to our level because that is easier than us raising ourselves up to the standard of God. We water down the word of God to make it easier for everybody to follow. Let's be clear right now. Not everyone will be able to make this walk. All are called, but only a few will choose to follow.

There is nothing easy about making this walk with God. I have not read the Bible word for word, but from what I have read, I have not found the word *easy* anywhere in the word of

God. God's desire is to raise us up to His standard, for us to want to live our lives through the word of God, for us to walk a higher life, for us to walk in a better way.

Look at the world today - all the corruption, all the immorality, all the abuse, all the hatred - and tell me who we have helped by watering down the words of Jesus. These preachers preaching this watered-down, middle-of-the-road version of Christianity, Christianity the easy way, Christianity that only tickles your ears, and does not preach the true message of Christ, they preach a brand of Christianity that teaches nothing; it just makes you feel good about yourself. Cotton candy Christianity. It's sweet tasting and looks good but there is no meat on the bone. That's why you are still hungry five minutes later. And that's how you can leave the church, and five minutes later, not remember one word from the pastor's sermon. The pastor taught you nothing; he just made you feel good for a minute. Truth be told, these preachers have only managed to give aid to the enemy.

Most people I speak with today think, and I mean they really believe, that the teachings of Jesus are impractical for today's world. Because they have convinced themselves that the teachings are impractical, they have come to a belief that they can pick and choose which teachings in the Bible that they will follow. And they really believe that this bartering is ok with God!

People justify not living a Godly life because they say that no one can be perfect. No one can live up to God's standards. We are able to live with the sin in our lives because we have given ourselves an excuse. Our excuse is that no one can do it. No one can ever be perfect. We use this excuse over and over again to save us from having to take responsibility for the lives that we choose to live. We use this excuse for not showing the world perfect love. We use this excuse for not showing everyone the love of Christ. You just can't expect me to do all that!

It's easy to justify not following the Bible word for word when we have already given ourselves a built-in excuse. Do you not realize how happy we are making the devil with all of our excuses? We make the devil's job so easy.

So therefore, if I slip; that's ok. A little sin in my life; that's ok. I told a little lie; that's ok. A little deceit; that's ok. If no one knows that I told that lie; that's even better. It's ok; everybody is doing it. Just because everyone is sinning, does that make the sin in our lives ok? At what point does a little turn into a lot? People try to justify their lack of integrity, their lack of morals because they say, "It's ok; everyone is doing the same thing." Have you heard this before; "But I only did it once." Does that make the hurt that you caused ok?

These thoughts and feelings are also shared by many church people. Let me say this again: the Bible is not a buffet line where you get to pick and choose what you like and what you do not like. The Bible is the word of God and is to be followed in its entirety. Every word. Word for word. God meant every word that He wrote in His Bible and God meant for us to live and follow every word. Every word!

When we want God, we want all of God. When we need God, we want all of God to show up - not fifty percent God, not ten percent God, we want all of God. But when it comes to the word of God, we only want to believe and follow half. Some of us do not even want to follow that much.

Can you really expect that God is ok with you only believing Him fifty percent of the time? We believe God only half of the time, but expect all of God to show up when we have a problem. That's exactly how the majority of us treat God.

The Bible is not up to our interpretation. When the Lord said to love you enemies as you love yourself, then that is exactly what He means for us to do, love everyone! Exclude no one!

When you begin to follow the Golden Rule, you are living and doing as God does. When the devil sees you doing the work of Jesus, living the Golden Rule, the devil believes that it is Jesus Himself. Jesus came to live in the flesh as the example to what we can do and what is possible for us to accomplish in our lives. We can do as Jesus did.

Why must we see only the differences in each other? When will we stop looking at each other as colors and start seeing each other as God sees us? Just like Him. When God looks down upon us, all He sees is souls. No gender. No race. No religion. No color. Just souls. To God, He made us all the same. Every one of us is created in the image of God. That single fact alone makes us all the same.

What makes the Golden Rule so hard for most of us to follow is that the person you want to love may just be that same person who is hurting you the most. Every one of us has hurt someone in our lives, but God still showers us with His love, abundantly and unconditionally.

In order to do as God does, we must wipe away the hurt, no matter how deep the pain, and love that person who has hurt us, as much as we want God to love us. Every one of us has done things to another that we are not proud of. Things we have done that we may not even tell another person. All of us have hurt someone and all of us have been hurt by someone. We will hurt people and hurt people until someone breaks that cycle. That cycle is broken only with the love of God.

"But I say to you who hear, love your enemies, do well to those who hate you, bless those who curse you, pray for those who abuse you.
To one who strikes you on the cheek offer the other also, and from one who takes away your cloak; do not withhold your tunic either. Give to all who beg from you and from the one who takes away your goods do not demand them back. And as

you wish that others would do to you, do so to them. (Luke 6: 27 - 31)

So many people in the church today have the mistaken idea that you can accept Jesus as your Lord and Savior without making any changes in your life. The church has completely failed its people in teaching "the teachings" of Jesus.

God is all about transformation. If God had a business, then his business would be in transformation. We think that we take the doctrine of Jesus Christ as a set of rules and principles that we can either accept or reject without changing our own life. This idea is so far from the truth.

If you believe that you can bring Jesus into your heart without changing your life, then you are still living in the darkness. You have not seen the truth about yourself or the truth about the life that Jesus is offering you. A true repentance, and the transformation that is to follow, requires the changing and the renewing of one's mind.

The teachings of Jesus Christ define a whole new way of life. The Apostle Paul writes, "I have come to show you a better way." Jesus came to show each of us a better way, a new way to live life. To repent and accept the Lord as your savior means that you must make a change. You must turn away from the old and accept the new.

When you repent and ask God into your life, you are asking God to change you from the old man who lives in the darkness to the new man who lives in the truth and the light. When you choose to walk with Jesus, a whole new meaning of life opens up to you. You begin to choose new activities, new friends, and new places to go. New words come out of your mouth. You are very different from the person that you used to be.

Jesus came to teach us about love: how to love, how to show love, how to be love. This is another area in which the church has failed. How can it be that if the church knows the love of God, then the divorce rate inside the church is exactly the same as the divorce rate outside the church? It's because the church does not know, and worse yet, cannot show the love of God.

What makes God's love so different from the love that you think you know all about in the world? Many, many things, but in one word, it's SACRIFICE! The love that the world teaches will not sacrifice day in and day out.

Jesus came to teach us how to love each other. You cannot even begin to know love if you cannot have love for everyone. You cannot even begin to know love if you are not willing to sacrifice for everyone. You cannot even begin to know Jesus if you are not ready to sacrifice for your fellow man. We profess that we know Jesus. We praise Him. We worship Him. We sing to Him. We dance in the aisle every Sunday morning, but we really do not know Jesus. We do not know Him because we know not His love. We know not His love because we will not sacrifice.

You can read the entire Bible all you want and you still may not know Him. You can quote all the scripture you want and you still may not know Him. You can attend church all you want and you still may not know Him. You can pray eloquent, lofty prayers all you want, and you still may not know Him. But when you learn to love as Jesus loves, and then you will know Him. When you feel the love of God, when you become full of the love of God, when you begin to give the love of God away to all, then you will know Him. When you love as God loves, then you will know Him. And if you know Him, then the Kingdom of Heaven is at hand.

But if you cannot love as God loves, then the kingdom you will never see.

Not everyone who says unto me, lord, lord shall enter into the kingdom of heaven; but he that doeth the will of the lord which is in heaven.
Many will say to me in that day, lord, lord have we not prophesied in thy name? And in thy name have we not cast out devils? And in thy name have done wonderful works?
And then I will profess to them, I never knew you; depart from me, ye that work inequity. (Matthew 7: 21 - 23)

Start by building your relationship with your heavenly father. Live your life as Jesus lived His. Align your life with the will of the Father. Align yourself and your life with the way that Jesus lived His.

Forgiveness. The easiest way to not fight evil with evil is to live a life of forgiveness. I may start to sound like a broken record, but the church has not taught us forgiveness. In so many areas, the church is failing the church-going public. And because the church is not a place of teaching, the church is failing the world.

This is the real failure of the church: it does not teach. The unsaved world looks at the church as a place that only preaches "at" people. Everyone wants to be the preacher on Sunday morning behind the pulpit. This is what I want you to think about. How many times when Jesus lived did He preach behind a pulpit on Sunday morning in a million-dollar building? The good news of Jesus Christ was not meant to be delivered behind a pulpit, but we think that is what it is all about. Becoming a preacher and delivering the word on Sunday morning behind a pulpit.

Jesus taught His message to all the people. There is a major difference between preaching the word and teaching the word. And in these days, we need many more teachers of the word.

In the world today, we want to be forgiven but we do not want to forgive. Or when we do decide to forgive, we put conditions on our forgiveness. Or worse yet, we forgive but we will not forget.

If you are not willing to forget, then you are not willing to forgive. The bigger part of forgiving is in the forgetting. Forgiving without forgetting is not forgiving. The two go hand in hand, and for true forgiveness to take place, the two happen at the same time. Jesus forgets our sins as quickly as He forgives our sins. Jesus was, and still is, the great teacher and the teaching of forgiveness by Jesus is demonstrated many times in the New Testament.

Love is the act of endless forgiveness.
Endless forgiveness.

Without forgiveness, life is governed by an endless cycle of resentment and retaliation.
                              -- Robert Assagioli

Then Peter came up and said to him, "Lord, how often will my brother sin against me, and I forgive him? As many as seven times?" Jesus said unto him, "I do not say to you seven times, but seventy times seven." (Matthew 18: 21 -22)

YOU WILL NEVER LOVE AS GOD LOVES CARRYING ANY UNFORGIVENESS IN YOUR HEART -- TOWARDS ANYONE

There are a countless number of powerful scriptures found within the Bible, such as:

We love because he first loved us. And if any man says he loves me but hates his brother; he is a liar. (I John 4:19-20)

Very powerful words said by God directed at every one of us. God's words do not say that you have a choice. I hear every day how much people say that they love God. If you really mean that you love God, then God gives you no choice but you must love everyone you see. And for those whom we say that we love, we only want the highest, the best in everything for every one of them.

We say we love all the time. We say the words, but to those same people that we say we love, we can do some of the worst evil. And very often, we justify the evil that we do. They hurt me first. They deserved it. They attacked me. I have to respond or I look weak. How many times have we ourselves said that one? How many times have we listened as someone said those same words to us? And we did nothing!

Why are we so quick to anger?
Why are we so quick to judge?
Why are we so quick to fight?

Do we really believe that fighting is the best answer? That fighting is the only answer?

What causes the quarrels and what causes the fights among you? Is it not this, that your passions are at war with you? You desire and do not have, so you murder. You covet and cannot obtain, so you fight and quarrel. You do not have because you do not ask. You ask and do not receive because you ask wrongly, to spend it on your passions. (James 4: 1 - 3)

No one wants to say "I'm sorry." We especially do not want to be the first to say those words. We think that when or if I show meekness, I'm showing my weakness. I think the entire world would say that Jesus was a meek man. Would you also call Jesus a weak man? Being meek has nothing to do with weakness. Actually, meekness is controlled power. There is great strength in showing another your meekness.

IT TAKES GREATER STRENGTH FOR YOU TO BE MEEK
IT TAKES GREATER STRENGTH FOR YOU TO FORGIVE

IT TAKES GREATER STRENGTH FOR YOU TO SHOW HUMILITY
IT TAKES A GREATER STRENGTH TO STAY LEVEL-HEADED
THAN TO LOSE YOUR COOL

A newborn baby can lose their cool. No strength there!

By no means am I saying that to put any of these principles into action in your life will ever be easy. On the contrary, they will be difficult. In some circumstances, very difficult.

Who is wise and understanding among you? By his good conduct let him show his works in meekness of wisdom. But if you have bitter, jealousy, and selfish ambition in your hearts, do not boast and be false to the truth. This is not the wisdom that comes down from above, but is earthly, unspiritual, and demonic.
For where jealousy and selfish ambition exist, there will be dishonor and every vile practice.
But the wisdom from above is pure, then peaceable, gentle, open to reason, full of mercy, and good fruits, impartial and sincere.
And the righteousness is sown in peace by those who make the peace.
(James 3: 13 - 18)

What those scriptures are telling you is that we who say we walk with Christ must strive on a daily basis to live in holiness. If you are going to say that you are a Christian, then you everyday goal is to be holy. "Be ye holy for I am holy." Through you, the world should see the holiness of Christ. Evil cannot thrive where holiness is. The evilness of the world and the holiness of God cannot ever occupy the same space. The holiness of God is always greater than the evilness that is in the world.

Evil survives in the world today because of two basic reasons. First, we are not open to reason or suggestion. We refuse to listen to the other side. We refuse to admit that the other guy might be right or the other guy might have a valid point. We are so hard-headed that we always think that it's my way or no way. That stance alone causes so much friction and conflict in the world. We just cannot see that there might be a better way outside of our way. The second reason is that mercy in our world no longer exists. We have become such a vindictive society. We have become so selfish that we can no longer think of anyone else but ourselves. Mercy must think only of others. Mercy is to show more kindness than what justice requires. Mercy is compassion beyond what justice expects. When was the last time you saw that kind of mercy?

Holiness to our Lord is so very important. That is why God says over and over again in the Bible, "Be ye holy for I am holy." To live as one with Jesus Christ is our goal. As we walk through this life that we are living, every day we should become a little more just like Jesus. Every day, your goal is to live a life just as Jesus lived His. To strive for that perfection. To strive for that oneness. To strive to do as Jesus did.

Jesus came to Earth to show us the life that we can live. To show us the life that we should be living. A greater life of holiness must be the goal every morning we wake. It must be our prayer. For the world to see our Jesus in each of us. That is the life we are to live.

Blessed is the man who remains steadfast under trail, for when he has stood the test he will receive the crown of life, which God has promised to those who love him.
 (James 1: 12)

The other point I want to make is that, in America, seventy-five percent of our population say that they are Christian.

If everyone who reads the Bible,
If everyone who attends a church,
If everyone who professes their love for Jesus,
If everyone who says that they are a Christian,

would only put God's principles into practice, then how much better, kinder, gentler, more peaceful, and a more joyful world would we be living in right now. Could evil even exist in such a world? How much easier would it be for all to follow the teachings of Christ, if seventy-five percent of the people were showing the way? What kind of world would it be if God's ambassadors were everywhere you looked, every day you looked? You could see an ambassador of God twenty-four seven, instead of only on Sunday coming in or going out of a building.

RESIST NOT EVIL WITH EVIL

What kind of world would we live in if we would only put that statement into practice? No harsh words. No unkind actions. No degrading speech. We would go out of our way only to do what is best for each other. Only uplifting each other.

Only applauding each other's efforts. No pass. No fail. No hatred. No jealousy. No backstabbing. No sabotage. Each of us does only the best for each other. How great would this world be if everyone only wanted to help? No one tries to hold you back. No one ever tries to hurt you.

This is my pledge. Will I always be successful? Maybe not. But my pledge is to always keep this in mind; I will only have a positive, uplifting word and action for everyone that I come into contact with. It is my hope that, in doing this, I can contribute to making this world a much better place for everyone.

The way we speak today is so full of negativity. For most of us, we do not even realize how hateful and cruel our speech has become. We throw words out of our mouths with no regard, or without a single thought, as to who may hear the words that we speak.

So often our speech is full of offensive and hurtful words. For most of us, we feel it is our right to say what we want where we want to who we want. We do not realize how are speech escalates and advances the evil in the world. Whatever happened to the days when if you had nothing good to say, you said nothing at all?

We have never realized how powerful our speech is. It is the primary way in which we communicate with each other. It is also the primary way in which we praise or criticize, and it seems as if the world today is so much more critical than positive, especially in the way we deal with each other. In a world full of evil, the primary way in which we spread that evil from person to person is through our speech.

Our speech is so full of evil. The hatred, the anger, the bitterness, the jealousy, the rage, the profanity, the intolerance towards each other that is expressed in our speech only fans the flames of the evil in the world today. The degrading remarks that we make to each other, so many times just in passing, only allows that evil to spread from person to person to person. We feed poison to each other with the words that we choose to use on each other. I am often hurt by the way I hear people talk to each other; quite often, their speech is never directed at me, but it still hurts me to see how deeply we can injure someone just by the words coming out of our mouths.

We talk this way every day and most of us think nothing about it. The way I speak does not bother me, so why should it bother you? I am afraid that the evil we speak is becoming too acceptable to too many. The fact alone that many of us, in our normal everyday speech, cannot even form a sentence without using profanity should be a sign that there is a problem. But profanity is becoming more and more an acceptable way to speak in public. It doesn't bother me, so why should it bother you? The evil that is spoken out of our mouths we don't even see anymore.

WHAT HAS BECOME ACCEPTABLE TO THIS GENERATION WILL BECOME THE NORM FOR THE NEXT GENERATION

Are we really that uncaring, that selfish, that we do not care that evil becomes the norm for the world that we are leaving to our children?

Death and life are in the power of the tongue: and they that love it shall eat the fruit thereof. (Proverbs 18: 21)

We speak death into our own lives. The way in which we speak keeps us from living the full and abundant life that God desires for each of us to have. The way we speak keeps us from that purpose and that destiny. It is our speech that keeps us stuck exactly in the spot where we find ourselves today.

We speak negativity and we wonder why we did not get that job that we wanted. We speak negativity and we wonder why our lives never seem to be going anywhere. We only shout out to God when we need Him, and we wonder why it seems as if God is not listening. Let me say this to you: God always hears you!

We speak death into our own lives, but by changing your speech, you can change your life. Changing your speech can change your outcome.

The fact that so many people today feel that it is ok to say whatever they want, to whomever they want, whenever they want; the fact that, today, the public use of profanity in our speech almost offends no one; the fact that so many of our youth feel they can say the "N Word" wherever and however they want; the fact that we just do not care today about what we say - I believe primarily comes out of the music that we are choosing to listen to.

We see rap musicians making millions of dollars, living large lives, getting away with saying whatever it is that they want to say, doing whatever it is they want to do, and we want to be just like them. We want the fame. We want the money. We want the large life. We want the success that they have.

Because they said it, it must be ok for me to say it. We make these rap stars our role models because we want their lives. We grow up wanting to be just like them. We imitate and emulate them. We practice to be just like them. And that includes the way they speak.

People say this to me all the time: "But Paul, everyone talks that way. It's just the way it is today. It doesn't mean anything. I'm just expressing myself."

Music has and always will play a major role in the life that we live. It did when I was growing up. Music can influence us and it can play a major role in our development as we grow up. Musicians will try to tell you that it's just music. They try to tell you that they are just expressing themselves.

But do not be fooled by the major influence that music plays in our lives. Music speaks to us. Music moves us. Music can even help to shape and form the way we think. Music, many times, reflects the mood of our society. Look back through the history of this country. We have used music to vent frustrations and to start change in the world. So be careful when a musician tells you that he is only making music.

For many of our youth, and it seems that it is this way today, they only see the money, the fame, the women, the status, the power, and they want the same. They emulate. They do not see the fact from the fiction in the music.

Music can be used in very positive ways, but music can also be used to destroy. Let me ask you, how can any music be good that degrades another person? That calls women vulgar, profane, and degrading names? How can any music be good that tells us that women should only be used as objects of pleasure?

The Devil comes to kill, steal, and destroy by any means possible. (John 10: 10)

At one time, who was in charge of the praise and worship in Heaven? Lucifer. And today, the devil is up to his same old tricks by using the music that we listen to. Through music, the devil continues to spread his brand of evil throughout the world.

How can any music be good that glorifies the making of a dollar at someone else's expense? That glorifies gang violence? That glorifies drug usage? That glorifies the use of a gun. That glorifies death? That glorifies the physical abuse of someone? How can that music be good? How does this music make our world better?

Is there any time or any reason to glorify violence, and then to hold that lifestyle up to the next generation as acceptable? Do you remember what I wrote a few paragraphs ago?

WHAT ONE GENERATION FINDS ACCEPTABLE THEN NEXT GENERATION WILL MAKE THE NORM!

Through the music we are listening to, we are teaching that money is power. That through the power of money, you have the right to say and do whatever it is you desire. Is that the world we want to teach our children about? Is that the world that we want to leave to our children? Is this really the world we want our children to grow up in? Me first. My wants, my desires, my needs, my selfishness. I want what I want and I want it now. Is that really how we want our children to grow up, or do we really not care about the children that we are bringing into this messed-up world? If we do not stop it now, it will only get worse with each following generation. Is this the norm we want for the next generation and for the generations to come? Is this how we want to be remembered, as the generation that only cared about themselves?

The power that comes from money is really called "bullying". We use money to force people to do what we want them to do. Sounds just like a bully. Sounds like intimidation. Not much difference between money and a gun. We intimidate people with both of them. People will do what we tell them to do with both. We control people with both of them. We can even kill people with both of them. The evil that comes from both can and will destroy people's lives.

RESIST NOT EVIL WITH EVIL

Before I leave this chapter, there is one more thing that God is leading me to write about. My pastor said something in one of her sermons that has stuck with me ever since she said the words:

"There is no group with greater power to destroy a person than their own family."

I really do not believe that a greater truth has ever been spoken. Until I heard her speak those words, I never realized what a powerful statement that was. You may know a truth in your mind, but it's not until you hear the spoken words, that the truth really becomes real to you. Think about my pastor's statement. Think about your own experiences with that statement. Then, think about your children.

Anyone who has children must be stopped by that one statement. I was! I have a son. Immediately, I began to think about his life and my life, and our life together. What were the things that I had done? I began to think about everything that I might have ever said or might have ever done with my son. I became scared and afraid. I thought of the scars that my father had left upon me. What scars had I left upon my own son's life?

We destroy each other every day, not with guns or knives, but with words. My father used the belt when I was a child, but my father never laid a finger on me to leave one of the deepest scars I have from my childhood. He just made me feel that he did not love me anymore. You can say words to a person that they may never, and I mean never, forget. We destroy lives forever with the words that we say, with just a word. You say that you are sorry. You say that you never meant it. You say it was just a slip of the tongue, but once those words are out there, once you have spoken those words, very rarely can we ever get them back.

Most of us never forget the harsh words that are spoken to us. Think back to your own childhood. What memories do you still carry? What scars will you carry with you all the way to your grave? Who hurt you the worst? Those negative words and phrases cut deep, and for most of us, those wounds never heal.

The words you say can carry the worse evil and those words ring in people's heads for their entire lives. Have you ever heard it said that the words you speak are your truest thoughts? Once those words are out there, it's virtually impossible to get them back. You do try to apologize, and even at your sincerest, most people say that they forgive you, but do they really ever forget?

We cripple people. We crush and take away their dreams for life. Most often, these are the same people that we say we love the most. The wounds from the words we speak may never go away. We carry the scars for our entire lives. I know; I have scars.

Relationships are lost over the words we speak. Relationships are lost for life. The hurts and wounds are so deep that these relationships cannot be repaired here on Earth.

Fathers lose sons
Mothers lose daughters

Brothers lose brothers
Brothers and sisters are lost forever
Families are shattered
Friendships are destroyed

People once so close that their lives were inseparable.
Marriages destroyed beyond ever being repaired; all over the
words that we speak.

So often, these words are spoken out of anger and in the heat
of the moment. Words we might not ever really mean, but
because of the anger, they just fly right out of our mouths;
once these words hit the atmosphere, very rarely can we
retrieve them back. So we lose the one that we love. The hurt,
the damage can never be repaired. The words we speak, once
spoken, cannot be erased.

As a child and as a young man, my life was molded and my
future set by the words that were spoken at me. In my case,
more negativity was spoken over my life than the positive
words that I so desperately needed to hear. Especially as
parents, we need to and must speak positive, uplifting words
to our children. We can inflate or deflate our children simply
by a word. We must begin to use words that build and inject
encouragement into our children's lives.

Always remember your children. Just because you may not
see them, they can still hear you. What words are you
speaking into their lives? What words do you need spoken
into your life? The words that you like to hear are the same
words that you must be speaking to others.

We must become more encouraging towards each other.
Instead of finding reasons why one can't, we must go out of
our way to find reasons why one can. We are so fast to tell
someone why they can't live their dreams. As we give them
all the reasons why they can't, we wind up killing their
dreams. Is that what you want to do with the words coming

out of your mouth? Be the dream killer! Not me! How many dreams have you already killed?

We need to become cheerleaders in each other's lives. If you really love them, then you only want the best for them. Is killing their dreams the best that you can do? Support each other in the pursuit of each other's dreams.

RESIST NOT EVIL WITH EVIL

The evil in the world comes in many different packages.

As I leave this chapter, let me leave you with a scripture from God in which God tells us pretty plainly how He feels about the repaying of evil with evil.

Finally all of you, live in harmony with one another; be sympathetic, love as brothers, be compassionate, and humble. Do not repay evil with evil or insult with insult, but with blessing, because to this you are called so that you may inherit a blessing.

For, "whoever would love life and sees good days
Must keep his tongue from evil and his lips from deceitful speech.
He must turn from evil and do good;
He must seek peace and pursue it.
For the eyes of the lord are on the righteous
In addition, his ears are attentive to their prayer,
But the face of the lord is against those who do evil." (I Peter 3: 8 - 12)

CHAPTER NINE

THE BATTLE BETWEEN YOUR EGO AND YOUR SOUL

There is a battle raging this very minute! There is a war going on in every corner of this world! It is completely up to you whether you will believe those two statements or not. However, whether you choose to believe or not, believe me, it is true!

There are two spiritual forces battling right now to control your very life. This is the very battle between your ego and your soul. I know that you feel it. You can kid yourself all you want, but when you want to face the truth, the truth is that you feel this war. I felt the war inside of me all the time. I know that there are many times when you too feel this war going on deep inside of you. You feel conflicted. You feel confused. You are never sure what to do next. You are not sure which way to turn. You are never sure what decision to make. You are always second guessing yourself. I never knew before what was really going on inside of me. Why could I not be more decisive? Why was I always so unsure of myself? I now know today that it was all because of the battle and I now know how real this war is.

This battle is being fought for your very life. This is the battle for your eternal life. It is the battle between heaven and hell. It is the fight that the devil is waging with you every day for your very soul. In addition, for the vast majority of us, the wrong side is winning the battle.

Beloved, I urge you to abstain from the passions of the flesh (your ego) which wage war against your very soul. (I Peter 2: 11)

I like to look up definitions of words, and for the most part, I find that the definitions that Webster gives us are usually somewhat inadequate; however, for *ego*, Webster was right on. Webster defines the ego as seeking the welfare of oneself only! Selfishness. Talking too much about oneself. Conceit. Excessive use of the words *I, Me,* or *My.* It is the habit of thinking, writing, or talking too much about oneself. How many of you did I just describe? How many people do you know whom I just described? Like me, I am sure it was way too many.

Before we go any further, as you read this chapter, God desires transformation. God wants to transform the life you are living today. Our God is a God of complete transformation and restoration.

Reflect upon the words of God that you are about to read. Many of the ideas you are about to read, for the majority, you may never have heard about before. Many of the teachings to follow will be brand new. They were new to me.

For a few of you, the words to follow will be confirmation of the way that you have felt for probably a very long time. Maybe it is still the way that you are feeling even today. These words may also be conformation to you about the people around you: why they treat you the way that they do, or why you do to them the things that you do. Take this teaching and let it transform your life to the life that God has always desired for you to live.

God wants to make a change in your life. Change comes through knowledge, and in that knowledge, you become exposed to the truth. When you find the truth by seeking knowledge, your life can change. It is by no accident that you are reading these words. God let you read this for a very particular purpose and a very particular reason. Let God do the work that He so desires to do in you. Read slowly, digest this teaching, contemplate the words, see the truth for the truth, and see what change happens in your life.

I would like to start with a very brief history lesson. How did the ego (your flesh) and the soul actually come into being?

In the beginning (and when I say this, I am talking about when God created man_), we were created in the image of God. Every one of us has been created in the image of God, no man excluded.

In addition, the lord God formed man of the dust of the ground and breathed into his nostrils the breath of life and man became a living soul. (Genesis 2: 7)

In the beginning, the soul was to be the true part of us which was to be life itself. We believe today that life is all about our bodies. When God created us, life was meant to be all about our souls.

Even though a doctor cannot pinpoint where your soul lies in your body, we all, every one of us, know that we do have a soul. God created us all as souls; we are all living breathing souls.

We think that it is our hearts or our minds that should be in charge of our lives. We are taught to listen to our hearts, to follow our hearts. We are taught to think about what we do and to think things through. We are taught that our hearts and our minds should dictate and control how we act, how we feel, what we do, and what we say. However, in all reality, it was our souls that were to have all this control.

The soul is that part of us where our lives with God, our father, originate. Our lives, our thoughts, our feelings, our emotions, our actions, everything that we do; God's intent, when God created man, was for our souls to have total control over everything. Our souls are completely spiritual in existence. Our souls belong to God. Our souls are God's soul. Through our souls, we commune (speak intimately) with God as spirits.

Behold all souls are mine; as the soul of the Father, so also the soul of the son is mine: the soul that sinneth, it shall die. (Ezekiel 18: 4)

At the creation, when God created Adam, man did not have a soul. Adam became a living soul when God breathed the breath of life into him. We share souls with God. At the time of our birth, God puts a small piece of Himself inside of each of us. Whether you believe in God right now at this very moment, every one of us at our creation was given a piece of God, no exceptions. No one is left out. We, every one of us, were all created in the exact image of our Father. That means we are all created as souls.

When your soul is in total control of your life, all you long to do is to have a deeper, more intimate, and constant (twenty-four hours, seven days a week) fellowship with God. That is exactly what God created man to do: to praise, to fellowship, and to have an intimate one-on-one relationship with God. God desires a relationship with you.

We are all created as souls and put into these bodies to live upon this Earth. Just as your car transports you from one place to the next, your body was made as the transportation that carries your soul from place to place.

God's will is for your soul to have total control over your life. God made us all as souls in a physical body. We live our lives so confused as to who we really are. We are taught that we are this skin, these bones, a heart, lungs, blood, hands, arms, legs; we have been taught so wrongly, and for some of us, we have not been taught at all. There are so many things that we have been taught wrong, for so many years, about God.

For as long as I lived in my parents' house, we children were raised in the church. As for so many of us as children, we had no choice when we went to church. Our parents went, and therefore, so did us children. Most weeks, we went twice on Sunday and then again on Wednesday night. For all the churchgoing, at least eighteen years' worth, I never remember anyone ever once teaching me about my soul. I always knew that I had a soul; just as most people in the world know that they have a soul. It was not until last year that I began to learn what God's true intent was for my soul. What purpose that my soul was to have and what part my soul was supposed to play in the life that God desires for me to have.

God's will is for our souls to control our everyday lives - every part of our lives, even in the world that we live in today. Our flesh was never to have a voice. We were only to have one voice: the voice of our souls. The serpent gave our flesh its voice.

When Adam gave into temptation, your flesh came alive and took control over us. Adam had no idea that his flesh even existed until he chose sin over the life he had with God.

Then the eyes of both were opened, and they knew that they were naked. In addition, they sewed fig leaves together and made themselves loincloths. (Genesis 3: 7)

Sin gave birth to our flesh and sin continues to give our flesh the control and power over us that it now has even today. Because of man's sinful nature, our flesh has become extremely powerful. The greater our appetite for sin, the more powerful our flesh becomes. Along with your flesh came your ego, and that ego has evolved over the years into the selfish people that we know ourselves to be today. Your flesh and your ego are a package deal. They are one and the same.

From the moment you were born, you have become locked into a contract with the ego. Our lives are dominated by the words "I, Me, and Mine." Just watch the actions of a little child if you need an example of the ego at work. A little child throws a fit to manipulate you to do the little child's will; that is the ego doing what it does at its very best. Your ego is the part of you that tells you that you are the most important person on this Earth and that everyone else is here to be of service to you. Your ego tells you that the planet Earth, and everything that lies within, does totally and completely revolve around only you.

Believe me when I tell you this: everything about you is either controlled by your ego or controlled by your soul. How you think, how you act, what you decide to do, moment by moment, every thought, every action, how you treat the people in your life, how you show your love, who you decide to give your love to, what you do with your time, how you spend your money, what type of relationship you have with God, whether you have a relationship with God or not - all this and more is either controlled by your ego or controlled by your soul.

Your ego tells you that you have needs and that your needs and your wants are critical to your survival. Your ego also convinces you that your survival in this world is dependent upon you finding happiness. Your ego will have you believe that you will not survive in this world if you cannot find some happiness.

We spend and waste so much of our time, our energy, and our resources in the search of this thing called "happiness". We really believe that if we can find happiness, then our lives here on this Earth will be perfect.

Your ego tells you that this search, the search for happiness, must be the top priority in your life, nothing else. No one comes ahead of what you need or what you desire in order to achieve your happiness. Finding happiness depends on you getting the things in life that you desire the most.

That pursuit of happiness, the world will have you to believe, is owed to you. Everybody must be happy. What is it that the world constantly tells us? Life, liberty, and the pursuit of happiness; doesn't the world tell us that we are owed at least that? It is our right to find happiness. We are born believing that we must find this thing called "happiness". It is definitely owed to us all just because of the fact that I was born. My happiness is the most important thing. This is the first entitlement that we come to know, happiness. It's owed to me. Better yet, you owe it to me.

We truly believe the life that we are living is solely about feeding our own desires to achieve our own happiness. If I can feed all my desires, then I will certainly be happy. We really do buy into that statement. That is exactly what your ego is telling you: feed your desires, find your happiness. Your ego whispers those words in your ear over and over again, day in and day out. You deserve to be happy. The world owes you your happiness. Go out and find your happiness. Go get your happiness.

If I marry the right man or woman,
If I can get the right job,
If I could only make x amount of dollars,

I will be happy!

Most of us have come to the belief that this is the only reason and purpose for us to even get up in the morning: to feed our own desires. We wake up every morning with only one goal for that day in mind:

What will I do today to fulfill my desires?
What will I do today to find my happiness?
What will you do today to help me fulfill that mission?

Remember that when your ego is in charge, it is only concerned about serving you and fulfilling your need to be happy. This is why:

We desire money to be happy, so we get up and go to work at jobs that most of us don't even like.

We desire even more money to be happy, so we get up every morning and put our bodies through undue stress, crazy hours, lack of sleep, emotional turmoil, headaches, backaches, heartaches, to achieve raises and promotions at those same jobs that we don't even like.

Some of us desire money, but we do not want to work, so we take what we want from others.

We scheme, we lie, we cheat, we steal, we do not care whom we hurt in the process of feeding our desires to find happiness.

Some of us wake up in the morning and desire a hit, a snort, a toke, a drag, a needle, a bowl, a pill, a drink. We have to have these things because that is what happiness has become for us. But as we take more and more and our needs, or should I say that craving, becomes greater and greater, we find that with every hit, happiness grows further and further away, and more difficult for us to ever attain.

Many of us wake up and head straight to the bar, because we believe we can find happiness in that drink.

Many of us spend our day lying, cheating, and deceiving another, trying to feed our own sexual desires; not ever realizing that we are the one being used to feed the desires of the other.

For so many, the fear of loneliness has such a grip in our life, the craving for acceptance and love is so desperate, that we allow ourselves to be used in unspeakable terms, telling ourselves that to be used is an equal trade just not to be left alone.

Many of us treat love and sex as the same thing so we spend our day in pursuit of the hookup only to find that after the sex the love is gone, and the empty feeling you believed your sexual partner had the answer for has only grown one size larger.

The world spends the majority of its day and all of its night in the sole pursuit of feeding needs and trying to satisfy that desire for happiness.

For the vast majority of the world, we wake up every morning with a desire and your ego tells you that it's your right to go out and fulfill that desire. Our ego is never concerned with who we hurt or who we use in order to get our needs and desires met. Just go and do what you have to do in order to satisfy your desire so that you will be happy. Don't worry. Whoever you hurt, they'll get over it. Anyway, remember back to the last time when you got hurt. You're just getting even. Your ego loves to justify.

It's your ego that says to you that you are entitled to get your needs fed. It's ok that you hurt her feelings. It's ok that you broke her heart. It's ok that you used her. Everybody uses a little manipulation from time to time. It's ok that you stole from her. It's ok that you went out with her best friend. Welcome to the real world. Welcome to the big leagues. Don't worry about other people's feelings. They are just being too sensitive. Remember that it's all about you and what you need. Fulfill your desires and find your happiness. Your ego is only concerned about you, no one else.

As young adults, we have grown up with this feeling of entitlement. I'm owed certain things. The world owes me. People owe me. These are rights of mine for just being born. I don't have to do anything. Just give me what is owed to me. The world owes me. How many times have you heard that before? Or maybe you have found yourself saying those very words. If you have never said it, then have you felt that way before? Do you feel entitled? That's your ego talking to you. It's your ego that believes in entitlements. Your ego, at its best, wants to work for nothing. Just give me.

Your ego leads you to believe that every need and desire that you may have can be satisfied. If you can think it, then you can have it. Your ego constantly leads you to believe that your happiness is just around the next corner. Don't give up yet. You're almost there. You can have everything and anything you want. If you work hard enough, then you can have it all. And for those of you who do not want to work, then you can just go out and take it. The world is yours just for the taking.

Your ego tells you that if you want it, then you can have it, and you can do that all by yourself. You can have it all, the good life. You need no help from anyone else. It's just you and your ego. That's all the team that you need.

Your ego will tell you that, as long as you follow its advice, you can and you will find your own way to the happiness that you deserve. Your ego will lead the way. It's your ego that tells you that you and you alone control your own life. You need no advice from anyone else. I'm my own man. I can find my own way. Sound familiar?

It's your ego that tells you that you have all the answers. In the '80's, Shell Oil had a television commercial that had a man whom they called "The Shell Answer Man." He could answer any question. For a time in my life, I would tell people that I was "The Shell Answer Man." I really believed it. That was my pride, my vanity, but most of all, that was my ego speaking out of me. Your ego, when in control, will have you believing things just like that. You know everything. You need no one. You need nothing from anyone. I'm old enough, smart enough, and tough enough to do what I want, when I want, because I want. That is the ego at its very best! I can do it all on my own! How many of us have ever made that boast before?

Your ego bases all of its decisions on satisfying the desires of your five senses: taste, smell, feel, sight, and hearing. Happiness for your senses is based upon two basic principles:

1) Avoiding Pain
2) Finding Pleasure

Be true with yourself and you will realize how the decisions in your life come into being.

That tastes really good -- Can I have more?
What you are doing feels really good -- I want you to do more.
She looks super good -- I want to have more.
You're telling me what I want to hear -- Will you tell me more?
That smells wonderful -- How do I get more?

When you get to the bottom line, your ego is just that basic. It's all about keeping your senses happy. It's just that simple. You think that you are some complicated multi-level, really deep individual, but every one of us being led by our ego is just that basic. And the opposite is also true. If what you are doing is not making your senses feel good, then you are out of there. Your pursuit of happiness is all about fulfilling the desires of your senses and it's your ego's job to make sure that happens any way possible!

As long as you let your ego run your life, I will always be more important than you! And I will always feed my needs and fulfill the desires of my senses way before I even begin to think about what you need. Wonder why marriages fail? I'm too busy taking care of me to even spend one moment thinking about you. How many people do you know where life is all about them? Life is only about them. They will let you in as long as you have something they want, need, or desire, but once you have nothing to give them, they are out the door. How many times have you heard this one?

We're not together because we just grew apart.

No you did not. No one just grows apart. You took everything from them for your happiness; they no longer have anything left to keep you happy, and so now, you are out looking for another to feed your happiness. That's what we call today, "growing apart."

Your ego is an enormous burden. Your ego has to be constantly fed. Your wants and desires have to constantly be met. Your ego can cause you as much pain and suffering as it will bring you in the ways of pleasure. Your ego with all its wishes, fears, high ambitions, likes, dislikes, wants to - no, your ego has to - dominate your life. Your ego has to be in charge and that ego must be fed.

As your ego's appetite grows, your ego places many needs upon you with great force. As you begin to fulfill your desires, your ego is the addict within you that demands more. More possessions, more sex, more status, more title, more power. We must climb the ladder higher, taller, and faster. Your ego is never satisfied with what it had yesterday.

It's your ego that tells you that you must hoard. Your ego tells you that you never have enough, and by the way, what you do have, you can lose in a second. That's why we are a nation of hoarders. We do not know the word *enough*. We fear that what we have today will not be enough tomorrow. We fear that someone could have more than us. Especially when it comes to money, we do not know the word *enough*. When was the last time you heard someone say that they had enough money and they really don't need any more? I don't know if I have ever heard someone say those words.

It's your ego that causes you to crave. Your ego constantly wants more. Your ego tells you that you must have these things in greater amounts in order to continue to be happy. And the more you have, the more demands your ego places upon you to get more. Cravings are the demands that your ego places upon you. You must have more power. You must have more quantity. You must have it more often. You must calm these cravings or your ego grows louder with its demands until you feed these needs.

Your time, your energy, your health, and your family all become pawns in this game that the ego is playing with your life. And what do we do? We give up every one of the things above to our ego and give them freely in order to gain the things that our ego tells us we must have in order to be happy. What is the cost of your happiness? What will you trade away, thinking that you are going to find happiness?

It's your ego that constantly has to be fed. Once you start feeding your ego, you alone cannot stop the demands.

I was completely caught up in money, status, career, and the power that goes with those things. I had a need and a desire for more and more and more. I had to make more money every year or I was not happy. I had to be promoted every year in the company or I would not be satisfied. My appetite to achieve and possess more was growing beyond my control. I just had to have. I had to be the boss. I had to be in charge. I had to be the one that everyone looked to and I was willing to risk my health. I was willing to give it all my time; I was willing to not be there for my family just so I could have more. I had to feed my ego and gain whatever my ego told me that I had to have in order to be happy. I really believed that the more I had and the more I could give the people around me, then the happier I and everyone else would be.

It's your ego that tells you this is the way that it is and you have no choice. This is the road to happiness. I remember my father telling me, over and over and over again: graduate high school, get into a good college, graduate college, get a good job, find a wife, settle down, have some kids, buy a house. That's the road to happiness. That's what my father taught me. Live by your ego. Fulfill your desires and you will be happy. No matter what you have to sacrifice along the way. And I bought into that - hook, line and sinker.

Once the snowball got started, it grew and grew and grew, and I could not stop it. Once on the train, there was no way of getting off. All I could do was try to outrun the need. Stay ahead of the snowball. Fill the needs. Fill the desires. Give my ego the things that it told me that I had to have.

The huge demands the ego can and will put upon you to achieve, will lead you into making many terrible decisions, and the demand will have you living a self-destructive life. You think that you are having this wonderful life, but the addictions your ego has fed you have secretly taken over your life. You really believe that you are in control, but secretly, your ego has taken control of your life.

Sex addictions, power addictions, money addictions, greed addictions, abuse addictions, control addictions, alcohol addictions, drug addictions are in the world today; your ego will have you addicted to anything and everything. It's the ego's way of staying in control of your very life. As your ego grows more powerful, the addictions become overpowering. Your appetite can never be filled. The snowball is catching up to you.

We think that we are doing well. We think that we are having this great life because of all the stuff that we have. We think that we are having fun. We just can't get enough. We really believe that we are a success. Look at me. Look at how successful I have become. Look at my life. Look at everything that I have. That was my life. Instead of keeping up with the Jones, I had to be the Jones. I wanted everyone to keep up with me. Look at how well I'm doing.

In all actuality, as long as your ego is in charge, we are only one step away from having the house of cards, which we have built over the course of a lifetime, collapse all around us. While your ego is in charge, your life is actually teetering on the edge of disaster. Every day you are only one step away from finding out the truth about your ego.

What your ego does not tell you is that after you have accumulated all that stuff, there is nothing else. All the money, all the cars, all the property, all the promotions, all the women, all the drugs, none of it fills that emptiness inside of you. Next time you are at the supermarket checkout line, just look at all the covers of the magazines on display. Each of those people has boatloads of all the possessions in the world, but they all are also miserable. Possessions will bring you pleasure, but only for a moment, and after that moment, we all - every person, it does not matter who you are - will ask ourselves the same exact question:

IS THAT ALL THERE IS?

And then one day, the big lie hits you. The truth about your ego hits you like a ton of bricks.

ALL THE POSSESSIONS OF THE WORLD CANNOT BUY YOU THE HAPPINESS YOU SO TRULY SEEK!!

I had built my entire existence around my career and all the stuff that I owned. I was known to others as my wife's husband, my son's father, the boss at work, the guy who owned the two-story house on the corner. I was known by what I did and what I owned, and when all those things were taken from me, so was my identity. Who was I if not a husband, a father, the boss, a home owner? To me, I was nothing. I had completely lost who I was. I had built my life on the sand, and when the storm came, my life just crumbled all around me. My life fell apart. I had no one and nothing to turn to, and this was when I tried to end my life for the first time.

My entire life was built upon the person who my ego said I was. My life had no foundation. No concrete. There was no substance to my life. My life was all flash, or in today's world, they would say my life was just all bling.

Nothing that I had built my life around was bad. Most of what I had was actually quite good: a wife, a son, a home. But when the stuff of the world is all that you have, you can lose everything that the world gives to you in the blink of an eye.

Anything that the world will give to you, the world also has the ability to take it back. The world will never give you any guarantees. There is always the chance that you could lose it all.

And when you do lose it all that quickly, without any warning, it is in that loss that you can find yourself in some very scary places in your own mind. And it is in that loss, and because of that loss, that you are able to do damage to yourself. Sometimes, that damage has deadly results.

We all either feel it now or have felt it in our past, that emptiness inside. You feel a hole in your gut. You know that something deep within you is missing. When we have finally achieved the desire, instead of feeling complete, we still feel the hole.

We drink to feed the need, but it doesn't fill the hole.
We drug to feed the need, but it doesn't fill the hole.
We have sex to feed the need, but it doesn't fill the hole.
We buy possessions to feed the need, but it doesn't fill the hole.
We surround ourselves with people to feed the need, but they can't fill the hole.

There is only one that I have found first hand that can fill the hole. In this battle between your ego and your soul, there is help that we can call upon. There is someone who can tip the scales of the battle in our favor. As your life is racing out of control, as your life is teetering on the edge of disaster, you can cry out to God for His help. It's your ego that always wants you to be more important than anything or anyone. And it is your ego that will always do everything in its power to keep you away from God.

"I will always be more important than you." That one statement alone will keep you from ever walking and talking with the Lord. Your needs, those being the most important thing, will stop God's will from ever taking the forefront in your life. Your mind will be so focused on your own needs that you will be completely unable to focus any attention on

God. Your ego always has to have all of your focus, all your attention, all your energy, all your time. Your ego is an all-or-none proposition. Your ego must be top priority in your life, and when your ego achieves that status, it is at that point that your ego has become your God.

No man can serve two masters, for either he will hate the one and love the other, or he will be devoted to the one and despise the other. You cannot serve God and money. (Matthew 6: 24)

And he said to him, "You shall love the lord your God with all your heart and with all your soul and with all your mind." (Matthew 22: 37)

YOUR EGO WILL ALWAYS GIVE YOU WHAT YOU THINK YOU OUGHT TO HAVE, BUT THAT SAME EGO WILL KEEP YOU FROM RECEIVING WHAT GOD KNOWS IS BEST.

Your ego is deadly when it comes to your walk with Christ. Your ego is an enemy of God, and because your ego is an enemy of God, your ego is also an enemy of love. Your ego only knows selfishness. Your ego only loves your ego. As long as your ego rules your life, you will never walk in the love of God.

Your ego wants to edge God out of your life and anything and everything having to do with God.

Your ego has to be first. God can only be found where the ego is not. God's love can only be found where the ego is not. God and your ego can never live together. The two will never coexist. Your ego is only devoted to the world and all of the world's demands. You must get beyond your ego to truly find God.

Do not love the world or the things in the world. If anyone loves the world, the love of the father is not in him.
For all that is in the world--desires of the flesh and the desires of the eyes and the pride of possessions--is not from the father but is from the world
And the world is passing away along with its desires, but whoever does the will of God abides forever. (I John 2: 15 - 17)

Your ego will not just give up and go away. Prepare for a fight. Just because you now say that you have accepted Jesus into your life, your ego is just not going to pack up its tent and go away. Your ego must dominate. Your ego will not share. It has not shared you up to this point, and your ego has no plans of starting to share you now. It cannot have things any other way. Your ego has had pretty much all the control in your life up to this point, and your ego likes it that way. Prepare for the fight.

The longer you were in the world allowing your ego to run your life, the more powerful your ego has become. Taking back that power will not be easy. Prepare for the fight. Your ego is very strong and extremely deceptive. Your ego has developed many tricks to keep its control over you, but as long as your ego is in control, you will only act out of greed and selfishness instead of love. You must take back control. Take back the power and decide what kind of person that you want to be: selfish or loving. You can only choose one.

There are many sides to your ego. It's your ego that will try to convince you that you can have it all. You can be selfish and loving. You can be both. No, you can't! Really think about it; a selfish person only loves themselves. That is your ego at its best.

When your ego feels a change in you, your ego will pull out all the stops. Your ego has many tricks up its sleeves to try to win you back to its side, to try to keep control over you. Let me talk to you about one of those tricks that I know well, because it is how my ego keeps attacking me.

We have been talking about how your ego places your needs above everything else, even God. But when you get over your own neediness, when you get over believing that you have to have all this stuff in order to survive, and when you get over the fact that the world does not really revolve around you, then your ego will come and attack you in another way. Your ego attacks your mind.

As a babe starting to serve the Lord, your ego will come at you, telling you that you are lacking. Your ego tells you that you do not deserve. Your ego tells you that you do not know enough to be doing whatever it is that God really desires for you to do. You lack the knowledge. You're not educated. You never went to school for this. You don't know enough scriptures. You really don't even know the bible that well. Your ego really lays it on thick and tells you that you really don't know God all that well. Why would people even listen to you anyway? What do you know about ministering the word of God? Your ego tells you that all you are going to do is embarrass yourself because of your lack of knowledge. You lack, so what do you think that you are doing?

Your ego fills your head full of doubt. And when you almost think that your ego is done, your ego throws down its ace card. Your ego fills your mind full of fear. It's your ego that makes you afraid. Afraid of really embarrassing yourself in front of everyone. Afraid that someone will laugh. Afraid that you will say something stupid or you will say something wrong. Afraid that if you do say something stupid, they will never ask you to speak again. Your ego tells you that you have to be perfect and you know that you can't be perfect.

That fear will paralyze you. That fear will stop you dead in your tracks and that is exactly the goal of your ego: to stop you. Your ego is sure that if it can fill your head with enough fear and doubt, then you will just give up. And when you give up, you will give all the power back to your ego. Your ego is sure that you cannot function without your ego being in charge. Through your own fear, you will just give up and quit, and then your ego wins.

Your ego will not back down. Your ego will keep coming at you, again and again and again. Your ego will tell you that your praise, your worship, your prayer is not good enough for God. Just look at how they pray. You can't pray like that. You'll never be able to pray like them. So why should you even try? Your ego will work on you to get you to not even try. You lack. This is how my ego attacks me even today, with that Spirit of Lack.

Your ego will even come at you and tell you that you do not deserve God's love. How could God ever love someone like you? All the things that you have done. Just look at you. Do you really believe all that talk that God could really love someone who has done all the bad that you have done? There is just no way. Grace and mercy are for the people who have been in the church their whole lives. Not for guys like you and me. Your ego really lays it on thick. It's powerful and it does not want to lose the control it has had over your life.

Your ego always wants you to be a people pleaser. It's your ego always looking over your shoulder to see who is watching you. What are they saying about me? What are they whispering about? I know that they are talking about me behind my back. Is anyone laughing at me? Why do I always say the stupidest things? That's your ego's way of teaming up with your mind to keep you in fear and to stay in control. Look at you; here you go just embarrassing yourself again.

Your ego wants to keep you in chains, chained to your ego for life, to keep you away from ever being free. Your ego always has to know what another is thinking about you. What did they say? Who said that about me? It's your ego always looking towards man. Your ego always has to please man. It's your ego always seeking acceptance. Your ego always has to be in control.

Still another trick your ego will use to keep that control over you is intimidation. This is another trick that my ego uses on me even today, the Spirit of Intimidation.

You will never be that good, so why even try? No matter how hard you try, no matter how hard you work, no matter how hard you study, you will never be that good. Look how they preach. What makes you think that you could ever do that? You can't do better than that. You have nothing to say. Your ego will use every trick to stay in control, even the dirty tricks. Your ego will even use your past failures to reinforce this idea of what you cannot do. You could never do better. You could never be the best, so why even try?

These feelings that my ego was using against me were first brought on by how my father treated me as a little boy. Your ego knows all your fears and every weakness that you have ever had. My father never made me feel like I was good enough. No matter how hard I tried, there was always someone better and I could never measure up.

My father's love was quite often given and taken away based upon my successes and failures. His love was also based on doing what he wanted you to do. If you did what he wanted and did it well, then my father loved you. If you decided not to do what my father wanted, then the opposite was also true. If you went against my father's wishes, then he could make you feel as if he never knew you. Let alone that he might have ever loved you. What a way to live as a little child and what a confusing way to learn about love.

Why do we always have to be the best? Why do we always have to be in competition? What is it about being number one? Why is that so important to us? It's your ego that always has to be in competition. It's your ego that tells you that you deserve. You deserve to be the best. You deserve everything that you can get. Go ahead and show them. You can do better and you can do better than they ever could.

Let me stop and tell you something right now. There is no best, better, or even number one with God. There is only what is pleasing to God. God does not judge us on a rating system like man does. Man will tell you: "you are a one" or "you are a six" or "you are a ten". There is no rating system with God. There is only what God finds pleasing. My goal every day, as I live my life, is to only do the things that God will find pleasing.

What is pleasing to God?

Your smallest turn towards Him
Your simplest shout out to Him
The honesty in telling God how much you love Him
A pure prayer from your heart

It is just the simplest of things.

What is pleasing to God?
God only wants you to trust in Him.

You must put your ego into check. The devil will continue to use your ego as the door to enter into your mind whenever he wants to attack.

This is exactly what the devil tries to do to me. Stop me from doing God's work. Stop me from living the life that God has for me. The devil loves to whisper into your ear: "You are not worthy of God's love." First shackle. "How could God ever love somebody like you?" Second shackle. "You are not good enough to do the work of the Lord." Chains around my ankles. "You have no training to do this." Tied my arms behind my back. "No matter how hard you try, you will never be good enough." Thrown into the dungeon. The devil uses the voice of my father to tell me that I will never be good enough. The prison door just slammed shut and locked. Now

I am completely trapped. Bound, chained, and trapped. That's just how the devil wants us.

It is very powerful and almost convincing how the devil gets into your mind and plays his games. The devil uses every trick to keep you away from God. I tried to show, with the illustration in the above paragraph, how the devil will chain you, shackle you, and put you into your own prison, in your own mind. Your ego never wants you to get a taste of freedom. You ego does not ever want you to get to know God.

Your ego is not going away without a fight. Your ego wants to keep you dominated through fear and intimidation. Will your ego ever go away completely? No. But you can reverse the power and put that ego that once controlled you under your thumb.

Once you push past all the fears, once you can push past all the wants and desires of your ego, once you realize that your ego is not the true and authentic you, once you realize that there is another way to live other than through the voice of your ego, then fear leaves you and you begin to get your first taste of what it is like to be free. Really free.

- WHEN YOU CAN STOP LISTEING TO YOUR EGO,
- WHEN YOU KNOW THAT YOU NO LONGER HAVE ANYTHING TO PROVE TO ANYONE,
- WHEN YOU KNOW THAT YOU ARE NO LONGER IN COMPETITION WITH EVERYONE,
- WHEN YOU KNOW THAT THE WORLD IS LOOSING ITS GRIP UPON YOUR LIFE,
- LIFE BECOMES MUCH SIMPLER
- AND DESPERATION FADES AWAY.
- IT IS THEN THAT YOU WILL FIND THE ABILITY TO MAKE THE VOICE OF YOUR EGO A LOWLY WHISPER INSIDE OF YOU; INSTEAD OF THE LION'S ROAR THAT IT HAS BEEN YOUR ENTIRE LIFE.

The place that is beyond your ego is your soul, the other part of you. The true you. The real you. The you that has been lying dormant inside of you since you were born. Remember at the beginning of this chapter I told you that everything about you is either controlled by your ego or by your soul? The authentic you is your soul. The life you really want to live rests in your soul.

No fear only freedom. Freedom is what awaits you in your soul. Within your soul, you know that life has a higher calling. There is a higher purpose to your life. Do we not all feel that we are called to do something meaningful while we are here? That there is something worthwhile that we are to accomplish?

Your soul knows that you have been called to this higher purpose. And if you are honest with yourself in your heart of hearts, you have always felt - deep, deep inside you - that you have been called to a higher purpose, also. You feel that you have been placed on this Earth to accomplish something. Something that no one else can do. You know there is a reason why you are here. You know it!

It is the soul that makes us all the same. When God looks down upon us, all that God sees is souls. I cannot stress this point enough. This one point alone is enough to save the world from all its suffering, from all its hatred, from all its jealousy, from all the discrimination that we attempt to put each other through on a daily basis. God sees us all as one. But we, on this Earth, may never understand that one simple fact. We were always meant to be one.

God does not see man or woman. God does not see Muslim or Jew. God does not see black or white. God does not see Baptist or Catholic. God does not see Asian, African, German, or Irish. God only sees souls!! We are all the same to God. We are all the same!!! And we must become all the same to each other.

We are all souls. You are either one of two people! These are only two choices. All of us on this Earth are only one of two people.

Right now, as you read this, you are one of the two following people:

YOU ARE EITHER A PERSON WONDERING RIGHT NOW IF YOU REALLY DO HAVE A SOUL, OR YOU ARE A SOUL WHO KNOWS THAT BEING A PERSON IS ONLY TEMPORARY.

We are not physical creatures having a spiritual experience, but we are spiritual creatures having a physical experience! We have completely failed in understanding that our souls have been in existence since the very beginning. When I talk about the beginning, I'm talking about when God created the Earth. God knew who you were; God knew your soul before you were even born!

Before I formed thee in the belly, I knew thee; and before thou camest forth out of the womb I sanctified thee, and ordained thee a prophet unto the nations. (Jeremiah 1: 5)

God knew our souls before God ever put us into the womb of our mother. God knows you. God has a purpose for you. And God placed you in this time and in this particular place because God has an assignment that only you can accomplish for Him.

We are so confused and we have no idea who we are or what we are doing. For the last two thousand years, we have been taught (and a lot of us have even been taught this by our church) that the life we are supposed to be living is a physical life. For the vast majority of us, we completely believe that the life we are living today can only be enjoyed through the physical. We have been brainwashed into believing this and most of us know no other way to live life.

I enjoy life because of the kind of car that I drive. I enjoy life because of the house that I live in and all that it has to offer me. I enjoy life because of the job that I have and the money I make from my job. I enjoy life because of the hobbies that I have and how I spend my time with my friends and my family.

Wrong! The best part of your life is to be enjoyed spiritually, through your soul. And the sooner you realize this, the sooner you will begin to really enjoy your life here on this Earth. The abundant life, which God so wants all of us to share, is rooted in your soul. God's abundance cannot be found physically. The life, which God so wants you to have, can only be found spiritually.

We in the church read and read and read, and then we quote this particular scripture over and over again: Jesus came to give us life and he came to give us this life more abundantly (John 10:10). We keep looking for that abundant life only in the physical and we wonder why we cannot find the abundance that Jesus promised us. Now, I am never going to tell you that the abundant life cannot come to you in the physical, because we all know people who have been blessed physically. But what I do want to tell you is that the greater, the more intense, the more fulfilling abundant life comes to you spiritually. To gain in spiritual blessings, these are the blessings that no man can ever take from you. When God blesses you spiritually, you have truly been blessed, and these are treasures that will go with you to eternity. These are the blessings that I pray for God to continue to rain upon my life: His love, His peace, His joy, His meekness, His temperance.

Let me take a moment to speak about another message that so many church folk have become confused about. Lots of preachers like to talk about prosperity and I have heard many so-called prophets of God speak a word over a person's life about their upcoming prosperity. We hear the word *prosperity* and our carnal nature automatically believes that God is about to bless us with great wealth. Of course, for the majority of us, when we think wealth, we think money. That's your flesh talking to you. Once again, I am not saying that some people will not be blessed by God with money, but the prosperity message is not about cars, houses, possessions, or money.

Beloved, I wish above all things that thou may prosper and be in health, even as thy soul prospers. (III John 1: 2)

How is it possible for a soul to prosper? Let me say something that most people refuse to recognize. Your soul does not care about material wealth! Let me add this: Your soul really does not care about worldly things. My soul only desires to prosper in the ways of God. Your soul was around at the beginning and your soul will live somewhere in eternity. Your soul desires to prosper in the things that will travel with it from the beginning to eternity. Let me break the bad news to most of you: your car, your bank account, that house are not able to travel with your soul. When your soul leaves your body at your death, your soul wants to take with it the things that your soul has prospered in: the character of God, the nature of God, God's holiness. My soul wants only to prosper in the teaching of and the giving away of The Fruits of the Spirit.

This is spiritual prosperity and this is the prosperity that your soul so desires. This prosperity, this kind of wealth when given to you by our Lord, you can never lose. This type of prosperity only grows and grows and grows. This prosperity, when given by God, is the only type of prosperity that, when given away, comes back to you in greater amounts. And as I said before, this prosperity is eternal. This prosperity will never leave you.

Thomas said to him, "Lord, we do not know where you are going, so how can we know the way?" Jesus answered, "I am the way and the truth and the life. No one comes to the Father except through me. If you really knew me, you would know my

Father as well. From now on, you do know him and have seen him. (John 14:5 - 7)

Jesus tells to all of us that He is the way. Jesus offers the way to everyone, but not everyone will choose this way. Jesus is the way to eternal life with His Father. Jesus is the only way to enter into the kingdom and we must enter into this kingdom if we are to have eternal life with the Father. But for many of us, our souls are asleep. As long as we live in sin, we are spiritually dead to God. To God, our souls are dead.

Another of the disciples said to him, "Lord let me first go and bury my Father." and Jesus said to him, "Follow me, and leave the dead to bury their own dead." (Matthew 8:21 - 22)

Leave the spiritually dead to bury the spiritually dead.

The only way that your spirit can become fully revived and come back to life is through the teachings of Jesus. Jesus is the way, the truth, and the life. There is no other way for a spiritual revival except through Jesus. And it is critical that your spirit must be born again.

Jesus answered, "Truly, truly, I say to you, unless one is born of water and the Spirit, he cannot enter into the kingdom of God." (John 3:5)

Your first birth was into flesh. We are all born into sin, and therefore, we are spiritually dead to God. Our second birth must be into spirit and through our soul. Through this rebirth, through your soul, you can then begin to have a personal relationship with God your Father. This is the relationship that God so desires to have with each of us.

Your soul comes to life as you feed your soul the word of God. As your soul is taught and begins to receive the fruits of the spirit, the life you are living starts to be soul-led. Your soul is alive. You have been born again. You are walking in God's love and you have found your way into the kingdom.

Eternal life is awaiting you. That is what your future looks like when you put your soul in charge. You are achieving spiritual prosperity, which is the prosperity that the bible is all about.

But we still have a life here on Earth. God desires for each of us to live and have an abundant life while we are here. But what is the best part of that life that we can find while here on Earth? To be free! The kind of freedom that I am speaking of here can only be found spiritually. Only through God can real freedom, complete freedom, be found. All the elements that make up this freedom can be found in your soul. Freedom has been with you the entire time. God place this incredible gift of freedom inside you when He created you as a soul. Freedom has been resting inside you, just waiting for you to release it.

Do you remember how I defined *freedom*?

WHEN YOU CAN WAKE UP EVERY MORNING WITH NO EXPECTATION UPON THAT DAY TO COME, YOU HAVE RELEASED FREEDOM UPON YOUR LIFE!!

You can only find this freedom in the life that you give to God, the life that you share with God through your soul. Through your pure praise, your pure worship, your complete admiration for your King of Kings and your Lord of Lords, your soul becomes linked with God's soul, in spirit and truth, and God begins to fill you with all the abundant life that we are meant to have here on this Earth.

When you have completely surrendered your soul to God and you give God complete control, God will reward you with an unimaginable freedom. Freedom you have never tasted. And once tasted, you will never want to go back. For the vast majority of us, we will never surrender to this level, so we will never taste the type of freedom that only God can give to us.

Your ego is battling your soul for control of the life that you are living this very moment; the war is being fought for your eternal life. There are no prisoners being taken by either side. This is a winner-take-all war. When the war for you is over, you will either be on one side or the other. You will either be going to heaven or you will be going to hell. There is no middle ground. Never be fooled! Never think, for one minute, that you are exempt from this war. Every one of us, and I mean all of mankind, is in this war for our eternal lives!

Your ego is all about you. Your soul is all about the desire to serve others. Jesus came to serve, never to be served. Our souls are linked to Jesus, which means that we are meant to also be of service to all man.

Even as the Son of Man came not to be served but to serve, and to give his life for the ransom for many. (Matthew 20: 28)

For you were called to freedom, brothers. Only do not use your freedom as an opportunity for the flesh, but through love serve one another. (Galatians 5: 13)

I am going to keep going back to this one point because it is so important that you understand what I am about to say. Trust me when I tell you this fact: you are one of the two following people. You are either living in the temporary right now - your life is completely ego-driven; your life is controlled by your sight and you live primarily for the pleasure of the moment - or you are living your life for the eternal. You are one of the few, the very few, small minority of people who, right now, know that they are living this life to live again. You are living your life right now completely led by your soul.

Every day, and yes, I mean every day, you are either one step closer to Heaven or you are one step closer to Hell. There is no middle ground. Every day you are either going in one direction or the other. This choice is yours. The choice has always been yours.

Your soul is always evolving. This process of evolution involves bringing a higher order of life into your being. It is from your soul that the deeper values of life come into being; love, creativity, and inspiration evolve from within your soul. The meaning of your life comes through your soul.

Are you loving?
Are you giving?
Do you show mercy?
Will you always forgive?
What are the values that you are creating through your soul?

Your soul carries the core values of the person you want to be. Your soul wants these values to be the way you live your life every minute: love, honesty, integrity, truth. As these values become your way of life, the soul wants to give these values to everyone and in every situation you find yourself in. For your soul, there is no middle ground. Your soul exists to bring an end to the pain and the suffering that people are enduring in the world today. You know that you are living through your soul because not only do you see the suffering, but inside, you feel the pain.

You are either loving or not.
You either give or you don't.
You choose to show mercy or you don't.
You either forgive or you don't.

THERE IS NO MIDDLE GROUND!

You either live the life or you choose not to. There are no sometimes, no maybes. There are no once-in-a-whiles. These are all-or-nothing propositions. You either walk the walk, or you don't. The life you live is measured by the things that you do and there is no middle ground.

You are either guided through the life you live by your soul, or you are driven through life by your ego.

Your soul loves and forgives.
Your ego only judges and blames.
Your soul takes responsibility.
Your ego finds fault with everyone but yourself.
Your ego feeds on stability.
Your ego loves the chaos and the drama.
Your soul feels good about who it is.
Your ego is never satisfied.
Your soul seeks humility.
Your ego feeds on pride and exaltation.
Your ego always has to have more.

Your ego asks the questions:

What's mine?
How much more can I have?
How do I achieve greater satisfaction?

Your soul asks the questions:

For what reason was I born?
What is the true purpose for my life?
How can I be of greater service to everyone?

Your ego is connected to two very powerful emotions: greed and fear. When your ego is in charge, these two emotions control all your thoughts and eventually determine the types of decisions you will make. Through the emotion of greed, your ego will have you believing that there is never enough. Everything is in limited supply and there is always the possibility that all things can and will come to an end. So you hoard. Your ego tells you that you can never have enough and that you must have more and more and more. So you hoard. We, especially Americans, have become a country of hoarders. As a people, we don't share very well.

It's your ego that makes you think that your needs will never be met without it in charge. That's the emotion of fear. You, as a person, lack, and so, you must give charge to your ego to get the things you desire. It's fear telling you that you will never make enough money to pay all your bills. It's fear telling you that with one mistake, you could lose your job. It's fear telling you that if I say something wrong, they won't like me anymore. It's fear telling you that without the right car and the right job, you will never get the right girl.

Its fear and greed that lead your mind into a state of worry. Worry is the cause of so many of our health-related problems. God never wants us to worry. Let your soul replace that fear and greed with faith and compassion.

Your soul exists to bring an end to the suffering and the heartache that the world has given to most of us in bucketfuls. The problem is that we have lost contact with our souls. We have lost that connection. Like I said earlier, I have always known that I had a soul, but I had no idea what my soul was for or how really important my soul was to me. Most churches are not teaching about the soul or teaching you about the spirit. We have no idea, because we are not being taught.

I am my soul!
I am who my soul says I am!

Our soul was never created to be useless. You and I have made our souls useless through our lack of knowledge and through disuse, and through the life that we choose to live away from God. Remember that we choose to either live our lives ruled by our souls or controlled by our egos.

Your soul holds the blueprints to God's higher intentions for our lives. Just as the blueprints hold the architect's intentions on how to build a building, your soul holds God's blueprints on how God would like for us to build our lives.

We still have the final say; it's always our choice, our free will. We choose between an ego-driven life or a life led by your soul. Once you have reconnected with your soul, God's guidance, God's hand comes upon your life to guide you into your higher purpose, into your higher calling.

Your most worthwhile life is spent discovering your soul and building your life upon that pursuit. If you do that, then you will be first in the eyes of the Lord, even if you are last in the eyes of the world.

Let me ask you a question. To God, what is your most vital asset? What about you should you value the most?

YOUR SOUL!

Just look at the twenty-third Psalm for the answer:
A Psalm of David

The Lord is my shepherd;
I shall not want.
He makes me to lie down in the green pastures.
He leads me beside the still waters.
He restores my soul.

God uses this psalm to teach us how to pray to ask for our soul to be restored. Why? Because the life that the Lord wants for you to live here on this Earth, the life that the Lord has made for you to live, that life rests in your soul. Your highest purpose, your true life, lives dormant in your soul, waiting only for you to bring it to life. Love, peace, joy, forgiveness, kindness, patience - all these qualities, all these higher virtues - live within each of our souls, just waiting for the moment when you will awaken them.

Besides all those things, the way to your eternal life is through your soul. God wants to restore your soul. Cry out to God and let your soul draw the breath of God again. God will bring restoration upon your soul. Through the restoration of your soul, your spirit is restored and the path to eternal life with your Lord and Savior can become yours.

We think that our lives are all about our minds and our bodies. But when you begin to understand the true purpose for your life, you realize that your soul is what your life is all about. Your body is in existence only to do the will of your soul. Your body walks, talks, breathes, and thinks only to do the things that your soul wishes for it to do. Your soul lives only for God. Your soul only wants God. Your soul desires that connection with its Creator.

For what is a man profited, if he shall gain the whole world, and lose his own soul? Or what shall a man give in exchange for his soul? (Matthew 16: 26)

Here it is that age-old question: "What are you willing to trade for your soul?" Would you trade your soul away for a million dollars? Five million? Ten million?
What would it take for the control of your soul?

You know that there are no guarantees. The fact that you have money guarantees you nothing. Just look at all the magazines the next time you are in the line to check out of your local grocery store. You do not even have to open the magazines; just look at the covers. All those people have boatloads of money. Boatloads of all the possessions you could ever think of. All the fame, fortune, status, and wealth that any person could want, but just look at the lives they are living. What a mess! Their lives are in such disarray, such a state of turmoil, such a state of confusion. We look at those magazines and we think, "How in the world could they make such a mess of their lives? If I only had their money, I would show them." But the real truth is that more money means a bigger mess. There is no guarantee on happiness or contentment or peace of mind, just because you have a ton of money. But yet, how many of us truly believe that money will and can solve the biggest majority of our problems, if not all our problems?

The life following Jesus does make you guarantees. By following Jesus and accepting Jesus as your personal Lord and Savior, Jesus will show you the way to eternal life in Heaven. Are you really willing to trade your soul, to give your eternal life in Heaven, away for only a few moments of pleasure here in the world? Would you trade your soul for only one night of folly? Would you trade away your soul for a pleasure that does not even last? Follow God, and God promises a life of eternal peace, eternal joy, and eternal love. These are promises from God made to you. Money cannot buy the things that God can and wants to give to you. And the things that God wants to give you are free.

If you give into the wants and needs of your ego, your ego will have you walking around as if you are the only person on this planet who really matters. Your ego has only one concern. Your ego is only concerned about its own physical survival. Your ego is only concerned about how it will continue to control the environment that it lives in to guarantee its own survival. Your ego, to stay alive, must stay in control. As you lead this ego-driven life, you acquire more and more to satisfy the wants and desires that your ego places upon you. Your ego gets bigger and bigger. How many times have you heard someone make a comment about how large a person's ego is?
For the vast majority of us, we are unable to keep our ego under control. This is the beginning of conflict in our lives and our ego is about to implode.

But there is a huge area of life that your ego has no answer for. For most of the world, there is an uncertainty of life that looms large in front of us. This is death. Your ego fears death. Death is really the only thing that brings fear to your ego. Why is it that the majority of the world truly fears death?

Death is certain for everyone. It is the one certainty that no one can escape. Fear of death grips most of the world today, because your ego has no answer for death. Your ego tells you that death happens to everyone else, but it will never touch you. You will never die. You can do that line of coke, you can drive that car as fast as you want, you can drink all the Jack Daniels that you can, you can sleep with whoever you want whenever you want, you can work eighty hours a week, you can eat whatever you want, you don't have to worry about taking care of yourself - death will not touch you. Death happens to everyone else, never you. You are untouchable.

Your ego tells you not to ever worry about death, because you are the one who will live forever. That's exactly the words that my ego would tell me. Don't worry about death; you're superman. And even if death is coming, it's a long, long time away. Don't even think about it.

But then, you do die. No one ever thinks that the next moment is never promised. That next breath is not promised to you. Tomorrow is promised to no man. So something happens and you do face death. What happens now? What happens to all those possessions, all that money that you traded your soul for? Are you aware of the fact that you can't take it with you?

When you die, no worldly possession is going to make the trip with you. I know that may come as a shock to a lot of you, but I have never been to a funeral where there were two hearses: one to carry the deceased, and the other to carry all the possessions that was amassed during the life that this person lived. Let me break this news to you: when you are gone from this Earth, someone else is now in control of all the stuff that was once yours. They are spending all your money; someone is living in your house; someone else is now playing with all of your toys, and quite possibly, someone else is now comforting your husband or wife. Everything you worked so hard to accumulate, someone else is now enjoying all those things that you just had to have. Someone has also taken your spot, almost immediately, in the corporation where you believed that you could never be replaced.

Now there is great gain in Godliness with contentment, for we brought nothing into the world, and we cannot take anything out of the world.
But if we have food and clothing, with these we will be content.
But those who desire to be rich fall into temptation, into a snare, into many senseless
and harmful desires that plunge people into ruin and destruction.
For the love of money is a root of all kinds of evil. It is through this craving that some have wandered away from the faith and pierced themselves with many pangs. (I Timothy 6: 6 - 10)

All that money, all your possessions, all that corporate status, those really important things that you thought made up your life, all the things that you so quickly traded your eternal life in Heaven for - someone else now possesses. And now that you are dead, what is happening to you?

Your ego was only concerned about today and never made one plan for you and your eternal life. We make more plans for the retirement from our job than we make plans for our eternal life. You just gave away your eternal life in Heaven for a few good years of folly. You traded your eternal life with God for the money, for the fame, for the possessions, for a few years of fun. Now you are dead and you have nothing. You don't have the money, but you do have an eternal life, but that life will not be spent with your Heavenly Father in Heaven.

Your priorities with the life that you spent here on Earth were all messed up and in the wrong order. When you put other things in front of God, your priorities are in the wrong order. Our first priority should always be to glorify God in everything that we do. The life that your soul wishes for you can never be defined through wealth, through power, through a title, or through any possession.

I will never trade my soul for anything that the world can offer, even all the money that the world could ever give to me! Why would I ever want to limit myself through the life that I could have with my ego, when I could live an unlimited life through the uniting of my soul and my spirit? All things - things that I have not even dreamed, things that my brain cannot even fathom, things that my mind has never seen as possible - can and do become possible with God.

The life that your soul wishes for you, your highest purpose in life, is the thing that can be accomplished when your soul unites with your spirit. When united with your spirit, it opens you to every possibility through God. Your soul, together with your spirit, opens you to everything and everybody. This union of your spirit and your soul expands your universe by leaps and bounds. The life, the life that God has for you, becomes limitless. The life that you can have with God in charge truly knows no boundaries.

Let me stop here for a moment and let's talk in depth about the spirit and the soul. So many people are confused when you begin to speak about spirit and soul. The church has done much to aid this confusion through its lack of teaching. Many people I speak with, and even those folks who have been in church for ten, fifteen, twenty years, think and believe that the soul and the spirit are the same thing. Nothing is further from the truth. Let us spend some time in these next few pages, and try to clear up some of this confusion.

In the beginning - and once again, I mean in the very beginning at the creation of Adam - God created man in His own image.

So God created man in his own image, in the image of God created he him; male and female created he them. (Genesis 1: 27)

God is spirit: and they that worship him must worship him in spirit and truth. (John 4: 24)

God's image is His spirit, His holiness, and His power. Each of us is created in that very likeness, in the image of God. God is spirit. We are spirit. Because we are created in God's likeness, we have the ability to walk in the same holiness and the same power as God. We have the spirit of God. This is the first part of who you truly are. God is three parts and so are we. That first part is His spirit.

As spirit, we are all created from the same stuff as God. Whatever God is, then so are we. We are not God, and we will never be God, but it is this spirit that you share with God that gives you the potential to walk as God walks. You can be just like God. That possibility is open and available to each of us. God gave us dominion over all the Earth, but we will not take our rightful place. For the vast majority of the world, we are spiritually dead.

Therefore be imitators of God, as beloved children.
And walk in love, as Christ loved us and gave himself up for us, a fragrant offering and sacrifice to God. (Ephesians 5: 1 -2)

Because of this spirit that God created each of us with, we can imitate God. Your spirit is always living for the eternal. Your spirit only wants you to live by faith and to view all things in your life through the Kingdom of God. It's your spirit that keeps you anchored to Heaven. When you are living spiritually, your mind never drifts far from God.

God created us with a heart and a mind and God gave every man free will. When we are living spiritually, it's our souls that are in control of our thoughts, our actions, and our decisions.

When God breathed His breath into Adam and made Adam a living soul, God downloaded all of His character into Adam. Adam walked in the nature of God. Adam walked as

God walked. The two walked together. Your nature is all the instincts or tendencies that direct our conduct. What is the nature of God? God's holiness. What is the character of God? His love, His peace, His joy, His longsuffering, His meekness, His kindness, His goodness.

Adam walked in the nature of God. Adam possessed all the same characteristics and the same nature as God. It's your soul that wants you to act as God would act, as you walk upon this Earth. Your soul controls your very nature. Your soul and God's soul are one soul. Your soul desires holiness, to be one with its creator. But for most of the world, our souls have been overrun and taken hostage by our egos. We let our egos take control of our natures, making us the selfish people that we have become today.

Your soul, which we have spent a lot of time talking about, is the second part of you. The third part of man is his flesh. Your flesh and your ego are a package deal. The two go hand in hand and the two operate as a team. When God created Adam and Eve, God created them as spirit and soul, and He placed those two parts inside a body: your flesh. As I said earlier, your flesh was never to have any control over you. Your body, your flesh, was only meant to be the transportation for your soul and your spirit. Your soul was to have the only voice. In the beginning, at creation, your soul was to have all the control over you.

When God created Adam, your spirit and your soul were connected, and the two controlled the life that Adam and Eve lived here on this Earth, the Earth that God had given to them. The serpent gave the flesh its control over your soul. Disobedience was the weapon used to overthrow the connection between your spirit and your soul. You must get and understand how powerful disobedience is to your walk with God. It was that disobedience that allowed the flesh to come alive. Sin came upon the Earth and your flesh flourished in that sin. Our flesh became and still is very powerful, and in that power, the holiness that we once enjoyed in the garden with God gave way to our sinful natures. The voice of our souls was trampled out and the flesh, because of our sinful nature, became the dominant voice inside each of us. That voice of your flesh is the same voice of your ego, and that voice has come to control your very soul. If you are not walking spiritually, then it is that voice of your ego which controls the very life that you live today.

The really sad part is that, for the last two thousand years, many of us have given not one thought to our souls. The majority of the world has just ignored it, denied its existence, lied to it, starved it, shut it up, medicated it, or we have just plain neglected it. Almost everyone, the world over, believes that they have a soul, but for the vast majority, we just choose to ignore it.

So are you getting this? Is it a little bit clearer to you? The battlefield is in your mind. This is exactly where your ego operates. When your ego is in control of your mind, your ego controls all of you. With your ego in control, you are only capable of thinking of yourself.

When your soul and your spirit line up with the will, then this alignment is called "being in God Consciousness". Being God Conscious is where your mind, your soul, and your spirit are all lined up together, and those three only desire to do the will of God.

Let's back up for one moment. For the vast majority of us, our souls, our spirits, and our minds are never lined up as one. For most of us, our minds are constantly aligned with our flesh, the ego. A thought comes into our brains and the mind has the free will to channel that thought through your ego or through your soul. Let me give you an example.

I am walking down the street. A person approaches me, asking me for spare change. They do look hungry and they could possibly be homeless. They ask me for help and that request automatically goes into my brain. My brain is now searching for the answer to the question. What do I do?

If I am led by my ego, then my ego tells me that I will always be more important than you. My ego tells me that I do not have enough. My ego tells me that my wants, my needs, and my desires are always more important than yours.

It does not matter that I just ate and my belly is full. It does not matter that I have a safe place to sleep tonight. I don't have to worry about the rain or the snow. It does not matter that I have a few bucks in my pocket and I'm getting paid on Friday. My ego tells me to watch out for myself. My ego tells me that I need everything that I have to survive. My ego tells me that if I help you, then I may be taking something away from myself. Remember that your ego is completely selfishly driven. Led by my ego, do I help you? Probably not.

But again, you ask me for help. Again, my brain is searching for the answer. But this time, I am living spiritually and I am being led through life by my soul. My soul has been taught that, in every situation, no matter how large the situation or how small the situation, I am always to ask myself only one question:

WHAT WOULD LOVE DO NOW?

Do I help? Yes!!!

This is exactly what I mean by your mind, your spirit, and your soul all being lined up together to do the work of the Lord. When you make the choice to renounce sin and when you choose to turn away from that sin in your life, then your spirit, which has been asleep inside of you, awakens and begins to take charge of your life. You begin to live by the spirit. You begin to live as God lives.

At this same time, you begin to feed your soul and you begin to renew your mind daily. You feed your soul the word of

God, and as your soul is fed and your spirit awakens, you completely surrender your will to God.

By taking the free will that God has given you and making all the choices above, you have caused your soul, your spirit, and your will to fall into alignment. This alignment, for the first time in your life, allows you to become fully alive. Up to this point, you have been spiritually dead to God, but with this alignment, you are now alive. For the first time in your life, you are alive! You become fully awake. You see the truth. You see the light. You see the world for what it really is. You see the world as a place full of lies, deceit, indiscretions, dishonesty, and lacking integrity. For the first time, the truth is awakened to you and you begin to understand.

THIS IS LIVING IN THE CONSCIOUSNESS OF GOD

As you feed your soul with God, the voice of your soul becomes louder and louder, and the connection between your soul and your spirit becomes stronger and stronger until that connection becomes unbreakable. Commit to feeding your soul every day. Begin every day with the renewing of your mind in the Lord Christ Jesus.

Your soul and your spirit, working together and feeding each other, become invincible and the voice of your ego becomes weaker and weaker. You will come to barely hear the voice of your flesh as you feed your soul everything you can about God. As you diligently seek your Father, you begin to get your first taste of the freedom that God has always had for you. You cannot believe the life that you used to live as God pours His character into your soul. "What took me so long," you ask yourself, "to find this life that has been lying asleep inside me. What took me so long to find and begin to live in the abundant life that God has for me?"

This is exactly what I mean to live in a total state of God Consciousness. When you are living in this state, when you are totally engulfed in this state of consciousness, you are living your life exactly as Jesus lived His, upon this Earth. You are living life at a higher level. No lies. No deceit. No schemes. You are living within and only by the truth.

I hope that you are, right this moment, asking yourself, "How can I achieve this level of God Consciousness? How can I find and experience this level of life? How is it possible for me to live a life completely through my spirit and my soul?"

FIRST: YOU MUST HAVE A MADE-UP MIND

When you begin your walk, and as you grow and continue to walk with your Heavenly Father, this fact is critical. You can never be wishy-washy with God. God cannot work with your "maybe" or your "I might." God cannot work with your indecision. In this walk with God, you are either all in or all out.

I know everything you have done, and you are not cold or hot. I wish you were one or the other. But since you are lukewarm and neither hot or cold, I will spit you out of my mouth. You claim to be rich and successful and to have everything you need. But you do not know how bad off you really are. You are pitiful, poor, blind, and naked. (Revelation 3: 15 -17)

The Lord is telling you, in point-blank words: in or out. One or the other, but do not straddle the line. If you are in, then be all the way in. If you want to be out, then be all the way out. There is no fifty-fifty with God. You want all of God and God wants all of you. These choices are yours.

If you chose in, then be zealous in your faith, trust, and belief in the Lord. Give all of yourself to God. If you are in, then speak of your Lord with fire and passion. Give the Lord your all. Give the Lord all that you have...

Obedience is so very critical. Be obedient to the Lord. Not sometimes, not only when it's convenient for you to do so, not only when it's comfortable, not only when the time is right for you, but be obedient. Listen for the voice of God, and then obey.

Behold, to obey is better than sacrifice. (I Samuel 15: 22)

For as by one man's disobedience the many were made sinners, so by one man's obedience the many will be made righteous. (Romans 5: 19)

Although he was a son, he learned obedience through what he suffered.
And being made perfect, he became the source of eternal salvation to all who will obey him. (Hebrews 5: 8 - 9)

Having purified your souls by your obedience to the truth for a sincere brotherly love, love one another earnestly from a pure heart. (I Peter 1: 22)

Going back to the Scripture in Revelations Chapter 17, Jesus is speaking about our pride. Jesus is talking about our desire to be self-sufficient and our want to live outside of the will of His Father. Jesus is speaking about our desire to live an ego-driven life. But remember, your ego is only interested in what it can do for itself.

If you want to live outside of the will of God, if you desire the treasures of the world, then you must realize that worldly possessions mean nothing to God. You can amass all the possessions you want. God does not care. And believe me when I tell you this not one possession of the world gets you any closer to eternal life in the Heavenly Kingdom.

In that same scripture, Jesus is talking about our complacency and laziness when it comes to our worship and when it comes to our delivering the Gospel to others. When it comes to praise, worship, and speaking about God, somehow, we have come to believe that all that is a Sunday thing. We can only talk about God on Sunday. We can only praise God on Sunday. And for sure, we can only worship God on Sunday, and we think that we have to have this special building that we can only do those things in. How did we get this idea that two or three hours on a Sunday morning is plenty of time for God? When did we get this idea that we have to have this special building that we call "church", to only praise and worship God in? We really believe that God is satisfied with this Sunday-only worship. We must because that's what the majority of so-called Christians do today.

Let me give you a very interesting statistic. I heard the other night that seventy percent of all Catholics ONLY choose to attend church on the holidays. This is the stat that I heard, but I am sure you will find the same number in just about every denomination. Do we really believe that we are pleasing God with that? Or worse yet, do you think that you are fooling God with your lack of sincerity? We want to be the most important thing to God, but we will not make God the most important person in our own lives. Everything else in our lives always comes before God.

God mirrors what you give to Him. If you want God to be crazy about you, then you must be crazy about God. If you want your life to be important to God, then you must make God important in your life. God will give you back everything that you give to Him. God will give you everything that you give to Him, but more and greater.

For it would be better for you not to have ever known the way to God, than after knowing the way, you choose to go back into the world. (II Peter 2: 21)

Read the next verse, verse twenty-two, and the Apostle Peter gets very graphic and writes:

What the true proverb says has happened to them: "The dog returns to its own vomit, and the sow, after washing herself, returns to wallow in the mire." (II Peter 2: 22)

Just imagine that picture in your mind. What a pretty picture of my life that statement makes. It would have been better for you to have never known, than to have known Christ, and then to make the free choice to reject Christ and return to the filth of the world.

You must have that made-up mind. You must know that I am on this road with my Lord and Savior, and that I will never, no matter what happens - and I mean, no matter what happens - ever let anything take me off this path. I will praise my Lord and Savior mightily, no matter what! I will constantly praise my Lord no matter what bump that I may hit along the way.

SECOND: YOU MUST BE DEVOTED.

DEVOTION LEADS YOU INTO OBEDIENCE

OBEDIENCE IS GREATER THAN SACRIFICE

Why do you call me lord, lord and obey me not!

It's your obedience to God that makes you a Christian!

You must find yourself only devoted to God. You must find yourself only becoming obedient to the voice of God. You hear other voices - the voice of your boss, the voice of your wife, the voice of friends - but the voice of God must be the loudest and the most prominent in your ear. When you become devoted to living a life of service to God, then your choices become apparent. You give your life in devotion, which leads you to giving your life to service. You love. You obey. You forgive. You give. You serve.

All begins with devotion to God, and then branches to the world.

This kind of devotion causes changes to occur in your life. When you devote your life in service to your Lord, you find yourself living in that higher consciousness. Devotion is necessary for your soul to really live the life of God Consciousness. Just as gas is necessary for your car to run, devotion is necessary for your soul to achieve this level of consciousness. The only way to stay at this level of devotion is to keep yourself in the light of God. The light of God is His truth. The only truth is found in the word of God. You must keep yourself in the word of God daily to maintain this level of devotion to the Father.

This higher level of devotion to God causes you to give up the outer control that the world has had over you. You give up the things that your ego desired and trade that control for an intimate relationship with God. God is calling you to devotion. Devotion is a power greater than self. Through prayer and reading the word, the Holy Ghost will come and be your ally to overthrow self and open the door for devotion.

DEVOTION IS THE DOORWAY TO YOUR SOUL.

THIRD: BE DILIGENT/SEEK COMPASSION

You must become diligent in your quest for God. God wants to be sought after. It is not a difficult search for God, but God does want you to make an effort. We must seek God every minute of every day. With all the distractions of everyday life, this becomes much harder than what it sounds. But that is the type of commitment that God wants from us and God rewards this type of commitment.

God is not a Sunday-only God. Don't fall into that trap; too many church folk are already in that mindset. God is not a God of: I worship Him only when I am in church. God wants us to praise Him, to worship Him, and to seek Him every minute that we are available. God tells us to praise, to worship, to seek Him no matter what the circumstances of our lives may be. Seek ye first the Kingdom of God. No matter what life is throwing your way, seek ye first God and His kingdom. Let God show you the way. Make God first in all things that you do and let God be the reward for your diligence; seek ye first God in all things that you do.

Diligence and longsuffering. Be diligent in your search after the truth, but be patient and wait upon the Lord. Even as you wait, continue your diligence but still wait upon the Lord.

We have such a bad habit, especially when we want something, to want it now or we have to put a time frame on it. We come to God, we ask God to help, we ask God to restore, and we ask God to heal; all great things and things that God is more than capable of doing. But then, we want to ruin things by putting a time limit on God. I need you to help me now. That's exactly how many of us approach God, and when the help does not come immediately, we begin to doubt God. Why, when the doubt comes, do we always point that doubt in the direction of God? When that second of doubt comes, that is the time for greater diligence. The worst thing that we can ever do to God is put a restriction upon God. Why would we ever want to restrict the one who created the Heavens and the Earth? Why do we want to limit the one who has no limits?

Diligence is that burning desire to put all that you are into a task. When I accepted God into my life, I was flooded with a hunger and a thirst. I was overwhelmed with this great thirst for knowledge about my creator, and at that moment, it seemed as if this thirst came out of nowhere. I became diligent in my seeking of knowledge, and to this day, I still have this persistent desire to learn more about God. To this very day, I read, I study, I listen to everything because I am still thirsty for God. I think that qualifies as being diligent. I just want to learn more and continue to discover the truth. This is the thirst of your soul and you will discover that the more you give your soul to drink, the more drink your soul desires.

Everything to quench this thirst can be found in the word of God. Ask God to direct you on this quest for knowledge. Ask God for wisdom and ask the Holy Ghost to direct your path on the search for the truth. Show me what to read. And as important as that is, when I would go to the library or the bookstore for more reference material, I would ask the Holy Ghost to show me what not to read or spend my time on. Open up your faith and let the Holy Ghost be your guide. Read everything that the Holy Ghost directs you to read. Stay connected to God and renew your mind through prayer and reading.

Seek compassion. Compassion comes by seeing the world through the eyes of our Lord. You cannot achieve compassion by looking at the world through your natural eyes. How can I see the world through the eyes of Jesus? Our Prophetess taught me something about how to read the Bible. Insert your name when you read. By inserting your name, you begin to see yourself in the Bible and the lessons of the Bible become personal. When you can see yourself in the Bible, you can begin to see the world through the eyes of Jesus and you develop compassion.

With compassion comes peace. With compassion comes joy. With compassion comes the love that Jesus showed to the world. When you truly have learned compassion, you will lose all the judgments that you have had towards the world. With compassion, there can be no judgment. Compassion allows you to live outside your ego. Compassion opens your soul to feel the hurt and pain of others.

But true compassion leads you to empathy. Compassion is a feeling of sorrow, but empathy is to truly feel as that person feels. Empathy is compassion doubled. Compassion allows you to ask yourself the question:

HOW CAN I SERVE THE WORLD TODAY?

But empathy not only allows you to ask yourself that question, but empathy moves you to action. Empathy asks, "What can I do for you?" And then empathy fulfills that answer. In order for us to do as Jesus did, we must have real compassion for everyone, but to really do as Jesus did, we must fulfill the need of everyone!

It's compassion that begs you to ask yourself the big question:

WHAT WOULD LOVE DO NOW?

Empathy leads you to the answer, and then moves you into action when that answer comes from your spirit.

FOURTH: PRAYER

Take everything to the Lord in prayer. Take everything. All of it. Everything. We are very hard-headed people, and when I wrote "everything", already some of you are trying to pick and choose. Yes, I read "everything", but I don't think that he meant this. Yes, I know he wrote "take everything to God", but God doesn't need to hear about this. Who are you to say what God needs to hear? Take everything to the Lord in prayer. You can't hide it, so why even try?

 So if God already knows why, do I have to tell God? Because God wants you to speak it. Deliverance is in the words that come out of your mouth. You cannot be set free until you speak it to God. You must speak it out of your mouth, so you can be made whole. God is waiting on you.

How do you build a relationship? You begin by sharing. God desires for you to share with Him. Share it all and share often. God does not want to only hear from you when you want or need something from Him. If you had a friend who, the only time you heard from them was when they had to have something from you, then what type of relationship would you call that? How long would that relationship last?

But that is exactly the relationship that we try to have with God. But then you say that God is never there. God is always there. The real question is: what kind of relationship are you building with Him?

Talk to God. Talk to God all day long. Tell Him everything that you would tell your best friend. God is your best friend; we have just not developed that type of relationship with Him. God wants to hear everything. Nothing is too trivial for God. Talk to God and be surprised what happens in your life when you let God in as your best friend. Tell God everything!

FIFTH: MEDITATE AND CONTEMPLATE

Contemplation is simply taking an idea, one idea at a time, and studying that idea with your mind. No television, no phone, no computer, no interruptions of any kind, just you and that one idea. We can't get close to God because we are not willing to devote the time. We are not willing to give some things up, even if only for an hour. That's exactly how selfish a people we have become.

If you become willing to break through that selfishness and allow the process of contemplation to take hold in your life, then contemplation will take you past the surface of your soul, where most people operate, and it will take you into the depths of your soul where God operates. What I am telling you is that contemplation can and will become very deep. This type of contemplation is life-changing. Through this type of contemplation, you can and will achieve a level of God consciousness that you never knew existed, let alone ever knew that you could live. But contemplation makes all that possible. When you choose the higher values of life to contemplate on, you find that living the life that Jesus lived is possible.

Meditation is all about taking back control; taking back control of a life that you have lost. Meditation is about taking back control of your life from the world. When you meditate you have taken back your rightful spot; no one is in control but you. In meditation, you have no thought, no music, no phone, no nothing, and no interruptions. Just peace. Just a blankness. You take back the control. It's just you. All you, and nothing but you. Listen to your breath. I like to go to the ocean and listen to the water. Listen for the voice of God. Be still and do nothing but listen.

For a lot of you, this will be extremely difficult, and for a lot of you, I am writing about a foreign concept. Be still and do nothing. I don't know if I can do that. Some of you may not even know how. But to do this, there is no greater liberating experience. Do this and taste freedom - real freedom, not that fake freedom that we have been taught out of books. Let God teach you His freedom. No greater freedom exists anywhere, and when you get that small taste in the beginning, all you want is more. Meditation is now a way of my life. Connect with God. Commune with God through your soul. Connect with that person that God created you, and you alone, to be.

Meditate every day if you can. If you can't, then do it two or three times a week. Same time. Same days. Same place. Find a place that works for you and go there. Meditation is sacrifice. When you have given God your time, you have made a sacrifice. God honors sacrifice. Remember what I wrote a few chapters ago about sacrifice.

SACRIFICE = LOVE
LOVE = SACRIFICE

There is no love, nor can there ever be love, without the sacrifice. I do not believe that there is a greater sacrifice that we can give than our time. You can tell God all you want that you love Him, and let me tell you, we have become really good with our lip service. But when you show and give God love through your sacrifice, then God will always honor your love and your sacrifice. Just listen for the voice of God. Will God always show up? No. But God will come. Wait. Be patient. Wait. Be still and listen.

But why is all this so important? Why are my spirit and my soul so important?

It is through your spirit that you can know God.
It is through your spirit that you hear the voice of God.
It is through your spirit that you develop an intimate, personal relationship with God.
It is through your spirit that you commune and have fellowship with God.
It is through your spirit that you share DNA with God.

Through your soul, you get to become the true you.
Through your soul, you learn boundless freedom.
Through your soul, you connect with your spirit.
Through that connection of soul and spirit, God consciousness flows.
Through the birth of your God consciousness, you are able to walk as Jesus walked.

As you achieve a greater depth of spirituality, your soul and your spirit begin to become one.

As you read, as you study, as you meditate, as you spend time in contemplation, as you talk with God, as you listen for His voice, as you diligently seek the will of God for your life, a shift occurs in you. Remember that when I started this chapter, I told you that God was looking for a transformation in your life. That transformation is right in front of you. The life that the Lord wants you to live is resting right in your soul.

Where your ego once controlled you, your soul has now started to take over. Relating to yourself as a spiritual being has begun to take hold. Because of the promises that God has made to you, you can now see yourself as the spiritual being that God created. You are becoming that person that God intended for you to be at creation. Your mind, your spirit, and your soul have merged into one. You have traded selfishness in for oneness.

As you grow more distant to the world, and the concerns of the world fade away, you find that:

1) You turn to God for all of your needs.
2) You have no fixed plans for life;
   it's God's time and God's will.
3) You begin to feel a deep compassion for the suffering going on around you, and you want to end it.
4) Nothing of the world satisfies the hunger of your soul.
5) The possessions that the world has to offer you no longer have any control over you. You realize that everything on the outside can come and go in the blink of an eye.
6) What becomes permanent in your life are all the qualities which God has downloaded into your soul.

But the fruit of the spirit is love, joy, peace, long-suffering, gentleness, goodness, faith, meekness, temperance, against there is no such law. (Galatians 5: 22-23)

God wishes for you to have and become all these characteristics. But you must first have love. You must become and continue to grow in the love of God in order to gain all the other fruits. Love is the base for all the other fruits to grow and flourish in. You will never be gentle without love. You cannot be meek without love. You will never forgive if you do not have love.

As long as we are talking about the fruits of the spirit, let me answer a question that I hear quite often. What is the most important, the gifts of the spirit or the fruits of the spirit? The fruits. You must gain and grow in the fruits so you will know how to handle and what to do with the gifts that God has given to you.

God gives us the gifts in order to give them away. So many of us have become clueless to this fact. We want the gift, we get a gift, and then we keep the gift to ourselves. God gives to you to give to others. Without the love of God living within us, we will live through our ego, and it is that ego that tells you to hoard the gift. Keep the gift for yourself. God gives us the gift freely. Without God's love, we will never feel the freedom to give the gift away.

You must renew your mind daily, and the best place to start every day is with the fruits of the spirit. As your soul feeds upon these fruits, your soul becomes restored to its rightful place in your life and your soul begins to generate:

1) The energy needed for love
2) The energy needed for compassion
3) The awareness for truth
4) The awareness for creativity

Your soul becomes like an engine feeding your mind. Your soul feeds your mind the above choices to live your life by.

The more you feed your engine (the soul) with the word of God, the closer you stay to God Consciousness, and the easier and more likely that, when confronted with a situation, you will act as God would act. You will not even realize you are asking yourself that one question that God always wants you to ask yourself:

WHAT WOULD LOVE DO NOW?

The question has now become second nature!
The question has now become a way of life!
You are now living your life as God would live upon this Earth!

As you become closer and closer to being conscious of God, the old you becomes smaller and smaller and you begin to feel only this connection to God. The connection grows stronger and stronger until an oneness begins to take you over.

At a certain point, wholeness prevails. This wholeness is to be full of the presence of God. There is no more going in and out. There is no more coming and going. No more moving in and then moving out. You have become one.

To you, the world becomes an empty place because the world lacks the presence of God. As you reach this level of God Consciousness, you become truly enlightened upon the ways of the world, and you know that you no longer have a personal stake in the comings and goings of that world.

As this oneness with God deepens, you have entered into God's identity. You have taken God's identity as your own. As you reach this way of thinking, there is a clearness that comes to your thinking and certain things become more real to you:

1) Your mind stops being frantic, restless, and obsessed.
2) You know that fear is only an illusion.
3) The threat of sin decreases in your life.
4) Material possessions have lost all meaning to you.
5) "Us versus them" thinking is no longer appealing - you realize that we are all one.
6) Self-importance is completely gone.
7) Issues of the world no longer have any importance - you probably no longer read or even watch the news.
8) Social status, money, and possessions have lost all importance to you.
9) You give love freely to everyone.
   The love of God becomes the supreme force in your life.

As your soul becomes linked to God's soul, as the Kingdom of God comes to dwell in your soul, God begins to reward you with the treasures of His Kingdom: freedom that you have never known before. This freedom brings you into the truth and the truth brings you into oneness with God.

You will feel love like you have never felt: God's unconditional love. A Love that never ends. A Love that will never fail. A Love that knows no boundaries. A Love that has no expectations. You will be in such peace that you have never experienced before. Joy will abound all around you and you will find joy in everything that you do.

You will feel these things more intensely and these gifts you will never lose. The peace that alone brings to you, knowing that you cannot lose these gifts, these gifts that God alone can give to you, is indescribable. God's presence is all around you and God will rain abundance down upon you.

Now that you have read and discovered your soul, it is my hope and prayer that you will feed your soul, and that your soul will begin to prosper. As your soul prospers, so you too will begin to prosper. Only through the love of God will your soul really know prosperity.

Let the true transformation begin. Let the presence of God rain down upon your life. God did come to bring you life and to bring you that life more abundantly!

CHAPTER TEN

HOW COULD I CHANGE?

When I left the life that I had in Cleveland, Ohio and came to Atlantic City with the purpose of ending my life, deep down, I did not want to die; I just wanted someone to love me. The fact that I was unable to find someone who could do that for me was leading me to do something that I really did not want to do. It was a decision that I did not want to make but I felt that I was left with no choice. How is it that most people fall into depression? They lose their choices.

It is through the lack of choices that desperation and loneliness set into our lives. When we become desperate and when we are all alone, these two factors will lead us into making some very bad decisions.

On Thursday, January 9, 2009, only through God's unmerited grace and God's endless mercy, I accepted Jesus Christ as my Lord and Savior. However, it was not really until a day in February when I met Jesus face to face that I knew, at that moment, that I had truly found someone who would love me for the rest of my life. On that day when Jesus walked with me, my faith was raised to another level and I knew, on that day, that I would never be alone again.

I also knew, at that time, that something extraordinary had happened to me on that day in February. It seemed to me that from that point on, God came to me to talk, and for some reason, I knew that I was supposed to write. God has been talking and I have been writing ever since.

There has been a recurring message from God ever since all this began. Go and tell all; tell everyone what you have seen and what you have heard. I know that these words are found in the Bible, but I hear the same words all the time. These words ring very loudly, over and over again in my spirit. Go and tell everyone who will listen. Even tell those who won't listen.

How could I have changed? Not by anything that I could do for myself. Only the hand of God upon my life could change me. Opening myself to God's presence and God's will changed me. God's hand has always been upon my life. God's hand has always been upon your life. You must open yourself to that presence in your life. I know what I know today and I feel what I feel today, because I feel the presence of God every day. In addition, I have made the choice to let that presence control my life every day.

I feel led to write my first writings here, now in these spaces. This was one of the first of the writings that God ever gave to me to read in public.

Minister Lea and I were in a prison one night, ministering to a group of men, and one of the men in the group asked me a question, "Why should I believe in God?"

It had only been a couple of months since I had accepted the Lord as my Savior, and when the gentleman asked this question, I did not feel as if I had given a good answer off the top of my head. Therefore, like everything else that I do now, I asked God what I should have said. "Teach me, Lord," and this was the writing and the answer that God gave to me and I now give it to you:

WHY SHOULD I BELIEVE IN GOD?

BECAUSE I NEED A SHEPHERD

Because believing in God allows me to be the person I really want to be. That word "BE" is very important. I want to "BE" just like Jesus. I want to "BE come" the fruits of the spirit. I know that I cannot "BE" these things without God. I need God to "BE" in charge of my life if I am to have any chance of "BEcoming" that person that I wish to "BE".

If I am left to my own desires, this rat race that we call life is not worth living. Life is cold, cutthroat, and devious. Life is dangerous, violent, and it is never fair. Life just does not work. In addition, life never worked for me. I tried so hard to live life my way, and through my will, making all my own decisions. And in the end, with all that effort that I had put into my own life, all that life gave me in return was two suicide attempts.

Now it is God's turn. I have turned everything over to God. God is now in total control of my life. I have surrendered all. Through God's will and in God's time, God is restoring my life. Through the grace of God, God is restoring my life to its fullest. God is restoring my life better than it was before. And the Lord started this process in my heart.

Am I a different person today than most people? I feel different and I think different; so yes, I am different! I think this is why the Lord tells us that the road to Him is small and only a few will find it. All are invited, but only a few will accept. Really, accept a true repentance. Repentance means to change. We should feel different because we are now different.

Worldly things no longer concern us. We no longer spend our time on matters of the flesh. When you truly become a citizen of the Kingdom, then money, job, property, bank account, things that once had importance to you are no longer a concern. People look at me strangely when I tell them that I do not have a bank account and I have not had one for over two years. I have no access to the internet. I had no phone for probably a year and a half, and if it were up to me, I would still not have a phone even today. Things of this world no longer have any control over me.

The will of the Lord and serving Him are your only concerns. You think of nothing else. God is the first thing you think of when you wake in the morning and God is the last thought you have before you fall asleep at night. This is the life that I live. This is the life that I want to have today.

What are you putting into your soul?

Our Prophetess, one evening during a Bible study, asked a question which has stuck with me ever since. "If your soul had the ability at this moment to leave your body and walk down this aisle to talk to me, what would your soul tell me?"
Is your soul empty?
Is your soul starving?
Is your soul asleep?
Does your soul live in darkness?
Would your soul like to see some light?

Maybe you believe that your soul is nonexistent. Do I even have a soul? Where can I find my soul? What is my soul even for? Alternatively, could your soul be the one that is being fed? Is your soul prospering? Do you know how to prosper your soul? Your soul really only wants to eat fruit - the fruits of the Spirit. Your soul wants to be the character of God.

Are you "BEING" or are you "DOING"? There is that word "BE" again. Doing is a function of my body. I do my job. Being is a function of the soul. I am becoming a more loving person.

Take a second and let that sink in. You do things with your body. You "BEcome" someone with your soul.

Your soul conceives, the mind creates, and your body experiences. Your body, your mind, and your soul are all equal. Your soul will never override the will of the mind or the will of the body.

The function of your soul is to indicate its desire, never to impose its desire.

The function of the mind is to choose from all the alternatives that your soul comes up with.

The function of the body is to act out the choice of the mind.

Without God in your life, your soul is empty. That is the hole that we all feel in our insides. That emptiness, that incompleteness that you feel is your soul not being allowed to live to its highest purpose. Without God to guide us, we are left to our minds and our thoughts to control our lives. Let me ask you, "How is that going for you?" With your ego in charge, that is exactly how we land ourselves in so many of the messes that we find ourselves in. When we are left to choose for ourselves, when we are left to our own devices, we have the ability to get ourselves into some real messes. In addition, the consequences that come with those messes are often life-changing, and not always for the better.

When we let God take control of our lives, God sends the Holy Ghost to live and be with each of us. Our soul begins to be fed with the word of God, and our soul begins to take over our lives. With our souls and our spirits lined up, working together, the two can keep our minds and our thoughts in check, and we begin to live our lives in God's will and for the glory of God. When you are living a life completely under the will of God, then your flesh and ego are always outvoted by the Holy Ghost and your soul.

Do not conform to this world, but be transformed by the renewal of your mind, that by testing you may discern what is the will of God, what is good and acceptable and perfect. (Romans 12:2)

God did not put you on this planet to produce anything with your body. You were put on this planet solely to produce things with your soul.

If you think that your life is all about the "DOING", then you do not understand what you are all about. We get so caught up in what we are doing and who we are. We get so caught up in statuses and titles. We get so caught up in wealth and power. These are all manmade and not of the Lord.

Your soul does not care what you do for a living. I know that many of you reading this may find that statement hard to believe. Remember that your soul is not into the "DOINGS" of your life. Your soul does not care what kind of car you drive. Your soul does not care that you can even drive. You soul cares less about the size of your house, how much money you have, how many women you have slept with, or how high up the company ladder you have been able to climb. Your soul does not concern itself with such trivia.

And let me really open your eyes with this next statement:

WHEN YOUR LIFE IS OVER,
 NEITHER WILL YOU

Your soul only cares about what you are being while you are doing whatever it is that you doing. Your soul only desires to "BE" not "DO".

Your soul only wants to be compassionate.
Your soul only wants to be kind.
Your soul only wants to be merciful.
Your soul only wants to be forgiving.
Your soul only wants to be humble.
Your soul only wants to love.

In your soul's highest form, what does your soul desire to "BE"?

GOD!!!

This is the life that I want to live. I want to be just like God. I want to imitate Christ. I want to live my life as Jesus lived His. One of the things I ask God for daily is to be just like Him. Please, God, as I walk through this world, let everyone see you in me. Fill my soul with the fruits, especially love. If I do fall short, please, Lord, help me to never fall short in the love that I show. Kill this flesh and let my spirit take control of the life that I now live. Let me walk in holiness as you have commanded, and continue, Lord, to teach me humility. I do so much love you, Lord, and let your will be done through me. This is one of the prayers that I pray daily.

I do so much wish that the world could find God the way that I know Him and love Him.

This was the first writing that the Lord gave to me after God began speaking to me on a regular basis. This was also the same time that I began to speak in public about my Lord and Savior. I was invited to go into a couple of different prisons to minister the Gospel and I began to take these writings and read them to the men. I never knew, at that time, that God was putting together a book, but every one of those writings is now in this book in one chapter or another.

God has been doing His work in me ever since that first day when I boarded the Greyhound bus and came to Atlantic City. How is it possible for a man, for any man, to make such a radical change in his life? Only through the grace and the mercy and the power and the love of a great God. A God who is, "THE GREAT I AM." God is so great, so powerful, so all-knowing that God can and will be whatever it is that we need for Him to be. Moving to a new city will not change you. Getting a new job will not change you. Finding a new girlfriend will not change you. Buying a new car will not change you. Only through the power and promises of our Lord can a man be changed.

The world tells you that if you change the outside, then you have changed. Another lie the world tells us. The world will tell you that if you change something in your life, that change will be good. You can change all the cosmetic things that you want, but your inside is still the same, and as long as your inside is the same, you are still carrying the old baggage into a new outside.

Only God can change your insides. God can and will clean you from the inside. True and real transformation has to start from your inside out. You awake your soul by trusting God. You align your soul and your spirit, which changes your heart, your mind, and your thought patterns - which all, in turn, change your actions. This is permanent change. This is the change that happens by believing and surrendering to God.

When this transformation began in my life, and the word of God really started to take hold for me and I could see this new man evolving in me, there were definite things that, looking back now, I know that God was showing me and teaching me, which really cemented this transformation in my life forever:

1) I felt love that I had never felt before, and then God taught me about that love
2) Jesus showed me a new way to live and He made me a new person
3) I learned to forgive and I learned to let it go
4) Jesus gave me peace
5) I have a made-up mind.
   I know what I know, and I know that I can never go back!

When I arrived in Atlantic City with the purpose of ending my life, I never wanted to die. I just really needed two things that I could not find in my world. I wanted someone to love me and I really needed a new way to live life. God gave me both. God gave me His love, and with the five statements above, God showed me a new way to live my life. I would like share with you a few things that God taught me concerning the above statements. They are in no particular order whatsoever; because each is equal in their importance to me as to how I live my life today. Each of the statements continues to play a vital role as they guide me in my walk with my Lord and my Savior.

We have no ability to change ourselves! The only way to accomplish change is through and with God. God is the only one with the power to affect a real permanent change in your life. God changed my life. In addition, God desires to do the same for you, today.

You cannot change until you are ready. Many of us speak of change, but they are just worthless words that carry no weight. You cannot institute any change until you realize that the world you live in does not work for you. Then you must even take that one step farther. The world not only does not work, but it will never work for you. Change will not come until you finally become tired of being sick and tired.

Why do you think that most of us call the life that we are living a "rat race"? Life is very much a race and you are on the track running. That was the life that I was living. I knew that my life did not work, but I also knew that life could work if I could only find that way. Close your eyes and just think of that last statement. If only I could find the way! Are you tired yet? Are you really tired?

Are you tired of this life that they call "The Rat Race"? The world has you bound to running in this Rat Race, lap after lap, with never a hope of the race ever ending. Actually, the world has you believing that this is exactly what you are supposed to be doing, running this race and trying your best to get ahead. With every lap that you run, someone is turning up the speed, so not only can you never get out of the race, but also every lap must be faster than the lap before. You keep running faster and faster and faster, but you never seem to get anywhere. Everyone else is getting somewhere, but you seem to just be standing still. You never get the big promotion. You never get the expensive, fancy, new car. You never get the recognition that you think you deserve.

Is this sounding like your life? Welcome to the life that the devil has for you. Welcome to the Rat Race. Never a hope. Never living life to its fullest. Never realizing the dream. Never living to your potential. Only running faster and faster to stay exactly where you already are. Only getting more tired and more frustrated. That was exactly my life.

I am here to tell you that there is a way out of this Rat Race. You no longer have to settle for being the Rat in the Race. There is a better way to live life. The way out of the world is through Jesus. Jesus saved me and Jesus wants to save you.

I know that this change in me is permanent and I will live the rest of my days here on Earth serving my Lord. With all that said, let me elaborate on a couple of the five statements that I said a few paragraphs ago:

1) JESUS GAVE ME PEACE

On January 7th, 2009, I accepted the Lord into my life. Immediately as I did that, I was overcome with an insatiable desire to learn everything that I could about God.

At this time, I had no job, which left me nothing but time, which I put to good use, spending hours in the public library, reading everything that I could get my hands on about God. At the same time, I attended Church every time something was going on, so I could hear more. I prayed and read the word of God. I began to meditate and I walked. I would take these long walks, and during these walks, I would talk with God, but mostly, I would listen. We, as a society, talk way too much. It is hard to learn and take things in when you are always talking. As I listened, God began to speak and I began to write.

In reading of the word of God, one of the first scriptures that God showed me was a scripture in Hebrews; it read:

And without faith, it is impossible to please God, because anyone who comes to him must first believe that he is God and that God rewards those who diligently seek him. (Hebrews 11: 6)

God rewards those who diligently seek Him and that was me. I took that scripture when I read it as a promise from God, and believe you me, I was diligently seeking God.

Everywhere I could. Anywhere I could. At any time I could. I was seeking after God. I had this thirst that just could not be quenched! I had a hunger that would not go away no matter how much I ate. This hunger and thirst for God I still have today and I pray to God that I will never lose it.

I am talking about seeking God and about God rewarding those who seek. Give me a second here to talk about the rewards from God. In our carnal mind, immediately when we hear the words *reward* or *treasure*, we think of money. In addition, if the reward is not in money, then it must be a possession. God is going to give me that new car I have been asking Him for. Alternatively, God is going to give us that bigger house that we have been praying for. Or God is going to give me that promotion at the job. Why do we always want the reward to be something from the world?

Yes, I do believe that God does and will reward people with these things, but are these the things that we should be seeking from God? Are these really the treasures that we desire for God to bless us with? I say no. I no longer desire the things of the world. What I am seeking from God are the spiritual blessings. What I am seeking and desiring for God to bless me with are the things that I can take with me when I go to live with Him in heaven. I always desire to be blessed and to grow in God's love. I always desire to be blessed and to gain more of God's joy, God's peace, God's strength. I want a deeper walk with my God, a greater presence or to be surrounded constantly with the presence of God, a greater anointing, to stay on the path to gain the greatest prize of all, to gain my salvation and my eternal life in Heaven. These, I believe, are the rewards that we should value the most.

The ultimate reward that we should always be seeking is to hear God say these words to us when our natural life has come to an end:

"WELCOME, MY GOOD AND FAITHFUL SON.
ENTER INTO THE KINGDOM. JOB WELL DONE."

Like I said earlier, I had no job during this time and I only had eight dollars to my name. Therefore, during this time, I had days where I was a little concerned about food and shelter. As I sought after God, and as I began to read the Bible on a daily basis, I would let the Holy Ghost direct my path and I would pretty much just open the Bible and read wherever the Bible opened to. In doing this, the Holy Ghost led me to a scripture that answered all my concerns - another promise from God. This promise was that if I would have complete trust, then God would provide for me. In addition, He would provide all of my needs; God did just that very thing.

Than Jesus said unto his disciples: Therefore, I tell you, do not worry about your life, what you will eat; or about your body, what you will wear.

Life is more than food, and the body more than clothes. Consider the ravens: They do not sow or reap, they have no storeroom or barn; yet God feeds them. And how much more valuable you are than birds!
Who of you by worrying can add a single hour to his life? Since you cannot do this very little thing, why do you worry about the rest? (Luke 12: 22 - 26)

I believed and I trusted God to keep that promise from; what God said, He would do. For three months, I lived on those eight dollars. I ate a meal every day - a very good meal every day, Monday through Friday. Saturday and Sunday, I was on my own. I had a place to stay. It was only a room, but it was a nice room. I had a bed and a roof. What more did I need? The Lord did provide and provided well. I trusted the Lord's promises and He delivered!

And then came the day. It was a day in February towards the end of the month. I had gotten up early and was heading out to take a walk. During this time, while I was not working, I did a lot of walking. We need to do more of that, walking. We get so busy rushing from here to there, losing track of time. Walking really slows things down. It puts you back in control of your life. Plus, walking is the best time for contemplation and listening for the Lord.

I was walking this morning up St James Place, going towards Pacific Avenue. I was very troubled on this particular morning; many things were on my mind and my mind just kept going back and forth. I could not find a job and I had no prospects on the horizon. I still only had eight dollars in my pocket, and even though I had this nice place to stay, my landlord was allowing me to stay on credit; the bill was starting to add up significantly.

I was very troubled and worry had taken over me on this morning. Fear was trying to creep up on me. I was having this feeling that I was digging myself into a hole that I would never be able to get myself out of. I owed money with no job and I had no car, so I was stuck. Fear and worry were looming over me like a big black cloud and I felt like the cloud was choking me. As I walked, depression was seeping in and I began to get scared. What had I done?

However, as I walked, I began to remember scripture from the Bible. As I walked, I began to remember things about God from the past few weeks of my seeking after the Lord. As I walked, I began to pray and my prayer turned into a cry out to God for help. "Help me, Lord! Help me! I do not know what to do. But help me, Lord!" And as I walked up St James, I just looked up to the Heavens and cried out to God.

I continued to walk and I began to feel something next to me. There was a presence. Someone was walking next to me. It was the Lord! You will never get me to say anything else. The Lord was walking right beside me. The Lord and I are walking up St James, side by side. We walked for a few blocks together in silence, and then the Lord turned to me and said three small words, "I got you."

"I got you." And with those three small words, I felt everything that I had ever wanted to feel. All the things that I had been searching for in the world that the world could never give to me, Jesus just did. Everything that was missing in my life, I had just found. The hole that was inside of me was, all of a sudden, filled. In a second, I was made complete. I felt security that I had never felt before. I was set free. I was made whole. I felt love. I felt peace. I felt a calmness come over me. I felt as if someone had just picked me up and put me in their arms.

"I got you." We walked together for a few more blocks, just Jesus and I walking together, and as we walked, Jesus spoke to me. Jesus told me that I would have another tough month, but at the end of that month, everything was going to work out. Jesus told me to never forget the words that He had spoken to me, "I got you and I will always have you."

Before He left me, Jesus put this air around me from the top of my head to the bottom of my feet. With that air of protection, Jesus took all of my cares. Jesus took all of my worries. Jesus took all my doubts. Jesus took all my concerns. Jesus took all those things away and He gave me peace - the peace that surpasses all understanding. I had never felt such a release of a weight and an influx of calm. At that moment, when Jesus filled me with the peace of God, I knew that everything was going to be ok. What a feeling! From that day to this very day, I have not had one worry, one concern, or one care. Jesus took all those things away when He spoke to me those three small words, "I got you."

Jesus took all my burdens and worries away. No one but God can do a thing like that. There is no man who can ever make you feel that secure. There is no man who can give you that kind of calmness. It is the calm that quiets every storm. Only God can step into life and give you such a gift.

And a great windstorm arose and the waves were breaking into the boat, so that the boat was already filling.
But Jesus was in the stern, asleep on a cushion. And they woke him and said to him, "Teacher, do you not care that we are perishing?"
And he awoke and rebuked the wind and said to the sea, "PEACE! BE STILL!" And the winds ceased and there was a great calm.
He said to them, "Why are you so afraid? Have you still no faith?" (Mark 4: 37 - 40)

This is the same peace that Jesus is offering you and it is the peace that Jesus gave to me on that day. In the midst of your storm, Jesus is ready and willing to say to your storm, "Peace, be still." But we are just like the disciples with our little faith, or with our shaky faith, or with our lack of faith.

You talk about feeling lighter. You talk about walking on air. You talk about a feeling of security; I was every one of those things in an instant!

JESUS GAVE ME PEACE

2) I HAVE A MADE-UP MIND.
   I KNOW WHAT I KNOW AND I KNOW THAT I CAN
   NEVER GO BACK!

When I came to Atlantic City to end my life, it was not the first time. I had put into motion a plan to end my life just a few years before.

It is truly amazing how we really think that we are in control. How we believe that we have it all going on. I am in charge. I have all the answers. I know everything. I do not need your help. That was me. I thought that I was in total control of my life. But in reality, my life was so far out of sorts that no one could possibly be in control of it, especially me!

It is so funny how we think that we can control everything. We make plans for tomorrow. We make plans for next week. We make plans for a summer vacation. We make goals for the next year, just as if all these days, months, and years are promised to us. We think that time is guaranteed. We really believe that our lives are forever.

You are not even in control of the next minute! Forty thousand people each year leave their homes, kiss their loved ones goodbye for the day, and tell them that we will see them later in the day - only to never return home again.

Car accidents take forty thousand lives every year. These were all people who were so sure that they were in control. These were all people who were so sure that life was guaranteed to them. These were all people who thought for sure that they would return home, at the end of their day, to see their loved ones. These were all people who had no control over their lives whatsoever.

YOUR VERY LIFE IS LIKE YOUR BREATH ON A VERY COLD WINTER'S DAY:
YOU CAN SEE YOUR BREATH AS YOU EXHALE FOR THAT SECOND,
BUT THEN IT IS GONE

Do not boast about tomorrow
  For you do not know what a day may bring (Proverbs 27: 1)

After my wife walked out on me, I began to lose control of my life. It felt like I was living my life on a treadmill that no one would ever let me off. That was somewhat ok, but I also felt like this same person kept turning up the speed on the treadmill. That was not ok. I kept having to run faster and faster just to keep up. The world was going so fast and it seemed like everyone was running right by me, passing me up, leaving me behind. I was running as fast as I could, but I was falling farther behind everyone else. No matter how hard I tried, I just could not keep up. I was getting so tired of running and running. No matter how hard I tried, I could not catch up with everyone nor could I slow life down.

I knew that I was stuck - stuck on this treadmill called life. No matter how hard I tried, life was going right by me and I was so tired. It seemed like my life would go in cycles. For a couple of years, I hung on and stayed in control. My life looked as normal as everyone else's, even though, in my mind, I was screaming for it to stop. For some reason, I got to that third year and something clicked and I hit rock bottom.

When I would get that low, in my mind, I believed the only way out was through suicide. You have really got to be on the bottom when you think that your only option is suicide. What I did know what that my life as it was did not work, and as long as I stayed in control, life would never work for me. I was also painfully aware that with me making all the decisions for my own life, I was stuck to keep going round and round and round, until one of these times, I would be successful in my attempts to end my life. Is it not funny how our lives only keep repeating themselves? What is it Dr. Phil always says? Past history is a good indicator of a future result. That is because we truly know no other way.

The peace, the joy, the love that God has given to me was never shown to me by anyone ever before. As I have said before, I never wanted to kill myself; I just wanted someone to love me. No strings. No expectations. No requirements. Not wanting anything from me. Not needing something from me. Not expecting me to do something for them. Not me being in constant fear. Always being afraid that I would wake up and that person would not be there. I just wanted someone to love me. I just wanted to be out of the rat race. I just wanted off the treadmill.

I did not want to die. I just wanted a new way to live my life. Not the same old, same old. I just needed someone to show me love. Jesus came and gave me that love, gave me His love - a love that mends all wounds, a love that restores you to wholeness, a love that gives purpose, a love that shows you reason, a love that makes each day brand new and worth living. Jesus came into my life and showed me what God's love is all about. No one loves me like Jesus loves me. No one ever can or ever will. No one loves you like Jesus loves you.

- When you can say that you have had enough of the lies of the world
- When you can say that you have had enough of all the trickery and the foolishness that the world has to offer you
- When you can say these words and really mean them once for all
- When you can say these words and know for certain that this is all the world has to offer you

ASK GOD TO ENTER INTO YOUR LIFE.

Ask God to come and show you a new way. Ask God to show you how to change the way that you are living. Ask God to flip the script.

The Lord gave me one more chance to say "yes" to Him. God gave me the choice. God looked at me and said to me, "On this day, you choose. Choose ye this day life or death." That's the choice that God gives us. If you are in the midst of a struggle right now, let me ask you one extremely important question:

HOW MANY CHANCES ARE YOU GOING TO GIVE THE DEVIL TO TAKE YOU OUT?

The Lord already knows the condition of your life. God will give you chance after chance to save your life. But you have to choose. The invitation is open to everyone, but you have to choose, Life or death, Light or dark, Heaven or hell. The road everyone travels or the road only a few have gone. It was always my choice. I could choose to stay right where I was forever. I could stay right on that treadmill, running the rat race, until I would destroy my own life. Or, I could choose a new way. I chose the new way. I chose to let God take control. I chose to surrender all to God and to let God lead my life. After fifty years of making all the wrong choices, I had finally made a right one.

However, I had to be able to say, "I had enough." When you have truly reached that point in your life, where you have had enough of everything and everybody, when you can truly say that you are ready to leave it all behind you, when you can truly say that you don't want it anymore, when you can truly say that it has no value to you, only then will change begin. The words that I have just written for most people are only just that, words. We say that we are tired. We say that we want to change. We say that we don't want it anymore, but the next time the opportunity presents itself, we are right there doing the same old habits. You have not hit the low of the low yet.

But if you are real and you know that you will not go back, then you can find that life that you have always had deep within you, that you have been searching for. You can discover what life is all about. You can find your true identity. You can discover who you really were created to be. You can discover your life with God. This is exactly the time when your soul and your spirit collide and take over. What do they take over? YOU!!!

For whoever would save his life will lose it, but whoever loses his life for my sake will find it. (Matthew 16: 25)

What is the purpose for our lives? Who among us has not asked ourselves that very question multiple times? Let me give to you what God has shown to me.

Life is twofold.

1) To spend every second giving glory to God

2) To enrich the lives of every person that you can touch
   I KNOW WHAT I KNOW AND I KNOW THAT I WILL
   NEVER GO BACK!

3) JESUS MADE ME A NEW PERSON

There are many promises that God gives to us in His word
once we accept Him as our savior. One of those promises that
has meant so very much to me is:

*Therefore if anyone is in Christ, he is a new creation; the old is
gone, the new has come.* (II Corinthians 5: 17)

That is exactly what I wanted: to be new. Not just to get a do-
over, but to be a brand new man, and to have a brand new
life. I wanted all the old to go away and I wanted a new life. I
wanted to get off that roller coaster ride that I had been on
and I wanted to find a brand new way to live life. I knew that
my life did not work, would not work, could not work, and I
needed to be shown a new way. God promised me just that, a
brand new life. To be made a brand new man.

But in order for this new life to work, you have to work for
this new life. Too many so-called Christians quote the word,
but have never worked the word a day in their lives. Let me
quote you a scripture. Faith without works is dead. You can
talk and quote all the faith you want, but if you never work
your faith, you are dead - spiritually dead. It is what our
Apostle calls, "Dead Man Bones." Let me tell you a reality. If
you are spiritually dead, then you have zero chance for
eternal life. The sad fact is that there are many so-called
Christians who attend church every Sunday, who can quote a
boatload of scripture; they might even sing in the choir, but
they are spiritually dead and have no chance of ever seeing
the Kingdom of Heaven.

The key words in the scripture above are being "In Christ." My old life does not just disappear overnight when I accept Jesus as my savior. As I read the word of God, the word must affect a change in my life. My life must change. Every day should bring me one step away from the old, and one step closer towards the new. As I grow into this new life "In Christ", my old habits should fade away and become less appealing. The things I used to do, I no longer desire. The people I used to hang with no longer appeal to me. Even the television shows I used to watch no longer attract me. The old has gone and the new has come.

In this new life, the goal is to grow in Jesus. We want to grow to be just like Jesus, to be an imitator of Christ. This is exactly what I needed and wanted. Now with God in control of my life, the rollercoaster ride has stopped. The ups and downs that were my life are gone. The emptiness that was huge inside me has completely disappeared and my life has become complete. For the first time in my life, I am whole and I am missing nothing. I have found everything in Jesus.

We are telling you what we have seen and heard, so that you may share in this life with us. And we share in it with the father and with his son Jesus Christ. (I John 1: 3)

What is it that I know? In this walk with my Lord and Savior, I have come to know four truths. We often say that we know what we know, but there are four distinct things that I have come to know:

1) I know that Jesus Christ, in this year, that He lives. He is alive!
2) That God is in control of my life.
3) God speaks to everyone. God speaks to me and He wants to talk with you.
4) I can never go back.
   The Devil may sting me, but he can never have me.

What is my purpose? To tell everyone what I have seen and what I have heard. I have done that in the writing of this book. But I will continue to do so for as long as someone is listening.

On Thursday afternoon - it was actually May 7, 2009 - I was sitting on the boardwalk just watching the ocean. I have found a very particular spot that I always go to and meditate while watching the Atlantic. On this day, God came to me, and at that time, gave me the initial instruction for writing this book.

At that time, God also told me to go out and tell everyone who would listen what I had seen and what I had heard. I thank and praise God for choosing me as His vessel in writing this book, for choosing me to be His scribe. I am a brand new creature in Christ and that is a promise that God makes to everyone. And that is a promise that you can live on!

CHAPTER ELEVEN

PEOPLE WANT A

DEMONSTRATION

THE ONLY JESUS THAT SOME PEOPLE MAY EVER SEE IS THE JESUS IN YOU AND THE JESUS IN ME.
-- JESSE DISPLANTIS

Just spend a few moments really thinking about that statement. If you truly are going to follow Christ, then are you beginning to see the responsibility that you have? Jesus charged us with a mission. To this date, we have failed in that mission. People die every day, lots of people, people right in your own backyard, people who do not know and people who have never felt the love of Jesus. They have heard of the name but have never met the man. We are failing!

If I could only know for sure, if I could only see Him - how many times has someone made those very statements to you when you are speaking to them about God? If I could only see a sign. If I could only know for sure. Please, God, show me something. If you show me, then I will know for sure.

God showed Himself to the Israelites in the Old Testament, over and over and over again, through multiple miracles. On their march to the Promised Land, God parted the Red Sea for His chosen people. I think that if I had been there, if I had seen God part the Red Sea and the children of Israel walk across on dry land, then I really believe that would have been enough for me. That sight alone would have been enough for me to believe that God is alive. However, for the children of Israel, that was not enough. They still would not completely believe, completely trust in the Lord their God. God's own chosen people doubted Him and would not believe in Him.

Jesus came in the New Testament, walked among the people, performed all sorts of miracles, healed the sick, casted out demons, and the people still would not believe. People saw and they still doubted. People saw and questioned the man. The point that I want you to think about is that even when

God shows Himself to us, we will still find a way to doubt His existence. We will still find a way to question whether God is real. We will still find a way to doubt that God is who He says that He is.

Walking with God, believing in God is all about building your faith and your trust in God. Establishing a personal relationship with the Lord is completely and totally built upon your faith in God. Faith is the foundation that your relationship is built upon.

WITHOUT FAITH, IT IS IMPOSSIBLE TO PLEASE GOD BECAUSE YOU FIRST MUST KNOW THAT HE IS GOD.

Each of us all starts with the same measure of faith given to us by God. What you do with that measure builds your faith. If your faith is never put to work, it dies. Faith without work is dead. You must put your faith to work every day in order to build and strengthen that measure of faith which God has entrusted to every one of us.

You begin building your faith by growing your knowledge in God and allowing God to be God in your life. You must know that God is the "GREAT I AM" and you must allow God to be exactly who He is in your life.

There are a few of us who I like to say go a step beyond that faith. We just know what we know. That faith is unmovable. That faith is unshakeable. That faith will not be swayed or compromised under any situation. I know what I know and it does not matter to me if you say differently.

That describes my faith. Moreover, from the time I wrote these words to today, my faith has only grown. I know that Jesus is alive today. Jesus has mended what I thought could never be put back together. Jesus has shown me what I thought I never would see. Jesus has given me what I never thought I deserved. I know that He lives because He is the only one who could do such things. Jesus speaks to me and I feel His presence daily. Nevertheless, beyond all the things that He has done, I have seen Him. Since I accepted Jesus as my Savior, I have seen Him. Therefore, I know what I know. I know that God lives, and never will anyone be able to tell me any different.

On this particular Sunday, Minister Cora was bringing the message and she said a couple of sentences that just stuck to me. The first statement she made was, "People today want to know that God is real," and then she said, "People want to see the demonstration. People need a demonstration."

The demonstration. I left church that Sunday morning with that line ringing over and over again in my head. Did she know how right she was? A demonstration.

People need the demonstration.

I knew that she had hit the nail right on the head when she said how much people want to know that Christ is real. People want and desire to know the truth. They really want to know that Christ is alive. Alive right now, today! People do not want church. They do not want your brand of religion. People desire God! People today really do want God.

They want to feel God's love. They want to feel God's presence. They want to feel God all around them. However, they have put up so many walls. They have used so many excuses. They have so many reasons why they cannot accept and follow God. Why they cannot let God into their lives.

I talk to people all the time. Most of the people I speak with are in search mode. They are searching for what they feel is missing in their lives. They are searching for that purpose for the life that they are living. So many are confused and looking to find their way. They are searching for fulfillment, for completeness. They are looking to fill a hole. They are searching for God.

Why does it seem that people today are having such a hard time finding God? People have such a hard time following anything that they cannot see. People cannot follow what they cannot hold, what they cannot touch. In the world, it is all about satisfying your senses.

So I left that service on Sunday morning, walking home. As I walked, I could not get that one sentence out of my head:

PEOPLE WANT TO SEE A DEMONSTRATION.

Therefore, as I walked, I began to speak to God, asking for His help. All the way home, on that very Sunday morning, I started talking with God as to the words that I had heard Minister Cora speak.

Lord, I know that you are alive. I have no doubts and there is no one who can ever tell me different. If anyone dares try to tell me that you do not live, then I will tell them different. I have seen you. You speak to me daily. I know what I know. However, what about this thing, this demonstration? What can I do? What is it that I can do so that people will know just as I know? How can I get people to believe like me? What is it that I can show them? What do I need to tell them? I began to pray these same questions to God over and over again. I was seeking an answer and I was seeking that answer from the Lord with diligence.

Then, one morning, the answer came. I was in the shower a week or so later, and the Lord came to me with the answer.

The Lord said to me, "Paul, you are the demonstration. You must be the demonstration. They will see me in you."

What a monster responsibility to show the world Christ. Through me, people will see you. I must become the demonstration. That is exactly what this world is crying out for. This is what the people are searching for. A demonstration. In addition, this is exactly where we are failing.

People are searching. They are searching for Christ, the Christ who lives today. They are searching for the Christ who lives inside you and me. That is the demonstration. The demonstration lives in me!

We are the demonstration. We who say how much we love the Lord. We who say that we are followers of Christ. We who walk and talk with God. We are the demonstration. We are the ones who show the world that Jesus Christ is alive today!

The lost, the people who are in the world today, searching everywhere for the answer, they will only know that I live by watching the ones who say they love me.

THE ONLY JESUS THAT SOME PEOPLE MAY EVER SEE,
IS THE JESUS IN YOU AND THE JESUS IN ME.

You, who are reading this book, have to become that demonstration. You must be the one to show Christ to the lost. You must be the one to show everyone that I am alive. You must be the one to show the lost the way.

It is God's desire for us all to be the demonstration. God offers this life to everyone. All are called, but only a few will respond. All are asked, but only a few will answer. God wants us all.

If you say that you are living a holy and righteous life,
If you say that you wake every morning seeking the kingdom first,
If you say that you are living a life filled and led by the Holy Ghost,
Then you have no choice; you must be that demonstration.

You must demonstrate to this confused world that Jesus lives.
You must be the one to show God to everyone around you.

The world has many problems today, but we as Christians compound those problems because we will not be the demonstration. We will not, and we are not showing the world that Christ lives today. Many folks are going to church every Sunday, but not too many are the demonstration that Christ lives during the week.

The world so desperately needs that demonstration. The world is crying out for that demonstration and we walk right on by with deaf ears. The world wants to know God. The world wants to see God, but we will not show them. It is our obligation to show, to tell. It is our responsibility. We who say that we love God so much, we who say that we are so thankful for what God has done for us, we who go to church on Sunday and we sing and we shout and we praise the most high God - we have a responsibility to go out into the world and show the world, to demonstrate to the world that Jesus is alive. We must show and demonstrate why the world today needs God in their lives. We must become that demonstration. We must demonstrate God's love to the world.

"Truly, Truly I say unto you, whoever believes in me will also do the works that I do; and greater works than these will he do, because I am going to the Father.
(John 14: 12)

We forget so quickly who we are. The vast majority of us have never been taught or told who we are "In Christ". As young children, many of us were raised in the church and we were never once taught who we are or the power that we possess.

As a young child, we were told by parents, or schoolteachers, or grandparents who we could grow up to be in the world.

Some of us were told that we would be a firefighter, or a doctor, or a lawyer, or a businessman, or a teacher. We were told that we could grow up to be a football player, a musician, or a singer. We were told that we could be a winner, or a leader, or maybe very successful. Our heads were filled with all the things that we could become in the world. We were told that the sky was the limit. We could go as far as we wanted. However, not one of these things is who you really are.

Would it have been nice to be raised and taught, as that young child, who you really are? So who are you?

In order to begin to understand who we are, we must begin this discussion by talking about the Kingdom of God. We all know that God does have a Kingdom, and at the moment of creation, God did establish His Kingdom upon the Earth. Man's original assignment from God was a Kingdom assignment. God gave man dominion and authority over all the Earth. That was the assignment that God gave to Adam, to have authority over all the Earth. God's original plan was to extend His Heavenly Kingdom onto the Earth. Earth was just to be an extension of Heaven.

When Jesus taught the disciples how to pray, part of that prayer was:

THY KINGDOM COME. THY WILL BE DONE.
IN EARTH, AS IT IS IN HEAVEN.

Thy Kingdom come. It was always about the Kingdom. Establishing His Kingdom on Earth was the only intent; it was never about establishing religion. God has never been in, nor has ever had anything to do with, this thing that we call "religion". Religion is all about man. Religions are manmade. God creates. Man makes. As I write, I like to look up definitions for words. I looked up the word *religion* and the first word I saw was *institution*. When I think of an institution, my mind thinks of cold, and then my mind thinks of a machine. Neither one of these words would you ever associate with God, but I could use both of those words to describe many of the manmade religions found in the world today.

The kingdom is all about God. It is God's kingdom. Our only goal should be to become citizens of God's Kingdom. So then why are so many of us hung up on all these religions and denominations? We can talk for hours about our particular denomination, but we cannot find one word to say about God's Kingdom. We have spent time and energy studying our denominations, but we know nothing about the Kingdom of God.

From this moment on, I want you to think about the Kingdom of God and to begin to think of yourself as a Kingdom citizen. There is only one kingdom and that is God's Kingdom. We are all Kingdom citizens, not a bunch of individuals belonging to a hundred different denominations. What will it take for the leaders of all these denominations to understand that fact? It is only about God's kingdom and it has nothing to do with all these different denominations! For each of us, it is only about gaining entrance into the Kingdom. It should never have been about joining someone's denomination!

When Adam sinned, for a time, man lost his rights to the Kingdom. Because of Adam's disobedience, both he and Eve were expelled from the Garden. They were made to toil the land and suffered death, which had never been part of God's original plan; death became a part of life.

And to Adam he said, "Because you have listened to the voice of your wife and have eaten from the tree of which I commanded you, that you shall not eat, cursed is the ground because of you; in pain you shall eat of it all the days of your life; thorns and thistles it shall bring forth for you; and you shall eat the plants of the field.

By the sweat of your face you shall eat bread, till you return to the ground, for out of it you were taken; for you are dust, and dust you shall return." (Genesis 3: 17 - 19)

Only because of God's grace and God's mercy, God sent His son into the world with two tasks to accomplish. The first was to reconcile man back unto God. The second was to bring God's Kingdom back to Earth. Jesus had the mission of reestablishing His Father's Kingdom back upon the Earth.

When you read the Book of Matthew, all Jesus speaks about is the Kingdom. Jesus came to teach every man about His Father's Kingdom. Every chance Jesus had, He was teaching His disciples about the Kingdom of God. Establishing God's Kingdom back upon the Earth was a top priority for Jesus.

When you read the Book of Matthew, you will also notice that Jesus wanted nothing to do with the organized religion of the day. Jesus took every chance He had to distance Himself from the Pharisees, the so-called religious experts of the day. Even when choosing His disciples, Jesus could have chosen anyone, but Jesus chose a bunch of regular guys. Actually, Jesus chose a bunch of fishermen.

Throughout Matthew, Jesus gives us many examples of the differences between His Father's Kingdom and the religion being taught at the time. Jesus' coming was never about spreading any religion or developing all these different denominations that we have today. Jesus' coming was always and only about reestablishing the Kingdom of God.

Let me back up for a moment because I get the feeling that a lot of you are wondering where this Kingdom is. Where can I find this place that he keeps talking about, the Kingdom of God? Where is it on the map? The Kingdom of God is not a place. It is not a town or a country that you can locate on your GPS. The Kingdom of God is about a way to live your life. The Apostle writes, in the Book of Corinthians, "yet I come to show you an excellent way" (1 Corinthians 12:31).

That excellent way is in the Kingdom of God. To live in the Kingdom, it is about changing your lifestyle. The Kingdom is about how you live your life. The Kingdom comes to live within you. Remember: "thy kingdom come, thy will be done, in Earth as it is in Heaven" (Matthew 6:10). The Kingdom comes to live within you and you live your life according to Kingdom principles.

After Jesus' death, burial, resurrection, and ascension, being the extremely hard-headed people that we are, we went right back and got ourselves stuck into the same religion that Jesus wanted nothing to do with. We went back to the traditions and stuck ourselves into all sorts of denominations. We decided that it would be better for us to be stuck inside of buildings instead of being out among the people, seeking God's Kingdom. We stick ourselves inside these buildings instead of being on the streets, winning souls for God's Kingdom. We run and hide inside these buildings and we forget all about the Kingdom of God.

When we move into religion and tradition, we become stuck. When you are stuck, you cannot grow with God. Just look at the Pharisees. The Pharisees really did not want anything to do with Jesus, especially to learn from Jesus. They thought that they knew everything about religion already. They were educated, so what could anyone teach them? They were the teachers. You talk about being stuck. When you are unable to be taught, you are stuck! You will never move or live in your purpose or destiny if you become stuck.

God's desire is for everyone to live in the Kingdom right now, today! In the Kingdom, there is freedom - freedom that you have never known, nor will you find anywhere else. In the Kingdom lives the truth. In the Kingdom lives growth. In the Kingdom, there is your destiny. Your assignment lies, waiting for you in the Kingdom.

God's desire is for us to experience and enjoy all the benefits, promises and privileges that living in His Kingdom has to offer us. In addition, God wants you to have that fulfillment right now. God wants you to have everything that God has for you. All of the promises that God makes to every one of us who choose to live in His kingdom, He has written down in His book, the Bible. Moreover, each of those promises is available to us now.

One of God's priorities for us is to seek, discover, and enter into the Kingdom of Heaven while we are still living; yes, I said it, while we are still living here on this Earth. Many of you are waiting. You have been waiting for the Kingdom to finally arrive. Many of you are waiting for the day when Jesus will crack the sky and bring the kingdom to us. There are still many more of you waiting for your own death in order that you may be able to see God's Kingdom.

I am here to ask you right now, "Why are you waiting?" The kingdom is here right now for you to have. God wants you to have the kingdom. God wants you to live in His Kingdom while you are living right now, right here on this Earth. God's Kingdom is here for you, right now.

Always remember:

THY KINGDOM COME, THY WILL BE DONE
ON EARTH, AS IT IS IN HEAVEN.

Now that you have a better idea about the Kingdom of God, I would like to spend some time telling you about the person that you are in that Kingdom.

We call each other Christians, but what does that word *Christian* mean? What does the word *Christian* mean to you? When someone on the street uses the word *Christian*, what do you feel when you hear that word? If someone calls you a "Christian", does the word make you feel special?

If someone on the street asks you if you are a Christian, what do you tell them? What kind of image does the word

Christian bring to your mind? Are you proud? Do you shy away? Do you run and hide? Do you stand tall and give an answer? For me, the word *Christian* has become a very hard word to put an exact definition to.

The word itself, *Christian,* has become so watered down, so twisted, so confusing, that in today's world, the word almost has no meaning whatsoever. Most often, when someone says the word *Christian*, it has a negative vibe to it. People almost turn and run away from you even before the whole word can get out of your mouth. They act as if they cannot get away from you fast enough. The minute they find out that you are a Christian, most people look at you as if you either must want to preach at them or you must want their money. Either way, they are crossing the street to get away when they see you coming.

People are not sure what to think when you tell them that you are a Christian. I will tell you this for sure: their first thoughts are not of love, joy, peace, meekness, or humility. How sad that we, the church, have managed to confuse people so badly. Not only confuse them, but also completely turn them off from wanting to hear the true message of Jesus Christ - the message of love, hope, and salvation.

The word *Christian* started out to mean believers in Christ. As a Christian, we do very much believe in Christ, but as a citizen in God's Kingdom, we are a whole lot more than just believers. And the fact is that God created us to be so much more.

All this is from God, who through Christ reconciled us to himself and gave us the ministry of reconciliation; that is, in Christ God was reconciling the world to himself, not counting their trespasses against them, and entrusting to us the message of reconciliation.
Therefore, we are Ambassadors for Christ, God making his appeal through us. We implore you on behalf of Christ, be reconciled to God. **(II Corinthians 5:18 - 20)**

You are an ambassador for God who has been placed here on Earth to fulfill a Kingdom assignment. From this very moment on, as you read these words, I want you to think and believe that you are one of God's ambassadors upon this Earth. In the Kingdom, we have been given an assignment as an ambassador to deliver the message of Christ, the message of reconciliation to all the people of this world.

That is an awesome assignment from God Himself, but what exactly is an ambassador, and what responsibilities does an ambassador for God have?

When you look up the word *ambassador* in the dictionary, the word is defined as:

THE HIGHEST REPRESENTATIVE SENT BY ONE RULER TO ANOTHER RULER TO SPEAK AND ACT ON BEHALF OF THE ONE WHO SENT THEM.

You have been put here on Earth to speak and act on God's behalf! That is our responsibility as ambassadors. What an awesome responsibility we have been given in God's Kingdom.

Another duty of the ambassador is to be an official messenger with a special errand. That is the part of the ambassador that I feel that God has given to me. I am a messenger with a special errand. The errand that God has charged me with is in the writing of this book.

Saying only that we are Christians just barely touches the tip of the iceberg. Really, we are the ambassadors for our God. We are His messengers. We are His representatives. We are here on Earth to speak and act on God's behalf. We are to be the body for God while we are here on Earth. We are here to be God's arms and God's legs. We are here to show this world the example of our God.

When you say that you are a Christian, God comes to dwell inside each of us. God lives in us and God lives through us. Because we are God's ambassadors, it is our duty to show the world our God. We have a duty to let God, who is growing on our inside, be shown to the world through our outside. I have already written how the world wants to see the demonstration. The world wants to see the demonstration of the living God, who lives inside of all believers. Because you know that it was only God who carried you through, you know who God is. Moreover, all of us who know, believe, and trust God must demonstrate to this world who we know our God to be!

I was listening to a tape of Wynitta Bynum, and on the tape, she was speaking with Cindy Trimm. It was during this conversation that Cindy Trimm made a statement that was confirmation for every word that I just wrote. Cindy said that the only way God can come upon the Earth is in the body of a living person. God is a spirit, and in order for God to get the majority of His work done here on Earth, God needs a willing vessel. God does His work here on Earth through us, His ambassadors. How truly special does that make you feel.

"The Lord knows who are his," and, "Let everyone who names the name of the Lord depart from iniquity."
Now in a great house there are not only vessels of gold and silver but also of wood and clay, some for honorable use, some for dishonorable.
Therefore, if anyone cleanses himself from what is dishonorable, he will be a vessel for honorable use, set apart as holy, useful to the master of the house, ready for every good work. (II Timothy 2: 19 - 21)

The United States sends out ambassadors from our country to almost all foreign countries. The country that receives the ambassador may not know anything about the United States, but they will begin to form ideas about how the United States is by the way our ambassador talks, by the way our ambassador acts, by the way our ambassador treats them, and by the way our ambassador handles his business.

God's ambassadors work exactly the same way. God chooses each of us to be His ambassadors, and then God sends us out to be in the world, but not of the world. God sends each of His ambassadors out into the world so the world can see the physical example. Therefore, the world can see the physical demonstration of how God talks, how God acts, and what God does. God sends His ambassadors out so the world can see. Can you be that ambassador for God? So many of us ask God to use us. We tell God that we will go, that we will do whatever God wants us to do. Can you be the ambassador for His Kingdom that God created you to be?

Ambassadors! That is the very thing that the world we are living in today is missing so badly. The world is missing that physical example. The world is so desperate for the true people of God to show them and to be God's ambassadors. As an ambassador in the Kingdom, you do represent God here on Earth. When you tell the world that you are a Christian, people look to you to see what God is like. People form their opinions of God by watching you. The world comes to know God by your actions, your speech, by the things that you do. Look back and reread the definition of an *ambassador*. Can you be that representative? Can you be that example of a living God that this world so desperately needs?

Will you be loving?
Will you be giving?
Will you show mercy?
Will you always forgive?
Will you help instead of hinder?
Will you be able to show the world the King of Kings?

We are the ambassadors sent to this place and sent at this particular time. We have been sent by our King to represent our King. We have been charged with a duty to represent that King as perfectly as we can to show the world our King's perfection.

Remember, I will say it one more time:

THE ONLY JESUS A PERSON MAY EVER SEE,
IS THE JESUS IN YOU OR THE JESUS IN ME!

Millions of people go to church every Sunday, participating in so many religious traditions. How many are leaving those buildings and being the ambassador that God has charged them to be? How many people leave church and are living their Kingdom assignment? God desires and needs ambassadors, not Pharisees.

Then Jesus said to the crowds and to his disciples, "The scribes and the Pharisees sit on Moses' seat, so practice and observe whatever they tell you - BUT NOT WHAT THEY DO. FOR THEY PREACH BUT THEY DO NOT PRACTICE.
(Matthew 23: 1-3)

How many people do you know today that Jesus just described? Too many, I am sure. And people say the Bible does not speak about today's world. The Pharisees prided themselves on their talk. In fact, they were all talk because they chose to live their lives contrary to the way that they spoke. Sounds just like many of the people I see today. The Pharisees were extremely judgmental and held everyone but themselves to the letter of the law. Am I describing anyone that you know? Looks to me like the Bible is still very applicable to our society today.

Jesus taught us, over and over again in the Book of Matthew, that the way of the Pharisee is never to be our way. My question to you is, "How many ambassadors of the Kingdom do you see during the week?" How is it that so many people go into church on Sunday morning and praise God, but leave church and live the life of a Pharisee the other six days of the week? How can we sing, dance, say we are filled with the

Holy Ghost on Sunday, and then go the next six days and never mention God's name once. How can we go six days and never be a witness of our God to anyone? How can we walk by and never help anyone?

For I tell you, unless your righteousness exceeds that of the scribes and the Pharisees, you will never enter into the Kingdom of Heaven. (Matthew 5: 20)

It is not nearly enough just to call yourself one of God's ambassadors. There must be a change in your life. To truly be that ambassador, Jesus teaches us that there are three things that must become a part of your life every day, every day!

1) CONFESSION - Confess you sin and deny yourself sin. It is impossible for you to be an ambassador in the Kingdom and continue to embrace the passions of the world.
2) DENY SELF - You must begin every day by picking up your cross and following Jesus. As an ambassador, you must learn to forget yourself and learn that life is about the serving of others. Your life is about showing God's love to everyone. The sacrifices that you make are the only things that make love real.
3) FOLLOW IN THE FOOTSTEPS OF JESUS - Jesus tells us all, "I am the way, the truth and the light. The only way to my Father is through me" (John 14:6). Being charged as an ambassador of God's Kingdom, we can only follow one way. The Apostle Paul writes to us that we are to become imitators of God. We will only be able to show Christ to the world by following in the footsteps that Jesus left for us.

When you talk to people and the question of church comes around, their number one reason for not attending is that the church today is full of hypocrites. We church folk in today's church, instead of imitating Christ we have chosen to imitate the Pharisees. We talk one way on Sunday and we live our lives another way the rest of the week. We say that we are God's ambassadors on Sunday when we are in this special building, but how many of us are actually living, actually practicing the three teachings of Jesus that were listed above?

Beware of practicing your righteousness before other people in order to be seen by them, for then you will have no reward from your Father who is in Heaven. (Matthew 6: 1)

Was Jesus really talking about us when He was describing how the Pharisees lived their lives in the Bible? How many of us today refuse to see ourselves in these writings that were written two thousand years ago? Yet, we continue to tell ourselves how irrelevant the Bible is to our lives today.

The Pharisees were so full of talk. Actually, Jesus called them men of all talk and no action. Our society today so mirrors the society that Jesus lived in. We today have become a society of all talk. Actually, I am going to say it; we talk too much. We must earn the right to talk. You can only earn that right through your actions. You can only earn the right to talk through the actions that you exhibit seven days a week, twenty-four hours a day.

People will and do watch you. Not just on Sunday when you are all dressed up and in your special building, but they will watch you all the time. They want to see if your actions will line up with the words that are coming out of your mouth. When they see that you are aligned, when they realize that you are the real thing and not just a Sunday-morning Christian, not just someone faking it, not just someone with an ulterior motive, they will come to you and ask.

At that time, then and only then, have you just earned the right to speak a word into their life. Do not speak until that time comes. But when that time comes, when they come to you and ask, then and only then have you earned the right and they will not only hear what you have to say, but they will take every word to heart, because it was they who asked for you to speak words into their lives.

Why is the world not turning to God? It has nothing to do with the fact that the world does not want to believe. The world knows Jesus. The world wants to believe. People in the world are searching for answers to their questions. Just look at yourself. What were you searching for when you found God? What question did you need the answer to?

The rest of the world is exactly like you. They are searching. You were searching. The problem is that we are not showing God to the people we touch on a daily basis. People are not seeing God in us.

On that Sunday morning, when our Apostle said to quit thinking of yourself as a Christian, and to start believing in yourself as an ambassador for the Kingdom, for me, those words took me to a whole new level, a different level of faith, a higher dimension of responsibility in the Kingdom. Those words took me into a higher dimension as to who I am "IN CHRIST" and to what purpose I must fulfill in the Kingdom.

When I think of myself as the ambassador for God and that God chose me out of the world for this assignment, I know that I have found purpose. I have found destiny. I know how very special I am to my Father in Heaven and I know that I must walk in this purpose every moment of every day as God's example, as the demonstration of the living God to this world. This I must do!

Believe in who you are. You are an ambassador in the Kingdom of God. Walk into that purpose every day.

Take a minute before you move on to the next chapter and read Matthew 6 in its entirety. Jesus teaches us, in His own words, about how to be an ambassador for the Kingdom of God.

CHAPTER TWELVE

IS IT TOO LATE FOR THE
WORLD TO REALLY CHANGE?

Into the ground, I dug a hole
Without consent to tax or toil
There I stayed for days and years
Confronted and tortured by all my fears

When I lost purpose, I gave in
Forgetting every place, I have been
No place to go, nothing to show
How I live on, I just do not know

I like to stop but here I can't
I tunnel the Earth like worm or ant
I dug for hours without a pause
The deeper I went the more I lost

Isolated and all alone
I fought my fears and found a zone
I opened my eyes to realize
This is where my life lies

I sense reform with my new sight
The sun has dawned I see the light
I clench the walls with all my might
And brace myself for eternal flight

--- Paul Henry Douglas Schmidt III

But I say walk by the spirit, and you will not gratify the desires of the flesh. For the desires of the flesh are against the spirit, and the desires of the spirit are against the flesh, for these are opposed to each other, to keep you from doing the things you want to do.
But if you are led by the spirit, you are not under the law. Now the works of the flesh are evident: sexual immorality, impurity, sensuality, idolatry, sorcery, enmity, strife, jealousy, fits of anger, dissensions, divisions, envy, drunkenness, orgies, and like these. I warn you, as I warned you before, that those who do such things will not inherit the Kingdom of God. (Galatians 5: 16 - 21)

TO LIVE YOUR LIFE WITHOUT ANY EXPECTATION,
TO LIVE YOUR LIFE WITHOUT THE NEED FOR ANY SPECIFIC RESULT,
TO LIVE YOUR LIFE EVERY MOMENT OF EVERY DAY
RULED ONLY BY THE HIGHER DESIRES OF YOUR SOUL,
THAT IS HOW FREEDOM IS DEFINED!

THIS IS TO LIVE AS GOD LIVES.
THIS IS GODLINESS AND
THIS IS TRULY HOW I WISH TO LIVE!

I know that I must change! I know that I have to change the way in which I live my life. The world that I know now, this world does not work for me. Moreover, if I remain in the world as it is for me today, this world will destroy me.
I cannot stop the path that I am on, so my destruction is inevitable. I am unable to change myself. God, help me to change!

Only through the power of God can a life be changed. God can restore, God can transform, and God can turn you around and change your life. Only God can do this kind of work. Through God, there is a better way.

Do not conform any longer to the patterns of this world, but be transformed by the renewing of your mind. Then you will be able to test and approve what God's will is. His good, pleasing, and perfect will. (Romans 12: 2)

Since accepting the Lord as my Savior, everything in my life has changed. I am a completely different person from who I used to be. Jesus changes you on the inside - your heart, your mind, your soul, the way you think, and the way you feel towards everything. If you will surrender, Jesus will change every bit of you.

Many of my old habits I no longer have. One of those habits was how I used to watch television. Before, I would come in the house, hit the couch, and turn on the television. I would flip through all hundred channels until I found something that struck my interest. Unless we were going out, that was pretty much how I spent my evenings: the remote and me.

I was not very selective about what type of program I would watch. I would watch almost anything that came on. Now, very little on television appeals to me. The television I now have was given to me, and it only gets eighteen channels, and most of those I never watch. I do watch TBN. I never watched TBN before, and as I started watching it a lot, I was struck by how many movie stars, entertainers, celebrities, big-time singers, and athletes who come on and speak about their love for the Lord. That is great!

What is not so great is that many of these people are very famous and they are people that I have seen and heard for many years. Some of them I held in high esteem. Some of the athletes were role models for me and for my son. What really hit me hard was that if I had not seen them on TBN, I would have never have known about their love for the Lord. That is not good.

Remember how I wrote about the demonstration? These people of fame have the ability to be enormous ambassadors for the Kingdom. These people of fame have the influence to demonstrate to masses the greatness of the God that we serve, but because they are not living their lives as the living witness, the living testimony, no one knows. Because they only choose to demonstrate Christ in a very particular setting on a very particular day, the majority of the world will never know. So much wasted influence for the Kingdom of God.

The world needs this demonstration so badly. We need the demonstration of God in every occupation and that demonstration is needed so badly, every day of the week. The world is in desperate need for their demonstration.

Why won't the world ever change? Yes, that is the title of this book, and in one sentence, here is the answer to the question: because we have far too many Sunday-Morning Christians! The world will change when we, as the followers of Christ, choose to follow God seven days a week, twenty-four hours a day. When we stop following God when it is only convenient for us to do so. When we stop following God because of what we think we can get from God. When we stop following God with only the words out of our mouths. When we stop following God by imitating the lives of the Pharisees. And we begin to follow God by living the life that Jesus demonstrated to us while He walked the Earth. Until you do that, call yourself what you are: a Part-Time Christian.

The world will change when we, who say that we love God with all of our hearts:

Begin to take God to work with us.
Begin to take God to school with us.
Begin to take God out to dinner with us.
Begin to take God to the mall with us.

Begin to live,
Begin to breathe,
Begin to speak,
Begin to vote,
Begin to work,
Begin to play,
Begin to shop,
Begin to make choices,
Begin to make decisions,

Until we put God into every part, into everything we do in our everyday lives.

The world will not change until we begin to do everything in our lives for and to the glory of God.

I only wish that there were a way that I could say that with more force! We must do everything in our lives to the glory of our Lord.

Why does the church today have no impact upon the world? Because people see no difference in the life that they live and the way that the people who say they love Christ live their everyday lives.

We, church folk, have no impact upon this world. We drink, we smoke, we cuss, we lie, we cheat, we have affairs, we hold grudges, we gossip, we hate, we discriminate, as much and as quickly as the unsaved part of the world. We go to church on Sunday, but we still glorify the world. We go to church on Sunday, but on Monday, we bow down and do Satan's bidding as well as the person who has not attended a church in years. We sit in church on Sunday, quoting scripture, and then on Monday, we glorify sin. We glorify our fellow man instead of the God we were just praising on Sunday, and then we make excuses for our actions. People look to us for the demonstration and look at what we show them.

Our presence, wherever we go, because we are filled with the Holy Ghost, should change the atmosphere. The world's aura should never affect us, but we should always be able to influence the atmosphere in any room we enter. We are the conquerors because of Christ who lives in us, and that includes changing the atmosphere wherever we go. Wherever we go, people should feel the presence of the living God. The world must start seeing the Christ who lives in you. The world needs that demonstration. To begin to save the world for Christ, we must be the demonstration. The world is crying out for that demonstration. The world needs Christ's ambassadors to stand up and be Christ's ambassadors.

We need lawyers who are ambassadors.
We need bankers who are ambassadors.
We need secretaries who are ambassadors.
We need high school teachers who are ambassadors.
We need coaches who are ambassadors.
We need nurses who are ambassadors.
We need mothers who are ambassadors.
We need auto mechanics who are ambassadors.

In every walk of life, ambassadors for the Kingdom are needed.

We must teach the world of Christ by the lives that we live every day and we cannot wait for the world to come knocking on our church door. Jesus commanded us to go out into the world. That is exactly why we must become ambassadors for God's Kingdom in every walk of life. Our impact in the world must be dramatic. Our impact must be real and that impact must be sincere. Everyone can see right through insincerity. Our impact upon the world must be in love.

This is the key to returning America back to the God-fearing nation that we were founded upon. To do everything that we do for God! To glorify God in all things that we do.

Right now, we give the world our best and God gets the leftovers of our lives. We give the world our very best effort, for most of us five days a week, and for some of us, we work six days a week. For forty, fifty, and for some of us, sixty-plus hours a week, we give the world everything that we have, but my question is, "What are you giving God?"

God might get a part of the day if I am not too tired. God might get the end of my day if I do not fall asleep first. Maybe if I have a minute sometime during the day, I will pray.

I hope that before I fall asleep, I will read some scriptures. Probably if I am not too tired, I will go to church this Sunday.

Does this sound like you? Do you really think that God is happy getting the leftovers of your life? If you want God to make you first in His life, then you must make God first in your life. In addition, that means God must be first in everything. God does not work as a light switch. You turn Him on when you need Him and switch Him off when your life is going smooth. God is the light switch that you must not ever turn off in your life.

We have this thought that being a Christian allows us the right to pick and choose when we will follow God. We think that we can choose the time of day or the day of the week that we want to follow God. Or even the situation we are in, whether we will obey the commands of God or not. Think about your own life. Think about the week that you just went through. How many times during the week did you take a mental time out for God? Following God, being an ambassador, being a disciple for Christ cannot work that way, but we think that it does. Following Christ is an all-or-nothing decision. God does not want the end of your day; God wants all your day!

There was a good week to ten days when the Lord kept talking to me every day about a concept called, "The Circle of Influence." God was just whispering things in my ear, giving me things to think about. Then one afternoon, I was driving home and the message was coming at me so hard that I had to pull the car over so I could write. The following is that writing which the Lord gave me:

"The Circle of Influence"

Again, he asked, "What shall I compare the Kingdom of God to? It is like yeast that a woman took and mixed into a large amount of flour until it worked all through the dough." (Luke 13: 20-21)

By now, you might have gotten the idea that I like to look up the definitions of words. *Influence* I found has many definitions, but the one that the Lord was talking to me about is:

TO BE ABLE TO CHANGE THE NATURE OR BEHAVIOR OF ANOTHER.
TO HAVE AN IMPACT ON ANOTHER'S LIFE

This impact, the impact that you may have on another's life, may be either positive or negative, but it will never be neutral.

Let us stop right here for a minute because I want you to really think about the last statement that I made. I want you to think about the influence you have over the people in your life. Your impact is always - yes, it is always - either positive or negative, but your influence will never be neutral. I know what you are asking yourself right now, "But Paul, what about when I do nothing?"

How many of you know the word *tacit*? This is the same word that I spoke of in the first chapter. *Tacit,* for those of you who may have skipped the first chapter, is your unspoken approval by doing nothing. Unspoken approval. Just think about those two words. You can, and yes, you do give your approval to many of the things that go on around you because you do nothing.

Let me give you a real example how tacit approval works. You have probably found yourself in this real life example many times. How did you react? This is such a good example because it shows both my circle of influence and how tacit works every day.

When I first went back to work, foul language was constantly being spoken at my job all around me. It truly amazes me how we are bringing up a generation of people who are completely unable to form sentences without a cuss word in them. Nevertheless, back to my example. With all this foul language going on around me, I had two choices. One choice would have been to say nothing, and give my approval to their speech tacitly. The other choice I had was to say something politely, to explain to the people around me my feelings about their choice of words. I chose to speak up.

The restaurant I work in has now been open for a year. I would like to say that no one uses foul language at all, but I cannot. What I can say is that the use of such language has dropped off dramatically and when someone slips around me, they automatically apologize without me having to say a thing. It is not perfect, but I will keep influencing the atmosphere at my job for my Lord and Savior. By choosing to speak up, I took positive control of the circle that I have influence over. By not saying anything, by not standing up for what I know is right, the influence that I have over that circle would definitely have been negative.

Each of us, everyone reading this book, has a circle that they influence - a circle that is unique only to you. Your circle is made up of the people that you see or that see you on a daily basis. Some examples of those people could be coworkers, family, neighbors, friends, relatives, and you can even expand your circle to include that cashier at the local supermarket, the person who cuts your hair, the salesperson at your favorite department store, your mailman, anyone that you have visual contact with.

Some circles may overlap with others. Someone in my circle could be in my family, but in your circle, they could be your friend. However, in every circle, there will be those people that you, and you alone, have influence over. There will be people who are unique to you and your circle, and people that you alone have the ability to impact their lives either positively or negatively.

I want to take a quick second here and mention the circle of influence that you are in. Who is influencing you? Whom are you listening to? We all have a circle of influence, but we also all belong to a circle of influence. Everyone belongs in someone else's circle. Whether you will admit it or not, someone does have influence upon you. Think about that. Really think. Who is influencing the decisions that you make? What type of influence are they having upon your life? Do you always seem to gravitate to the negative influences?

The idea is to influence your decisions through the word of God. The idea is for you to get yourself into God's circle of influence. Let God have influence over every decision that you make. Limit the number of people who have any influence over you. Limit the number of people who have access to your ears. This book wants to guide you to allow God, and God alone, to become your only influence. By allowing God to influence you, you will become God's influence to all the people in your circle. Remember the chapter on being the demonstration.

How do we influence the people in our circle? The greatest influence we have over the people in our circle, which people will pay the most attention to, is what you do! Your greatest impact upon another's life is through your actions.

Don't you dare judge anyone about their language
    when you just dropped the "F" word out of anger.
Don't you dare judge someone about not helping another
    when you just walked by the homeless man asking for a
    dollar.
Don't you dare judge someone about their unforgiveness
    when you are holding your own grudges in your heart
 Don't you dare judge someone about their anger
    when you just blew up at someone
Don't you dare judge someone about their marriage
    when your own home is in a mess

Your greatest impact on somebody will always be through the life that you are living. So many people look for the examples that are walking among them, for examples of living a holy and righteous life. God said, multiple times in His word, "Be ye holy for I am holy." If you are one who says they love God, then holiness is not an option; it is a command from God! Living a life of holiness, that is how we influence another.

We do not realize it, but people are watching each of us. We like to watch each other. When I was a young boy, my parents called it "people watching". I used to hear them say, "Let's go to the mall and watch some people." If you do not think that we are still watching each other, then where did reality television come from and why is it so popular?

Especially when people know you profess a life for Christ, people automatically begin to watch you. Most often, they watch you for the wrong reasons. They want to see you fail. They want to see you fall. They want to see what it is that you are going to do in certain situations. They want to see your reaction.

However, if you are truly striving to live a life in Christ, then that someone who has been watching you will eventually notice that there is something different about you. Something has changed. The you that you once were, you are no longer. They will see, and that something new about you, they will want to know about. You have something they need, something they want, and now they will ask you.

When they ask, you have earned the right. Through the life that you live, you have earned the right to speak the words. When you have earned the right, your words will carry an amazing weight. The person who asked will hang on your every word. They now want to hear what you have to say. Where before they could care less about God, now they want to hear everything, all because of the demonstration that you showed to them. All because you chose to live a Holy and Godly life. They now have this desire to hear your words. This cannot be stressed enough; you must earn the right to speak.

That is a major problem with us today. We are all talk. I do not know where this thinking came from, but this belief has spread like the plague. We have a society full of "Know It Alls". We think that we know everything about everything, and we are not bashful about giving everyone our opinions. We want to tell everyone what we think, what we know, and what you are going to do. We are going to tell you, whether you want to hear it or not. We do all this with our words, even though we cannot get our own lives straight.

Our society has become a world full of talk. We do not sit down and write anymore, and we sure do not want to listen. However, just because talking is the easiest way to communicate does not always make it right or the best way. Moreover, in this instance of influence, talking is definitely not the right way or the best way to get the message across.

We, as people, speak way too much. We speak before we think. We speak with no consideration for others. We speak about things that we cannot even do for ourselves. We give advice as if we were the experts when our own life is in ruin.

PHYSICAL EVIDENCE WILL ALWAYS HAVE GREATER WEIGHT THAN ANY PERSONAL EXPRESSION

What you do will far outweigh any words that can come out of your mouth!

The Poet Edgar Guest writes:

I'd rather see a sermon
Than hear one any day
I'd rather one would walk with me
Than merely show me the way
The eye's a better pupil
And much sharper than the ear
Fine counsel can confuse me
But the example's always clear
The lectures you deliver
May be very wise and true
But I'd rather get my lesson
By observing what you do

While the Lord was still speaking to me, God told me there were a couple of things going on in the world today that God really wanted me to start thinking about:

1) NO ONE IN THIS GREAT COUNTRY SHOULD BE HOMELESS *700,000 PEOPLE IN AMERICA ALONE WENT TO BED LAST NIGHT WITH NO ROOF OVER THEIR HEADS*
2) NO ONE SHOULD EVER GO TO BED HUNGRY
3) NO ONE SHOULD LIVE IN POVERTY *75 MILLION AMERICANS ARE LIVING IN HUNGER AND IN POVERTY*
4) EVERYONE SHOULD WORK *AT THE MINIMUM, 15 MILLION AMERICANS ARE UNEMPLOYED*
5) NO ONE, NO ONE SHOULD NOT BE LOVED BY SOMEONE *33,000 SUCESSFUL SUICIDES IN THE UNITED STATES ALONE LAST YEAR REMEMBER, IT'S*

EXACTLY BECAUSE NO ONE LOVED ME ANYMORE; THAT WAS WHY I TRIED TO COMMIT SUICIDE THE SECOND TIME

The Lord then said to me, "Let me make this easy for you. My definition of your circle of influence is everyone in your own backyard."

I am going to give the words to you exactly the same way the Lord gave them to me on that day. God said to me, "Why do you feel this great need to feed the world, when you can't even feed the people in your own backyard?"

And the King will answer them, "Truly, I said to you, as you did it to one of the least of these my brothers, you did it to me." (Matthew 25: 40)

How is it possible that we could help someone thousands of miles away, but we can walk right by the same people who need our help every day? Do we not even see the people living in our own backyards? Or do we just not care? We can mobilize for every foreign nation across the globe, but we cannot help the person on our own streets every day during the week. For the majority of us, it is sad but true; it takes a disaster for us to pry open that wallet to help someone.

We must begin by taking care of the people in our own backyards. If you want to really save the world, then begin in your backyard. As I take care of my backyard and you take care of your backyard, the collection of all our backyards becomes the world. We save the world one backyard at a time. You can save the world and you do that in your own backyard. If it is happening in your backyard, it is happening to you.

I may say something here that might upset a lot of people, especially church folk, but I said that I would give you the words the same way the Lord gave them to me. We get so busy trying to save the world that we leave behind and forget about the person living right next to us. We can see problems thousands of miles away, but we cannot see or fix the problems on our own city block.

Don't even begin to read this wrong. Saving the world is important, very important, and it is definitely one of the goals in writing this book. We have just gone about it the wrong way. People will not even try because they think that saving the world is a monumental task that takes millions of dollars. How wrong they are. Saving the world is about saving your backyard. Just look; I mean, really look at what is going on in your own backyard.

In Atlantic City, the city I now live in, we still have people sleeping under the boardwalk every night. How can that be? We get so wrapped up in the busyness of our own lives, we are so consumed with running from here to there, and we have become so worried about me, me, me - that I cannot even see you.

For the majority of us, we have become content just to sit on the sidelines and do nothing. But as I have already explained to you, by doing nothing, you are really doing more harm than good. By doing nothing, you are giving your approval that life all around you is just fine. Remember the word "TACIT".

We sit on the sidelines and we point fingers. It is not my problem. It is someone else's to fix. If it does not physically touch me, then I want nothing to do with it. I do not have the time to get involved. How many times have I heard that one? How many times did I myself use that excuse? I do not want to get my hands dirty. Someone else will fix the problem. You know what happened. Because everyone said that, and because we get so busy pointing fingers, finding excuses, and placing fault, no one fixes anything.

I hate to be the one to break this very real fact to you, but the world is not getting better. Actually, the world is getting worse, much worse. For the majority of us, we just say that we are too busy to get involved. If you say that you love God, if you know who you are in Christ Jesus, if you are ready to become an ambassador for the Kingdom, then you also know that you can no longer be a spectator. Deep inside you, you feel this desire to get involved. You feel a desire that you must do something. You feel this desire to end the pain.

This is exactly the way I feel today. I can no longer walk by without feeling the pain I see on the streets today. For fifty years of my life, I sat on the sidelines. For fifty years of my life, I did not see the pain and suffering of the world. For all those years, I told myself that what did not touch me really did not exist, and if it did exist, then it was someone else's problem to fix. Now I have this burning desire that lives within me to do something. I am not sure how, but I know the Lord has a plan for me to do something.

On that same day that the Lord was speaking to me about the "Circle of Influence", I was on my way to pick up Lea. I began to tell her all the things that the Lord had been explaining to me. When I was finished, she said something very profound.

We were driving through a neighborhood and she said, "It's sort of like these houses that you see here. You have four houses in a row; for three of them life is great, but for the fourth house, they are in a crisis. Maybe the father just lost his job and they are not sure what the future holds. The other three houses should come together and offer aid and comfort to the house in crisis." What a thought! So easy. So simple. The Circle of Influence in action.

That is exactly what the Lord was talking about when He was talking about your backyard. How few of us, if any, really take the time out of our day for another. When was the last time you even said hi to your neighbor? Few of us even know who our neighbors are.

The next day was Saturday and I had to work. We were scheduled to have a meeting at nine o'clock. I arrived at work and was met by our general manager, Justin, who told me that he had a great idea for today's meeting.

On this same morning, one of the other managers was moving. He was married and had two small children, so he really had no help. He was going to move his family all by himself. Justin suggested that instead of us spending our time in this meeting, we take the time and go help Mike move. What an excellent idea. What better way did we have to spend our time? We went and surprised Mike and his wife, and with those two hours, we were able to get all the big stuff moved. Needless to say, Mike and his family were greatly touched by our coming to help. A random act of kindness.

The Lord has guided me all the way through the writing of this book. God has shown me which books to read, which books to take out of the library, and what parts of what book would fit where into these writings. As I was reading last night, I came across a perfect example of how great a random act of kindness can be to someone.

It comes from a book written by Caroline Myss entitled "Invisible Acts of Power". It was a random act of kindness that someone showed to her. I hope that Caroline does not mind me writing about her experience, but it does fit perfectly. Thank you, Father, for the guidance.

The story goes that she was flying, and normally when she flies, Caroline always checks her luggage. She is physically unable to carry a lot of weight, and so, she never carries luggage with her onto the plane. On this particular day, her connecting flights were so close together that it was either carry the bags on the plane or take the chance of losing her luggage. Just the anticipation alone of having to accomplish this chore, carry her bags onto the plane, and then getting them stored for the flight properly, was enough to put her into a high level of anxiety. She began to sweat and her pulse was starting to race.

As she boarded the plane, all she could think about was the unavoidable dread that was facing her. A man waiting for the seat behind her just picked up the bags and threw them into the overhead compartment, as if it was nothing. To him, it was nothing, but to Caroline, he had just saved her life. He had helped without a word from Caroline. He had helped someone without even being asked. He never had any idea how much Caroline needed his help, nor did he ever realize what a huge gesture for someone else he had just done.

It was a gesture that Caroline would never forget. The gesture was so memorable in her life, and such a great example of a random act of kindness, that she included it in one of her books. The example touched me so much that I have included it in this book and the memory lives on. This random act of kindness, done by a complete stranger, left a lasting impression upon her for the rest of her life.

Like the stranger in this real life story, we may never know, nor may we ever realize it, but that small, random act could save, or at the very least, change someone's life. How little it takes from you to make an impact on someone's life. It does not take a large amount of money or a huge display on your part to change what is going on in your own backyard. Just do something!

What type of influence can you show through a random act of kindness? How often do you stop in your day to aid someone who really needs your help? We think that it takes so much, but it does not take that much to impact someone's life, in order to possibly impact that life forever. When you help, everything you do counts.

There is no such thing as a small act of kindness. In the eyes of God, there is only kindness. There is no small act of mercy. There is only mercy. God does not work in degrees. Man must be the one to measure everything. This is bigger than that. This is greater than that. I need this more than that. This is how man thinks, not God. God only wants you to respond.

When you give, just give. Give from your heart, not your brain. Do not over think, just do. Give what you can. Do what you can. Every act of kindness counts. The man who has ten dollars and gives a dollar has done the same deed as a man who has a thousand and gives a hundred. Do something. Do what you can and do everything that you can.

Giving your service to others is most often not about the one big gesture, but it is about the million little things that you do for others every day.

When you give your time, you have given something more precious than money. We give more respect to money than we do to time, and by far, it should be the other way around. If you give money, you can make money back. If you give time, then that time you can never get back. When you give someone your time, you have truly given someone a very precious commodity.

Are you getting this? As our backyards connect, as we solve the problems in our own backyard, the collection of all of our backyards is what saves the world. As our circles of influence connect all over this globe, we do fix and change the world.

But, Paul, I cannot change the world. I am only one person. The world is just way too big. So why should I even try? I hear this argument from people all the time. People always tell me that they cannot make a difference. Paul, you really cannot believe that you can change the world? Yes, I do believe.

But, Paul, the world is just too big. There is no way that just one person could ever make the difference that you are talking about. But I am not just one person. With God leading the way, I know that all things are possible and I know that one person plus God can and will make the difference that this world needs so desperately.

When you begin to think in terms of the world by the way the Lord defined "Your Circle of Influence," then the world suddenly becomes a lot smaller. When you look at the world as being your own backyard, all of a sudden, the world becomes a place that you can have influence over. Your world is whatever you find in your own backyard.

If everyone in my backyard is saved, sanctified, and doing the work of the Lord; and if everyone in your backyard is saved, sanctified, and doing the work of the Lord; and if everyone next to your backyard is saved, sanctified, and doing the work of the Lord, and when we connect all those backyards, then we can and will make a big change in the world today.

I heard a pastor say some very poignant words. This is exactly what he said:

"IF IT'S IN MY CITY
         THEN THAT'S MY PROBLEM."

I wish there was a way that I could say these next words with more force. We must begin to care for the needs of our community. It is not the government's job; it's the church's! Why is it that we have to have a disaster before we come together and offer aid? Why can we not take that same energy and effort that we put forth when there are disasters and fix our backyards? Do we care less for the hungry in our own backyards than the hungry in Haiti? Or do we just not recognize the hunger in our own backyards?

We should not have to wait for the next disaster before we will come together and help somebody. So many people are hurting right next to you. So many need your help. So many in dire straits are living right in your own backyard.

It is your duty, as an ambassador to the Kingdom, to do whatever you can to help and give aid to the people in your community. Do not wait. Help somebody today. As long as there is pain, suffering, loneliness, hunger, depression, loss, poverty, and homelessness in my neighborhood,
THEN IT IS MY RESPONSIBILITY TO DO SOMETHING

I AM ONLY ONE, BUT STILL I AM ONE.
I CANNOT DO EVERYTHING,
BUT I CAN STILL DO SOMETHING.
I WILL NOT REFUSE TO DO THE SOMETHING THAT I CAN DO.
                     --- HELEN KELLER

We have a restoration program on Thursday evenings, and on most Thursday evenings, the pain, the hurt, the loneliness, the depression, the lack of hope that files into that room from the streets is so thick. There are so many people in deep hurt. So many people walk the streets feeling that no one cares about them. So many people feel unlovable. So many people are not able to forgive. So many people don't know where to turn for help.

We must stop giving lip service, because truth be told, the majority of us, the vast majority of us, are doing nothing. Yes, I said it. We are doing nothing. Moreover, if you really want to tell the whole truth, most of you do not even care. In addition, this next sentence comes with much pause on my behalf, but if we are telling the whole truth, most churches are doing nothing but talk.

If every church in America took the attitude of the pastor a few paragraphs ago that this is my city, this is my neighborhood, these are folks who need my help, and I will help them; if every church in America went out, fixed their backyard; and if every church around the world took the same attitude about their backyard, then what kind of world would we be living in right now? I assure you, the world would look very different than it does right now!

It is not only our responsibility to win souls for the kingdom of God, but we must begin to care for the needs of our communities. That is exactly what Jesus did as He walked in flesh upon this Earth. Jesus brought souls into the Kingdom and Jesus cared for the needs of the people.

If you were sick, Jesus healed you.
If you were hungry, Jesus fed you.
If you needed a word, Jesus spoke to you.

Jesus never said, "I'll fix that tomorrow," or "wait on that till next week." Jesus cared for your needs on the spot. If you say that you love God, if you say that you follow Christ, then these are the same things that you must begin to do now. We must begin to care for the needs of our communities and we must begin now.

This is exactly what the Lord meant when He told me that one will touch one who will touch one who will touch one. Will you be the one that I touch who will go from here and touch another?

There is a story of a man who stood before God; his heart was breaking from all the pain and the injustice in the world. "God!" the man cried out "Look at all the suffering, all the distress in the world. Look at all the pain. Why, God, why? Why do you not send some help?" God responded to the man, "But I did send help. I sent you."

We are all here to make this world a much better place for everyone, not just the chosen few. Stop taking and see what you can do to give to another. Do you feel as I do that God is calling? "I did send help. I sent you." Will you respond to God's call?

Respond to the call of God. God calls us all, but only a small few will respond. Do the will of the Lord while we are still here on the Earth. Follow the example that Jesus set for us, "Not my will be done, but your will, Father." So often, when someone dies in the prime of life, we try to console ourselves by telling each other what a tragedy it is that another life was cut short. However, I was reading a book by Hank Hanegraff in which he wrote a very deep and profound sentence. He wrote, "The tragedy is not in dying young, but in living large, and never using any of that life for an eternal significance." It may take a while for that to sink in, especially if you are the one living the large life.

How many of us take great pride in the life that we have built? I did. I was so proud of all my accomplishments, all the stuff that I had collected, all my toys. I was so proud. We are so caught up in this life that we walk right by people in dire straits every day. We live our lives, and then we die, never doing anything to help; just a society full of takers. The challenge that I heard the Lord say to me one day was to help everyone that I could, and when you think that you have nothing else to give, then help one more.

I was preparing this message to deliver it to a group of men in one of the prisons that we minister to, and God came to me and said, "Tell the men, 'It's time to make a stand.'"

God was tired of the spineless Christian - Christians who have no backbone, Christians who have no voice outside the protection of their church building. God has had enough of your false praise. Actually, God told me to write for you to stop faking. God knows of your weak faith and so does the devil. Why do you think all hell keeps breaking out in your life? God says that it is time for you to make a stand. If the only time you can talk about God, or worse yet, if the only time you can praise God is on Sunday in this building, then you are spineless and your faith is worthless. It is time for you to make a stand!

There is a line that has been drawn in the sand, and you are either on one side or the other. Everyone, and yes, I do mean everyone on the face of this Earth, is on one side of that line or the other. When it comes to God, no one is on the line. You are either on the side of the Lord or not. There is no middle ground in this choice. Remember tacit; to refuse to choose means you have chosen against God.

The majority of us, as long as we are in the company of other Christians, will say that we are on the side of the Lord, but are you really ready to make that stand when you are by yourself out in the world? Remember what the Lord told me about being tired of spineless Christians. Can you stand up and be counted Monday through Saturday when you are out among the world, by yourself? Can you make the stand as an ambassador for the Kingdom? Do not fool yourself; the Lord already knows what side you are on. Are you able to show yourself the truth?

Enter by the narrow gate. For the gate is wide and the way is easy that leads to destruction. And those who enter it are many. For the gate is narrow and the way is hard that leads to life, and those who find it are few. (Matthew 7:13 - 14)

Remember when you used to run for the devil? Whatever he wanted, whenever he wanted, you were always there. You drank. You drugged. You lied. You slept with whoever, whenever. You stole. You stole from your family. You watched pornography. You gambled. You took advantage whenever and whoever. You did whatever you wanted whenever you wanted. You were a tool for the devil's use and you were very good. Let me not let you think that I am writing about you. I am writing about me. I did all those things and so much more.

I was bold when I was running and gunning out in the world. I was not even close to what you would ever call spineless for the devil. If and when I saw something that I wanted, I went out and got it.

You know, in the world, we are divided into two groups: the leaders and the followers. I always considered myself one of the leaders. In the world, we considered ourselves "The Man". We were "The Man" for the devil. Not only were you "The Man" but you took great pride in that fact. Let someone come along and try to call you a punk. Let someone come along and show you disrespect. If you called me a punk, punches were going to be thrown. Let someone call you a punk. No way! You cannot come in my backyard and show me no respect. You had better show me my respect. Isn't that the way we talk for the devil? We can be so tough and so bold all for the devil.

But let someone come along talking Jesus. Let someone come up and hear you talking about your Lord. Let someone come up and challenge you about the Bible. We shut right up. We close our mouths, try to shrink and hide, or we just put our tail between our legs and run away. Why do we find it so easy to become punks for God? Just a bunch of spineless Christians.

How could we be so bold and such tough guys for the devil, and then turn our backs on God? Be honest, because it is time to make a stand. Why do we, who say we love Jesus so much, why will we not stand up for the one we say we love? The devil is on every street corner. Where do you see God? We just let Satan run all over us and have his way. Why is that?

God did not choose you out of the world just so you could be a punk. You must know who you are. You must know the power that lives inside you. You must know that you are God's ambassador here on Earth.

You, who are reading this book, have entered into my circle of influence. Who is inside of your circle? Take time right now and think about whom you have influence over. Think about your circle. Everyone has a circle, everyone! You do not get out of this responsibility that easy. How are you choosing to use that influence? Are you using that influence to recruit for Satan or are you using your influence for the greater glory of God?

Remember your influence can only go one of two ways. You are either influencing the people that you touch for God or against God. Make no mistake here, because you too are being influenced one way or the other. Who is influencing you? Which way are you allowing yourself to be influenced?

People are watching you. A son, a daughter, a friend, your wife, a neighbor, maybe even your parents, and quite possibly someone you are not even aware of. They are watching what you do. Watching to find the true you. How you act. How you respond from day to day. What type of influence do you want to have over these lives?

Take this teaching and go seek opportunities to be an influence for the Lord. Get to know the people around you. Slow down, and get to know your neighbors. Be genuine. Start by saying hello to everyone as you walk by. We used to do that back in the day. Open yourself up to others and others will open up to you. List the people in your circle. Take a minute a really look at that list and seek out the possibilities to help. As you take stock of your list, continue to ask yourself the only question that really matters:

WHAT WOULD LOVE DO NOW?

When you feel the answer come to you from your soul, JUST DO IT!

Let me give you a scripture that the Lord gave to me:

Do all things without murmurings and disputing. That ye may be blameless and harmless. The sons of God, without rebuke, in the midst of a crooked and perverse nation among whom ye shine as lights in the world. (Philippians 2: 14 - 15)

We are always to be in the world but never of the world. We must be in the world to share our witness to the many unbelievers who are still in the world. You must share your testimony with all the people in your circle. Shine as the light in your circle. Yet while in the world, we should not succumb to the sin of the world. In this world, we should shine as bright as the stars in the night sky. That's exactly the way our lives must stand out. We must be the beacon of truth to all the darkness that thrives in the world today. Become that bright light over your circle of influence.

Ye are the light of the world. A city that is set on a hill cannot be hid. Neither do men light a candle and put it under a bushel, but on a candlestick and it giveth light unto all in the house. Let your light so shine before men, that they may see your good works and glorify your Father which is in heaven. (Matthew 5: 14 - 16)

It is time to make that stand. There is a line that has been drawn in the sand. Choose the right side. It is time for all those who are on the side of the Lord to get off the sideline and get into the fight. Stop being a spectator. Stop being a part-time Christian. Open your mouth and speak the truth. Get out of your buildings and let your voices be heard.

It's time for a unified voice to be heard. Jesus spoke of one body, not many different pieces all running off doing their own thing. It is that one unified voice showing the way that will bring this great nation back to God. It will never be done if that voice stays in the building. It will never be done until we all speak for one God. It will never get done if that voice continues to run and hide. The devil wants to divide and separate us so much. The devil wants nothing more than for us to stay in our separate denominations. Division only causes weakness. Don't let the devil tell you that it does not take all that. To win back America for the side of the Lord, it will take all that and even more.

How much longer will we, as ambassadors for the Kingdom, tolerate the immorality in this country? How much longer will you hide your head in the sand and pretend that things are really not that bad? People are dying every day, busting Hell wide open, because things are that bad. And that's people in the church. The world is that bad because the church is that bad. How much longer will you sit by and just watch the complete destruction of the family in America?

Our society mirrors our media so much. Just look at what is on television. Look at what is playing at the movie theatre. It used to be that television and the movies were the world of make believe. Today, what plays on television and what is happening in the world are identical. Television promotes all the immorality of the world. Every sin, every lust, every vice, all corruption, lying, cheating, stealing, murder, excessive violence, all this and more are promoted and even glorified on television.

Just look at the new rave on television. It's called reality T.V. Look at the talk shows being aired every day. Sex, drugs, violence, no integrity, the lies, the deceit, no morals, no honor; what you see on television, it's all about satisfying myself, and if you get hurt in the process, too bad. You really want to see what has happened to the family in America? Turn on "Murray", turn on "Springer". How low can we go?

Even the evening news only airs and promotes the bad in our culture today. Television has had the greatest influence on what is wrong with America today. We wonder why we say the world is going to hell in a hand basket. Our children are bombarded with pornography, violence, profanity, sex, drugs, anger, jealousy, hatred, racism, and all that is on the television. I have not even started in on what you can see on the Internet.

Let me give you a very hard fact. In the average American home, the television set is on six to seven hours a day and we wonder who is setting the example. You wonder who is influencing your children. Is your family in the circle of influence called the television set? Is this really the life you want to live? Is "Three and Half Men" really the life you want your sons to grow up to emulate? How you want your daughters to be used? Do we even think of such things as we watch or are you really the vegetable that the television hopes we are? What are you allowing the television or worse yet, the Internet to teach your children? I noticed there is even a new show called "Revenge". Is there anything that we will not promote for money? What is this show telling the young minds of America?

I see the devil everywhere. Wherever I walk, I see sin and temptation. Where is it that I see my God? Where are the people standing up for God? Why can I not see all the people on Monday who were in all these church buildings on Sunday? It is time. Now is that time. The line is in the sand. How much longer will you wait? The next second is promised to no one. How much longer can you afford to wait? How much worse does the world have to get? What will it take for you to make a stand and say that enough is enough?

Trust me when I tell you that the world is only going to get worse. I do not say that as a scare tactic. Just look at what the world has evolved into over the last fifty years. Can you say that things are really better? Is there more love in the world today? More peace? More forgiveness? More compassion? More mercy? What good do you see? Do you see real examples of people stopping to help another? Or do you see, as I do, that there is only more evil in the world today than ever before?

Our leaders lie. Our leaders steal. Our leaders cheat. Our leaders use deception to get where and what they want. And yet, we stand by and do nothing. When is enough going to be enough? Or will you do as most people do today, and say, "That's just the way the world is, so get used to it"? God has drawn a line in the sand. When will you not only stand up for God, but start to use that voice that God gave to you?

I was riding home on the bus one afternoon and God began to speak to me:

It was God's intention for the Earth to be the Garden. Not just one country, not just one particular area, not just one geographic region, but God intended the entire Earth to be the Garden of Eden. God made this Earth to be perfect and for man to have dominion over everything on this Earth.

It was always God's will for Heaven to reign upon this Earth. Once you get to know God, really get to know God, not just know of God, once you begin to walk in oneness with God's purpose, then you will want nothing more than to reestablish Heaven upon Earth. And you will want that for everyone.

Instead of war, instead of the hatred, the hunger, the violence, the separation, that we have come to know of on this Earth, your desire will replace those evils with God's peace, God's love, and God's joy. These are the qualities that you so desire to bring upon this Earth. All the qualities that existed in the Garden of Eden. The only qualities that existed in the Garden. When your purpose is only the will of God, then you will wish only for God's love, God's peace, and God's joy to reign again upon this Earth and in abundance. When God speaks of the abundant life, it is these life qualities that God speaks of. All you want to do is touch and bring these qualities to as many people on this Earth as you can.

You want to do the things that Jesus did when He walked this Earth - walking, talking, touching, and teaching as many people as possible about the ways of Jesus. In this day of all the technology, email, Twitter, Facebook, texting, we have forgotten that Jesus came and physically touched people. It will be the one who touches one, who touches one, who touches one that will change this world for the Lord. Will you be the one that I touch today with the word of God who will go out and touch another? This is exactly the way Jesus spread the word. No matter how much or how great the technology, love will never be spread through machines. Love can only be passed from person to person and in person.

Just as the Apostle Paul wrote:

AND NOW I WILL SHOW YOU A MORE EXCELLENT WAY (1 Corinthians 12:31)

I KNOW THERE IS A BETTER WAY AND THAT WAY IS TO LIVE IN THE LOVE OF JESUS

There is so much work to do. Too many people are just sitting in church; too many pastors are only standing behind their pulpits; too many people try to preach the word of God behind the comfort of televisions monitors. All these people think that they are doing the work of the Lord, but the Lord told me that they are not doing His work. Many pastors today are feeding their own agendas. They have their own reasons and motives for doing what they do.

It never has been a number game with God. It's all about finding that one lost sheep. It's about touching that one lost sheep with God's love and that sheep going out and touching another with God's love.

Is the Earth getting closer to Heaven because of their work, or is it just the same old thing, month after month, year after year, decade after decade. Many of these pastors are just preaching to the choir, if you get what I am trying to say.

It's the same message, to the same people, Sunday after Sunday. They have compromised the word of God only to fill their buildings. They have watered down the word to fit today's times. They tell the people what the people want to hear only to fill seats, to fill the plate. We don't preach about sin, or Satan, or Hell, or eternal damnation, or that there is only one way. We preach a middle-of-the-road, wishy-washy, one-size-fits-all Christianity, and look at the mess the world is in.

Actually, the world is in worse shape than ever before, and some of these so-called pastors have been preaching the word of God for ten, twenty, thirty, forty, or even fifty years. I was flipping between the Christian television channels and I kept seeing all these pulpits filled with people wearing black and white collars. You know what I am talking about. It struck me that I see all these people of God on Sunday, but why do I not see these people on Monday? Or why do I have to turn on the television to see these people? Where are they in real life, Monday through Saturday? How did this Earth fall into such a mess? What are all these people teaching Sunday after Sunday?

The true work of the Lord is in the field, in the street, in the inner city, wherever the torn, the beaten down, the broken, wherever the people are who have given up hope. We must get out of our comfort and go do as Jesus did. Too many churches are waiting for the broken to find them. Go out and do what Jesus did. Jesus touched people. Jesus touched broken people. We must touch the broken people with the love of God. You cannot do that unless you are out there!

We must offer hope and solutions to a world that we know today does not work. We know the only way to make life work and we must be out among the people, giving solutions to people's needs. There is a world out there full of hurt and we, who Jesus lives in, must be in the thick of that hurt, offering aid. It's exactly what Jesus did, and if you say that you follow Jesus, and if you say that Jesus lives in you, then you must do as Jesus did: physically touch people.

Let me tell you a sad, but very true story. I overheard one preacher speaking to another preacher. They were talking about the severe rash of heavy snowstorms that we were experiencing this year. One pastor said, "It really upsets me when it snows so heavily on Saturday. All that snow affects my Sunday service. The attendance on Sunday is way down and boy does that affect my finances."

That statement alone bothered me, but then he said something else that bothered me even more. He said, "I can't win any souls when the people don't show up for my service."

What did I just hear him say? Is Sunday the only day that souls can be won for the Lord? Can he only win souls inside his building? Does he really believe that the Lord's power only lives inside of his building, behind his pulpit? What happens to me if I never find his building?

This is exactly the wrong thinking held by many of our church leadership, which has led America to the state of emergency that we find ourselves in today. Souls are dying every day, all around us, busting hell wide open while we hide in our buildings on Sunday, waiting for the lost to find us.

How can the world be saved? How will the world ever come to know the love of God? How can the world ever come to know Jesus Christ if we never show the world the glory of God in us? For each of us, there are specific people waiting for your testimony so they can meet Jesus. You who say that Jesus lives in you will have to give account one day of how you used the testimony that God put inside of you.

YOUR BEST PERFORMANCE IS OUT IN THE WORLD AMONGST THE PEOPLE, NOT HERE INSIDE YOUR BUILDINGS!!

We have built these multimillion-dollar buildings that have become our golden calf.

We expect the sick, the hurt, the broken, and the lost to find us. You want God? Come and find me in my building. I heard another pastor pray, "Father, send to me all the broken people. If you send them to me, I will take care of them." My only question is: what if they cannot find you?

Maybe I'm the one who is confused, but didn't Jesus say to go out and find the one lost sheep? I though Jesus commanded us to go out, seek, find, and win that one lost sheep for our Lord and savior.

Let me take a moment and give you an example that may bring this all to light for you. Close your eyes and imagine that today is Wednesday. Jesus has just flown into the town that you live in. Jesus flies into your airport on Southwest Airlines, gets off the plane, picks up His luggage, and gets into a taxi. Where is it that Jesus tells the taxi driver to take Him? What sites does Jesus want to visit while He is in your town?

First, Jesus tells the driver to take Him to the poorest part of town. "Take me to where the people are in need. Take me to where the people are struggling. Take me to where the people are worn out and battered. Take me to where the people need me the most. That is where I want to go. Those are the people who need me the most. Those are the people I want to see. I'm looking for the lost and the wounded."

Where does Jesus not ask the driver to take Him? To the largest church in town. To visit the preacher whose church has the largest congregation. To visit the most beautiful church building.

Jesus gets back into the taxi; it's getting late into the afternoon. Jesus asks the taxi to take Him to a hospital. "There are people there who need me. There are people there who need to be healed. There are people there who need to hear a word."

It's now early in the evening; Jesus is leaving the hospital and returns to the taxi. "Is there a prison nearby? I want to visit and share a word with all the people in the prison. There are people there who need some hope." That's exactly how Jesus would spend a day in your town.

Get out of your buildings. Tear down your buildings. These buildings mean nothing to God. Get out and touch someone. Truly touch someone with the word of God. Change someone's life by introducing them to the kingdom. Make a permanent change in someone's life today.

God would say, "Do as my son would do if he flew into your city today. Bring freedom and salvation to the world. Bring my Heaven down upon this Earth. And do it now. Restore the Earth back to the way I meant for it to be from the beginning.

Do that and I will tell you, 'Job well done!'

IS IT TOO LATE FOR THE WORLD TO CHANGE?

We are God's greatest miracle. We are God's greatest creation. Each of us is special in our own unique way. Each of us is made in the image of God. From the moment we were born, God created each of us as His special creation. If only as children we could have been raised to really know God and how special each of us is to our Lord.

We are not raised or taught, nor do we ever hear how truly special we are to God. We are not told or taught that God has a predestined purpose for each of us. We never hear how God values us as His priceless treasure. I wish that I would have known all these facts a long time ago. I wish that someone would have taught me to look to God instead of looking towards man for all my answers.

How many of us look to the world to be special? We look for someone, anyone, to tell us how special we are. We waste so much time, so much energy, and for some of us, all our resources, looking and searching for someone who will make us feel special.

We spin our wheels, looking for acceptance and love in the world. We look and look and look, and the whole time, everything that we are looking for is right in front of us. God has everything that we are searching for, but no one is teaching us about God. No one is teaching about the kingdom.

Why do we always let people tell us what to do? Why do we listen to the advice of others? Because, as children, we are not taught to wait and to listen to God. Instead, we are taught that we must listen to our parents, our teachers, our grandparents, everyone but God. We take our problems to our friends, our neighbors, our boss, the neighborhood bartender, sometimes just to anyone who will listen to us. The problem with turning to man for our counsel is that they do not always give us the best advice. They have their own motives or agenda for the advice they give to us and their advice is not always right.

Why will the world not change? Because there are so few teaching. "Teaching what?" you ask. Teaching us to listen for God first.

It took me nearly fifty years to find everything that I had been searching for my entire life.

GOD LOVES ME.
GOD ACCEPTS ME AS I AM.
GOD KNOWS THAT I AM SPECIAL.
I AM GOD'S GREATEST MIRACLE.

There is nothing else that I need. God supplies all my needs just as He promised, and the best thing is that when God supplies a need for you, God supplies that need for your life.

IS IT REALLY TOO LATE FOR THE WORLD TO CHANGE?

As long as I stay on the road of me first, we cannot.

As long as I believe that my life is separate from everyone else's, we cannot.

As long as I believe that my needs are way more important than anyone else's, we cannot.

In order for the world to change, at some time, I must reach the point where I begin to see everyone on this Earth as ONE; Chinese, Japanese, Italian, African, British, American, Mexican, we are all one together. One people. One Earth. God created all the people on this Earth and God created everyone in His image.

WHAT YOU DO TO ONE, YOU DO TO ALL

You must begin to see all life as divine. You must see that God lives in everyone; let me say that again;

GOD LIVES IN EVERYONE!

And to harm one, you harm God; maybe then we will have turned the corner. You will no longer be able to harm one.

YOU WILL NO LONGER BE ABLE TO HARM ONE PERSON WHEN YOU SEE

THAT TO HARM ANYONE, YOU ARE REALLY HARMING GOD!

THAT'S THE STATEMENT THAT CHANGES THIS WORLD!!!!!!!

LET'S TAKE THAT STATEMENT ONE STEP FURTHER.

How can you be happy when another is sad?

How can you prosper when another lives in poverty?

How can you live in peace when another lives in violence?

How can you stuff your belly when another goes to bed starving?

Got the picture? Had enough?

THE ANSWER IS: YOU CANNOT!

When you begin to see all of what God has created as divine,
And when you begin to see all human beings as one,
Then

ONE MAN'S SUFFERING BECOMES YOUR SUFFERING.

And you will not rest until everyone lives as you live.

You will not rest until everyone can and does experience life as you experience life.

Living life to the fullest was meant for everyone. You cannot rest until everyone is as blessed as you are. We must raise each other up and get beyond the haves and the have-nots so that everyone can have.

NO ONE SHOULD EVER EXPERIENCE LIFE FROM THE BOTTOM!

**JESUS DID NOT COME TO SAVE YOU AND NOT YOU.
JESUS DID NOT COME TO HEAL YOU AND NOT YOU.
JESUS DID NOT COME TO LOVE YOU AND NOT YOU.
JESUS CAME TO GIVE EVERYTHING TO
EVERYBODY.**

And that is the exact mission Jesus left us with. Jesus came to give everyone life and Jesus came to give that life abundantly. Jesus did not say such a word to you and not you. Give everything you can to everybody.

**STOP EXCLUDING.
STOP SELECTING.
STOP JUDGING.
STOP MAKING SOME MORE IMPORTANT THAN
OTHERS.**

Just give. Give everything to everybody, and when you think you have no more to give,

GIVE TO ONE MORE!

MY PLEDGE

**I WILL SPEND THE REST OF MY LIFE GIVING TO
OTHERS**

**I WILL SPEND THE REST OF MY LIFE HELPING
EVERYONE THAT I AM ABLE**

I WILL SPEND THE REST OF MY LIFE GIVING AID TO
THE SUFFERING OF OTHERS

I WILL SPEND THE REST OF MY LIFE FORGIVIN AND
THEN I WILL FORGET

I WILL SPEND THE REST OF MY LIFE RESISTING
EVIL AND SPREADING PEACE

I WILL SPEND THE REST OF MY DAYS GIVING TO
OTHERS THE JOY THAT GOD HAS BLESSED ME
WITH

I WILL SPEND THE REST OF MY LIFE, EVERY DAY,
THANKING AND SERVING MY GOD

I WILL SPEND THE REST OF MY LIFE PRAISING AND
GIVING ALL THE GLORY TO MY GOD

I WILL SPEND THE REST OF MY DAYS GIVING AND
TEACHING THE LOVE OF GOD

PAUL SCHMIDT

WHEN THE MAJORITY OF US

BECOME THE LOVE OF GOD

IN THIS WORLD TODAY,

ALL THE PROBLEMS,

EVERY PROBLEM THAT WE KNOW OF TODAY,

ALL THE PROBLEMS

OF THIS WORLD

WILL DISAPPEAR!!!!!!

THANK YOU FOR READING.
PAUL SCHMIDT

REFERENCES

AU BIBLE SCRIPTURE TAKEN OUT OF THE ENGLISH STANDARD VERSION. PERMISSION GRANTED.

CHOPRA, DEEPAK. *THE THIRD JESUS.* NEW YORK: HARMONY BOOKS, 2008.

CHOPRA, DEEPAK. *WHY IS GOD LAUGHING?* NEW YORK: HARMONY BOOKS, 2008.

MACDONALD, WILLIAM, *BELIEVERS BIBLE COMMENTARY.* NASHVILLE: THOMAS NELSON, 1798.

MYSS, CAROLINE. *ENTERING THE CASTLE.* NEW YORK: FREE PRESS, 2007.

TOLSTOY, LEO. *THE KINGDOM OF GOD IS WITHIN YOU.* NEW YORK: CASSELL PUBLICATIONS, 1894.

WALSCH, NEALE DONALD. *CONVERSATIONS WITH GOD BOOK I.* NEW YORK: G.P. PUTNAM, 1996.

WALSCH, NEALE DONALD. *CONVERSATIONS WITH GOD BOOK 3.* CHARLOTTESVILLE: HAMPTON ROADS PUBLISHING, 1998.

WALSCH, NEALE DONALD. *HAPPIER THAN GOD.* ASHLAND: EMNIN BOOKS, 2008.

WALSCH, NEALE DONALD. *TOMORROW'S GOD.* NEW YORK: ATRIA BOOKS, 2004.

www.ingramcontent.com/pod-product-compliance
Lightning Source LLC
LaVergne TN
LVHW051449080426
835509LV00017B/1711